Smile Though Your Heart Is Breaking

PRESCOTT

Smile Though Your Heart Is Breaking

PAULINE PRESCOTT
with Wendy Holden

HARPER

HARPER

an imprint of
HarperCollinsPublishers
77–85 Fulham Palace Road,
Hammersmith, London W6 8JB

www.harpercollins.co.uk

First published by HarperCollinsPublishers 2010
This edition 2011

1 3 5 7 9 10 8 6 4 2

A catalogue record of this book is
available from the British Library

ISBN 978-0-00-733717-0

Printed and bound in Great Britain by
Clays Ltd, St Ives plc

This book is dedicated to John, the memory of my parents, and for my three wonderful boys: Paul, Johnathan, and David; and for my beautiful granddaughter Ava Grace

Smile, though your heart is aching
Smile, even though it's breaking
When there are clouds in the sky
You'll get by
If you smile
Through your fear and sorrow
Smile and maybe tomorrow
You'll see the sun come shining through
For you
Light up your face with gladness
Hide every trace of sadness
Although a tear may be ever so near
That's the time you must keep on trying
Smile, what's the use of crying
You'll find that life is still worthwhile
If you just smile

(John Turner and Geoffrey Parsons)

Prologue

I LAY ON MY NARROW METAL-FRAMED BED, HANDS ACROSS MY TUMMY, AND felt the life inside me stir. Relishing the silence of the dawn, I knew that Sister Joan Augustine would burst into the dormitory any minute, clanging her bell to get us up and bathed for morning prayers.

It was 25 December 1955. Enjoying a few more seconds' peace, I allowed my mind to drift back to the fifteen Christmases I'd already known or at least those I could remember. Each year, my mum and dad would roll the carpet back and dance across the living room to the songs of Fats Waller or the Ink Spots playing on the gramophone. Under dangling paper chains Dad would waltz me laughingly around on his feet, clinging to the back of his legs until I was giddy.

The best part was when my brother Peter and I were allowed to open the presents my parents had placed either side of the fireplace for us. Apart from the usual apple, orange and banana, there would always be some special gift they'd saved especially hard for – like my brother's bicycle or the sleeping baby doll I'd coveted ever since I'd spotted it in Garner's Toy Shop window. When the doll was replaced by another just before the school holidays, I cried all the way home. To my astonishment, there she was on Christmas morning, batting her long eyelashes at me. From Mum's wages as a part-time cleaner and my father's as a bricklayer a little money had been put into a savings club until there was enough.

Now aged sixteen, I was about to give birth to my own baby doll, the one I prayed would bring back its airman father from wherever he'd returned to in America. I'd written and told him about our child but he hadn't replied yet. Maybe once the baby was born, he'd divorce his wife and send for me to marry him as he'd always promised he would.

I thought back to Christmas two years earlier, the first that Mum, Peter and I had faced a few months after we'd watched Dad's coffin being lowered into the ground. That Christmas, I was invited to a party at the local American airbase for children who'd been orphaned or bereaved. A scrawny fourteen-year-old, I'd stepped nervously into that mess hall and thought I'd been transported to Hollywood. The scene was like something in the movies that transfixed me every Saturday afternoon at the Regal Cinema in Foregate Street, Chester. The hall was filled with clowns, balloons and entertainers. A trestle table groaned under oversized platters of exotic food. There was cream and frosted icing, the likes of which I'd never known because of rationing. Smiling shyly at the handsome men in uniform who reminded me of Rock Hudson or Clark Gable as they handed out gifts, I was star-struck.

Had that Christmas party only been two years earlier? Before my brother got sick? Before my widowed mother had her accident? Before I met the father of my baby? It seemed like a lifetime ago. The words of my favourite song, 'Unchained Melody', sprang unbidden into my head.

Oh my love, my darling,
I've hungered for your touch a long lonely time.
And time goes by so slowly and time can do so much.
Are you still mine?
I need your love … God speed your love to me.

The bell ringing in Sister Joan Augustine's hand snapped me from my reverie. Her long black habit making her seem taller than she really was, she stood in the doorway of our dormitory as she had every morning for the three months that I'd been a resident at St Bridget's House of Mercy, a home for unwed mothers in Lache Park. Apart from Mother Superior, whose office I'd tremblingly approached with my suitcase that first day, Sister Joan Augustine was the nun I feared the most.

'Come along now, girls!' she cried, clapping her hands together impatiently. 'Stop dawdling.' Dutifully, and in various stages of pregnancy, we twelve teenagers heaved ourselves upright, grabbed our wash bags and formed an orderly queue for the bathroom. With one bath shared between each dorm, we were only allowed a few minutes each before we had to dress and troop down to the chapel.

Because it was Christmas, the nuns had decorated a small tree in the room where we'd be permitted to greet family and friends later that afternoon. Its sparsely decorated branches were a bittersweet reminder of happier festivities beyond the former convent's walls. There would be no traditional gatherings by the family hearth for any of us that year. No pile of presents. No oranges or cute baby dolls. Instead, we'd quietly eat our breakfast cereal in the refectory, each lost in memories of Christmases past. Then we'd fall in for normal duties: peeling potatoes in the kitchen, working in the laundry or scrubbing the cloisters' floor. We were young, some the victims of sexual abuse, others (like me) too innocent to understand the consequences of what we'd done. All of us were waiting for babies we were expected to take home or hand over uncomplainingly for adoption.

In a few days' time, my turn would come. Excited and terrified in equal measure, I dreaded the birth but fervently hoped my baby would arrive before those of two other girls in my dorm whose babies were due imminently. Sister Joan Augustine had promised the first child a beautiful Silver Cross pram that had been donated to the home by a well-wisher. That pram was gorgeous, with its cream enamel paintwork with a silver flash and its grey cloth hood. Not since I'd spotted the doll in the toy-shop window had I wanted anything quite so badly.

What I longed for even more, though, was to gaze into the eyes of the infant whose steady heartbeat matched mine. I ached to hold its tiny fingers. I wanted to kiss its cherub face. I was convinced that one look at those innocent features would change my mother's mind. Setting eyes on her first grandchild, she would announce (I felt sure) that we couldn't possibly give it up and that somehow – even though we both worked full time and couldn't afford help – we'd manage.

Kneeling in the chapel that cold December morning, my swollen tummy pressed against the pew, I bowed my head. 'Please God, let me keep my baby,' I whispered, my knuckles white through the skin of my hands. 'Don't let them take it away.'

If my prayers could only be answered, that would be a million times better than any doll or any pram. It would be the best Christmas present ever...

One

I DON'T KNOW WHAT MY MOTHER'S CHRISTMASES WERE LIKE WHEN SHE WAS a little girl, but I don't suppose they were much fun. Christened Minnie Irene Clegg but known to all as 'Rene', she rarely spoke of her childhood except to tell me that her father Joseph had died of war wounds when she was three, leaving her mother Ada to raise four small children.

From a devout Salvation Army background, Ada met another man and had six more children by him, making ten in all, although some died along the way. Sadly, the man Ada ended up with was a violent and abusive drunk, so my mother, her younger sister Ivy and her two brothers were sent into a children's home and then into service. Auntie Ivy, who was known as 'Little Titch', was much taller than my mother who stood at just over five feet. Despite her diminutive height and the fact that there was only a year between them, Mum was 'the boss'. The two women were so in tune with each other that they could sense if the other was unwell or in trouble. If one had an accident, the other seemed to a few days later. We named them 'the Golden Girls'.

When Ivy moved to Southampton to take up a position in a country mansion owned by a lord, Mum had no choice but to remain in Chester where she had a job as a maid in one of the old houses owned by the Welsby family of wine merchants. She missed her sister terribly, even more so after Ivy married Len, a bus conductor and later had a daughter, my cousin Anne. In the privacy of her attic bedroom, my mum would shed tears for the sister from whom she'd never before been separated. Looking mournfully out over the rooftops, she'd wonder where Ivy was and what she was doing. On one such day, her eyes fell upon a good-looking young man clambering about on the roof of a hotel across the street. Spotting my mother in the window, he smiled and waved.

From that moment on, my mother's mood lifted. Every chance she'd get, she'd run up to her room, heart pounding, to see if the handsome bricklayer was still working on the roof. Each time she saw him, she'd wave happily and he'd wave back. Eventually, he waited for her by her employer's back door to ask her name. His was Ernest Tilston, and within a year they were wed.

Ernie was the youngest of twelve children, ten of them boys. Their father George, who was originally from Wales, became a Regimental Sergeant Major in the Cheshire Regiment during the First World War and sported a splendid waxed moustache. Ernie was such a good football player as a lad that he'd been offered a place with Tranmere Rovers but his father, a builder and master scaffolder, wouldn't let him take it up and insisted he got a trade. Ernie's brother Fred was a world-class boxer known as 'Little Tilly'. Ernie worked for his dad and lived with his parents but once he and my mother were engaged, they began saving for their first home, a red-brick terraced house in the village of Boughton Heath, in the suburbs of Chester. They married when they were both just turned twenty.

A few years later in 1937, my brother Peter was born. I came along twenty months after that in February, 1939. My timing was just right because when I was seven months old, war broke out. I was very young but I can still remember bombing raids in Chester; hiding in 'the glory hole' under the stairs with Mum and Peter; eating emergency rations by torchlight. As a pupil at Cherry Grove School, I'd run to the concrete air-raid shelter with my Mickey Mouse gas mask with its sticking-out ears whenever the sirens sounded. I hated that horrible-smelling rubber mask. It made me feel sick every time someone clamped it to my face. After the school day was over, I'd play on the bombsites with my brother and his friends, using wooden doors that had been blown off their hinges as makeshift slides. It was all good fun until I got splinters in my bottom and my mother had to pluck them out.

My father enlisted in the Royal Marines and was posted to Scapa Flow in the Orkney Islands where many of the British battleships were based. Albert, one of my mother's brothers, lived in Glasgow with his wife Nan and three sons so once, when my father was given leave, we took a train north to meet him there. German bombs rained on Glasgow too, especially the area round the river Clyde, but there was never a suggestion that we shouldn't go and what a time we had. Being in Scotland felt like being on holiday and we'd never had a holiday before. Dad brought us enormous duck eggs from the Orkneys, which were such a luxury after years of powdered egg. In the local sweetshop he treated us to pear drops, strips of liquorice and humbugs that changed colour as you sucked them. Because of the sugar shortage, these were things we'd rarely had except as a monthly treat from the family ration book. One of my happiest memories is climbing the hills outside the city with Dad to pick some heather for Mum, my small hand swamped by his as he lifted me squealing above the carpet of purple flowers.

People couldn't help but love my father. When he was in the Marines, he used to MC all the dances and shows, and was a popular member of their football team. He bore more than a passing resemblance to a young John Wayne and was a natural joker whose favourite comedian was Al Reed. Occasionally he'd repeat some of Al's jokes, which could be a bit naughty. Mum would nudge him then and scold him with: 'Ernie!' When the war ended and we knew for sure that Dad was safe and coming home, we celebrated at a street party held locally for VE Day. There was bunting and cakes and jellies. Trestle tables lined the lane at the back of our house. A few days later, Dad came marching proudly down the street to the music of the band of the Royal Marines, which still moves me to tears each time I hear it.

After the war, Dad was offered a job as a master bricklayer for British Insulated Callender's Cables, in the works' maintenance department eight miles away in Helsby. They not only wanted him for his bricklaying skills but for their football team. Each morning, he'd put on his overalls, pick up his haversack with his sandwiches, and whistle to himself as he got on his old bike and set off to work. On Thursday nights he'd come home with his little brown wage packet and wander into a corner with it, my mother peering over his shoulder. If she wasn't looking, he'd slip us a tanner each, especially if we'd done something to please him.

Once a month, Mum would check his pay packet and say, 'But you've already opened your wages.'

'Yes, Rene,' Dad would reply. 'I had to pay my union dues to the agent.'

Mum would nod and put the rest of his money away. I never knew what union dues were but I knew they were something my parents both took extremely seriously.

Although he seemed to like his job and got on well with his colleagues, my father preferred nothing more than to spend time with us. Every Saturday night he'd take us to the pictures. We always had to get there early and queue for the cheapest seats, right in the front row. He'd always buy us an ice cream in the interval and then we'd go home on the bus. Dad's hero was Fred Astaire, so we saw all his films like *Three Little Words* and *The Belle of New York*. My favourite star at the time was Elizabeth Taylor, who at seven years older than me was the most glamorous young woman I'd ever seen in my life. I think I saw *National Velvet* three times.

We never went to church as a family so every Sunday Dad would switch on the wireless to listen to a pianist called Charlie Kunz who played Gershwin, Fats Waller, and Cole Porter songs. The carpet would be rolled back and Dad and I used to tap dance or waltz across the living-room floor, laughing all the while. Dad loved to dance and would copy all the steps he'd seen at the pictures. I inherited that passion and his love for swing music. His favourite song was 'Ain't Misbehavin'' and even now when I hear it, it makes me smile:

I know for certain the one I love;
I'm through with flirtin', it's just you I'm thinkin' of.
Ain't misbehavin', I'm saving my love for you.

My brother preferred modern jazz, which he'd play in his bedroom. Listening to those songs drifting through the walls, I soon fell for artists like Gerry Mulligan, Dave Brubeck and the MJQ or Modern Jazz Quartet. I remember loving one song in particular by the Tommy Dorsey band which was called 'A Sinner Kissed an Angel'. For my birthday, Peter would buy me Ella Fitzgerald or Sarah Vaughan records. Being nearly two years older than me, Peter had his own friends and I was often just the kid sister who got in the way. It wasn't until we were grown up that we became much closer and now we're the best of pals.

Since I didn't have a sister to play with, my closest companion was Joyce Ashford, who lived in the same street. She and I used to put on dance and puppet shows in her garage. Her younger sister Barbara sometimes joined in, but she once spied on us rehearsing and put on her own version of our show before we could. I don't think we ever quite forgave her.

I never felt poor but in comparison with our family Joyce and Barbara were definitely better off. Joyce's father was a bookie who owned a car, a television and a garage, none of which we possessed. My dad only had a bike and we all used the buses. If ever I wanted to see something on television, I'd go round to Joyce's after school. We loved *Muffin the Mule* and watched all the important public events, including the Coronation in 1953. I remember holding my breath as the glittering crown was placed so solemnly on the Queen's head and thinking how incredible it would be to meet her one day. Aged fourteen, I never thought my wish might come true.

A tall, skinny kid, all I wanted was to be a television 'Topper' when I grew up: dancing in a troupe of glamorous girls in support of a main act. I couldn't think of a finer job than to be paid to dance. A proud member of Miss Eve's Morris Dancing Team, by my early teens I was touring all over the Midlands, Wales and the North to compete in regional finals. Mum would travel with me on the bus and we had such fun getting me into my costume each time, with its little skirt and frilly knickers. At Christmas, I'd put on my 'Fred and Ginger' outfit for the family (I was always Fred, in a top hat) and do a little routine bursting balloons with high kicks and the splits as Mum, Dad and Peter all laughed. I have such carefree memories of those years.

I was thrilled when my parents found the money to send me to the Hammond School of Dance on the Liverpool Road, which was the best in the North of England. There was a price to pay, though. When Peter was given a new bicycle one year I was told I couldn't have one as well as my classes. I didn't mind. As far as I was concerned, I had the better deal.

I loved school and there were several subjects I was good at, especially drama. I even played the Virgin Mary in the school nativity play. Having a vivid imagination, I was also good at English and would make up little stories in my head. Because of my dancing, I was sporty and my long legs were ideal for running and the high jump. I was always in the middle of my class academically, and only ever came top in needlework and cookery so I guess I was destined to be a housewife. It wasn't that I was thick, I just didn't apply myself. When I failed my eleven plus, which meant I couldn't go to the City High School in Handbridge with my friend Joyce, I was devastated. For the first time I felt the stigma of being labelled 'stupid', something my brother (who'd passed his eleven plus the previous year) took great delight in rubbing in whenever he could.

I was sent to Love Street secondary modern school instead, where my party trick was to do handstands against the wall with my skirt tucked into my knickers. I threw myself into athletics until I was made sports captain and finally felt I'd achieved something. Then, when the rest of my class voted me house captain I decided that I should try harder to live up to the little badge I proudly wore on my lapel, and – with a little application – I came second in the class that year.

Coming home on the bus with all the posh girls from Queen's School and City High, I was painfully aware that my differently coloured uniform defined me as 'not one of them', so I did all I could to blend in. I'd slip off my navy-blue blazer and try not to draw attention to myself. One day, I watched in horror as my father stepped on to the bus in his overalls, his haversack slung over his shoulder. I was sitting halfway down and shrank into my seat. Dad didn't see me so he sat right at the back, legs apart as always, chatting and laughing with everyone around him in that real working-class Cheshire way of speaking that he had. To my eternal shame, I can remember thinking, Please, don't embarrass me! I still hate myself for that, because the one thing I can't stand is snobbery.

I was thirteen years old when my father began to complain of feeling unwell. He had a bad back and other ailments and used to take all sorts of herbal remedies when the medicines the doctor prescribed didn't work. Unusually, he took time off work but he never seemed to improve, even with bed rest. I think, like us, he assumed that an aching back was something that went with his job. After a year of pain which nothing seemed to ease, he discovered a lump on his neck. Mum, who'd taken on extra cleaning to make ends meet by then, told us a few days later that Dad would need an operation to remove it.

'First of all, though,' she said, 'we're going on holiday!'

I couldn't believe it. We were to spend a week at the Middleton Tower Holiday Camp near Morecambe, Lancashire. Dad was to be admitted for surgery soon after we got back but I didn't worry about his operation in the slightest. All I could think about was our impending break, which was the first proper holiday we'd ever had. The camp was like nothing I had ever seen. Set in sixty acres with nine hundred chalets, its dining rooms and cafeterias could feed three thousand people. The main building, which had a theatre and a dance floor, was modelled on a Cunard cruise ship called the SS *Berengaria*. We were joined by my mum's mother Ada – or 'Nanny' as I called her, who was a traditional cuddly grandmother from Ellesmere Port. Then there was Aunt Bessie, who brought her daughters, my cousins, Barbara, Linda and Janet. My brother Peter, who was sixteen, brought along a couple of friends.

Even though my father wasn't very well he still drew people to him and he and my mother were so lovely on that holiday – like newlyweds. They danced together most nights and I can remember watching them on the dance floor and feeling a little jealous. Later, my lovely dad made sure to dance just with me. Best of all, he won a bingo prize of sixty pounds which more than paid for the holiday. He was so happy.

Soon after we came home, Dad was admitted to Chester City Hospital where he was expected to stay for two weeks. We were planning to visit him one night after school but Mum said there had been a complication and that he needed peace and quiet. 'He'll be home soon,' she told us, sensing our disappointment. I couldn't wait. The house felt so empty without his laughing presence.

The day he was due to be discharged I hurried back from school, excitedly skipping along in front of our row of terraced houses, the gardens of which sloped to the road. As usual, the other mothers were standing by their gates or leaning across their garden fences, chatting to each other as they waited for their children to come home. But on that particular afternoon, something unusual happened. One by one, the women stopped talking, turned, and walked back up their paths without saying hello to me. I remember thinking how strange that was as I danced on by.

Dad wasn't waiting at our garden gate as I'd hoped he might be. Swallowing my disappointment, I ran inside and found my mother in the kitchen. 'Is he home?' I asked breathlessly.

She bent down and took my hands in hers. 'Yes, Pauline, but he's in bed. He's still not very well. Why don't you go up and see if he recognizes you?'

I ran up the stairs two at a time wondering what Mum meant. Of course Daddy would recognize me – he'd only been away two weeks. But the man lying in my parents' bed hardly even looked like my father. The shock froze me halfway across the room.

'Dad?'

His eyes flickered open and he turned to look at me, but didn't respond. Taking a step forward, I reached for his hand. It lay limply in mine.

'Daddy? It's Pauline.'

He closed his eyes again and I stood stock still, uncertain what to do. If only he'd open them and say, 'Hi, baby.' He often referred to me as 'baby', which I loved.

My mother came into the room and sat on the edge of the bed. 'Something happened during the operation,' she said. Her voice was strange. 'It's left Daddy a bit confused.'

He remained 'confused' for the rest of the day and by evening Mum was so worried that she summoned a doctor, who called an ambulance. I stood silently on the landing as two men manhandled my father past me on a stretcher.

'Where are you taking me?' Dad asked them, his eyes fearful.

'To a lovely hotel, Ernie,' one of the ambulance men replied, giving his colleague a conspiratorial wink.

I was furious. How dare they talk to my father as if he were stupid! I wanted to push them down the stairs and out of the house.

Visiting the hospital over the next few days wasn't at all as I'd imagined it would be. When we got there we had to sit quietly at the side of the bed while Mum gently woke my father. Sometimes he would recognize us but often he didn't. The doctors said he'd suffered a blood clot on the brain during the operation. Only once did he seem to know who I was. He looked at me, turned to my mum and said, 'The baby's too skinny. She's doing too much dancing.'

He never called me baby again.

When Auntie Ivy came up from Southampton with her husband Len and daughter Anne, I knew things were serious. A week later, on 8 July 1953, my father died. We didn't have a telephone but they somehow sent word from the hospital. He had a type of cancer known as Hodgkin's disease, the doctors told my mother, although it didn't really matter that it had a name. His death certificate also cited cerebral haemorrhage as a secondary cause of death.

Dad did come home then, but in a wooden coffin that rested on trestles in the middle of the living room so that friends and family could pay their respects. I was terrified of that open box with the white gauze cloth draped loosely over my father's frozen expression. I was only fourteen years old; I'd never seen a dead body before. The room had a sweet, sickly smell, which I suppose was to mask the formaldehyde. All I knew was that the cloying scent stuck to the back of my throat.

For three days, people came and went. Whenever I was summoned by my mother to say hello to our guests, I would creep in and cling to the walls, walking around the edge of the room and averting my gaze. My mother finally asked me, 'Why won't you look at your father, Pauline?'

I hesitated before whispering, 'I'm frightened.'

Mum sat me down. 'He never hurt you when he was alive,' she told me, 'and he certainly won't hurt you now that he's dead.'

Dad had been a choirboy at St Mary's in Handbridge, so his funeral was held there. Mum bought me a lovely new skirt and top and everyone kept hugging me and creasing it. The church was filled with flowers and people, including fellow Marines and colleagues from the BICC factory where Dad had worked. The vicar, who'd known my father as a boy, said that he'd been an excellent footballer, a model member of the community and a good family man. My mum was more upset than I had ever seen her and kept dabbing her eyes behind her spectacles with a white lace handkerchief. I didn't know what to do to stop her crying. Peter was as white as a sheet and didn't say a word.

Dad was buried in the family plot at Blacon on the other side of Chester. As I watched clods of earth shovelled on to the lid of his coffin, I thought to myself, Well, he was forty. That's *really* old.

Going home to an empty house felt stranger still. No more coffin; no more sickly smell. People didn't come to pay their respects any more and it was just the three of us with no Dad bursting in from work to put on a record, roll back the carpet and pull my mother or me into a laughing waltz. It was peculiar going back to school without even Peter for company. I was the only child who'd lost a father in my class and that made me feel very different – older, I guess, and more lonely.

My mother had one really good black-and-white photograph of my dad, which she cherished. A few weeks after he died, she took me with her to Will R. Rose's, a famous photographer's studio in Chester. 'I'd like this hand-coloured and enlarged, please,' she told the man behind the counter, handing him the precious photo.

'Certainly, madam,' he said, studying the picture of my smiling dad. 'Tell me, what colour are his eyes?'

My mother faltered. 'He had the most beautiful blue eyes …' she said, trying to hold herself together. After that, she couldn't say another word.

Two

I THINK WHAT SAVED ME DURING THOSE FIRST FEW WEEKS AFTER MY FATHER died was my dancing. By practising daily and trying to ignore the pain in my heart, I managed to work my way to the top of my tap class and was all set to try for a silver medal. I already had my bronze, which was my pride and joy. I kept it in a special place in my bedroom, touching it like a talisman whenever I passed it.

Then one day my mother broke some bad news. 'I'm so sorry, Pauline,' she said, 'but you'll have to give up your classes. I can't afford them any more.' I knew that money had been tight since Dad had died and that luxuries were out of the question but nothing much else had changed; we still had a lamb roast every Sunday and it hadn't occurred to me that my dancing might have to stop. I was devastated but, looking at my mother's expression, I could tell that she had no choice.

Instead of tip-tapping my way through dance classes after school, I turned my feet in the direction of a house in Queen's Park, just over the suspension bridge in Chester, where Mum now worked as a cleaner. Wandering through the lofty rooms of that beautiful red-brick Georgian house, its silver and brass gleaming from all her polishing, I'd wonder what it would feel like to own such a place. Not that I ever imagined I would. I reckoned I'd probably stay in our little terraced home for the rest of my days, taking care of my mum and helping her pay the bills. I hated that she had to work so hard. As well as cleaning, she had a full-time job at the Ideal Laundry in Boughton Heath, which rented out linens to big hotels and restaurants. She operated the hot iron press and came home smelling of starch.

Peter, at sixteen, was now the head of our household. Still just a boy but trying to be a man, he took his responsibilities very seriously. My father had always teased him that he was 'the brainy one' and would never end up getting his hands dirty. Once Dad died though, Peter left school and went to work at the same factory, albeit behind a desk as a trainee in the sales department. The personnel welfare officer who'd offered him the job had been one of those who'd come to the house to pay his respects when Dad died.

Within just a few months of starting his first job, though, Peter started to lose weight and became quite poorly. He went to the doctor on several occasions but, as with Dad, no one seemed able to help. By the time he finally went to see a specialist, it was discovered that he had pleurisy and his lungs were filling with fluid. He was rushed to hospital and ended up in the same ward Dad had been in. My poor mother must have feared the worst. Peter's pleurisy then developed into tuberculosis and the doctors warned my mother that he'd 'outgrown his strength'.

Peter was sent away to the three-hundred-bed Cheshire Joint Sanatorium at Loggerheads in Staffordshire, where he remained on a 'fresh air and rest' cure for the next eighteen months. Every Sunday, Mum and I would take the bus all the way out to beyond Market Drayton to take him magazines, fruit and a fresh pair of pyjamas. He was very poorly, and so pale. TB was a killer in those days and was treated very seriously.

The nurses gave Peter enormous pills to swallow, as big as an old penny. Only one visitor was allowed into his room at a time, so Mum and I would take turns. Later, the nurses would wheel his bed out into the fresh air to help improve his breathing. All wrapped up in blankets over his striped pyjamas and dressing gown, he virtually had to sleep in the grounds overnight, so convinced were they of the benefits of oxygen. Mum and I would stay for an hour or so before making the long journey home to a house that felt emptier still.

I knew the day was looming when I'd have to leave school too and decide how to earn my keep. Because I was good with my hands I often made my own clothes. Dad had bought me a sewing machine a year or so before, although when he tried to mend his overalls on it once he'd broken it. Maybe I could become a dressmaker or work in a ladies'wear shop? My interest in fashion probably came from all the classic films I'd watched as a child. My parents had both been dapper and I loved dressing up in Mum's clothes, especially her hats.

There was a wonderful hat shop in Chester run by a lady called Mary Jordan. It was in the Rows, a sort of medieval shopping mall that I used to skip down as a child. The Hollywood actress Margaret Lockwood, star of *The Wicked Lady*, used to go there to have hats specially made for her. That really impressed me: a big star like her coming to our town. I dreamed of working in Mary Jordan's, making hats for film stars like Joan Collins, Audrey Hepburn or Jean Simmons. When I learned that the shop was offering an apprenticeship I wanted it with all my heart but another girl from my school was offered it so my chance was lost.

Disappointed, I heard from a school friend called Norma Hignett that a big new development was about to open in Chester as part of the

Lewis group, which owned the famous Bon Marché department store in Liverpool. There'd be a shop, a restaurant, a jazz club, a bar, dance floor and a hairdressing salon, all under the name Quaintways.

'They've got vacancies for trainee hairdressers,' Norma told me. 'You don't need any experience; I've been taken on already. The salon opens in a week. If you like, I'll see if I can get you in.'

Hairdressing, I concluded bravely, was fashion too. After all, film stars had to have good hair as well as fancy clothes. With Norma's help, I applied for a job at Quaintways and was signed up for a three-year apprenticeship with a starting salary of three pounds a week. I'd begin as a trainee learning how to wash hair and give manicures before moving up to the position of 'improver'. By the end of five years, I'd be a fully qualified hairdresser and manicurist with my own clients and the chance to make up my income with tips. Aged fifteen, I left school on the Friday afternoon and started work when Quaintways opened the following Monday morning. I could tell my mother was relieved. Although our house was like a new pin and she always kept a good table, she was undoubtedly struggling without my father's weekly pay packet and mine, though small, would make a difference.

On my first day at work I wore a skirt I'd made myself from a favourite Vogue pattern. Conscious of being so thin, I'd added layers of petticoats underneath to make it a dirndl skirt, which I hoped would make me look shapelier than I really was. To hide my overly long neck, I wore a high-necked polo sweater. The whole look was finished off with a little waspie belt and flat shoes. Oh, and a matching umbrella cover: I made one for all my outfits and they became my trademark.

I arrived at the salon on opening day with the ten other juniors who'd been taken on. We were all given pink overalls to wear and I slipped mine on. Because my skirt stuck out so much, the overall rode up and didn't cover anything. Miss Jones, the manageress of the salon, laughed. 'You'll never get near the wash basin,' she told me. 'You'll have to take off your skirt.' I was horrified. I knew that wearing the skimpy overall on its own would make me look thinner still but I had no choice. The next day I made sure to wear a less bulky outfit.

Try as I might, I couldn't gain weight. The film stars I most admired had curves in all the right places, none of which I possessed, although I did at least have a bust. Mum had already taken me to see the doctor about it. After examining me, he asked how much I ate. 'Like a horse,' my mother replied, which was true.

'Please, doctor,' I asked him, 'how can I get bigger?'

'Take more exercise,' was his reply. Mum and I looked at each other in disbelief. I had never stopped dancing and even after I'd had to give up my classes I kept practising at home. When my mother told the doctor this, he shrugged his shoulders. 'Being skinny must be in her genes,' was all he could suggest. It was just as I feared; I was a hopeless case.

Not long after I joined Quaintways, something happened that completely took my mind off gaining weight. I was told I had a telephone call at the salon, which shocked me. We'd never had a telephone at home and I'd hardly ever used one. Taking the unfamiliar receiver I listened as a woman from the Ideal Laundry told me that my mother had been taken to hospital after an accident at work. I threw off my overall and hurried across town to the same Chester City Hospital where my father had died and where Peter had first been admitted for pleurisy.

My mother's left hand was heavily bandaged and she was in a great deal of pain. She'd been working on the double press, smoothing down the sheets and tablecloths while another woman stood by operating the floor pedal which brought the hot iron thumping down. On this particular day, her colleague wasn't paying attention and she accidentally hit the pedal while Mum's hand was still smoothing under the iron. When they managed to extricate her hand from the machinery, her wedding and engagement rings were so flattened and embedded into her flesh that they had to be cut off. Her fingers were horribly disfigured and burned down to the bone. She was told that she'd have to endure a series of grafting operations, using skin taken from her thigh.

My great-aunt Mabel and my cousin Rita, who lived next door, helped look after me while Mum underwent her operations. Rita took me shopping or to the pictures, but I still remember feeling terribly lonely. My father was dead; Peter and my mother were both in and out of hospital. I couldn't help but feel abandoned.

Mum had trouble with her left hand for the rest of her life and was never able to do manual labour again. She eventually received compensation from the company after a drawn-out legal process. They didn't award her a huge amount, considering how disfigured her hand was, but it certainly seemed enormous to us. She took me into Liverpool on the train and bought me a beautiful fuchsia-coloured coat with a fur collar, which I kept for years. She bought herself and Peter something special too, and then put the rest of the money away. As soon as her hand was mended, she took a job behind the counter in Woolworths in Chester where she was brilliant at dealing with people. From there she went to work in a shop that sold raincoats and umbrellas. The manager couldn't believe she'd ever been a manual labourer because she was such a stylish little lady who could speak to anybody. My mother wasn't a snob, though. She'd take any work as long as it paid.

At around the same time as my mother was recovering from her accident, she began dating a local man called Harry Dawson, who was an inspector on the buses. I knew his two daughters Pat and Shirley from my dancing days. Harry was a widower and a lovely man. Although it had been not much more than a year since my father had died, I was happy that she had someone to share her life with, especially during such a difficult time. After all, she was only in her late thirties.

Everyone else around me seemed to have new interests too. Once Peter was discharged from the sanatorium after eighteen months, he was transferred to the Wrenbury Hall Rehabilitation Centre near Nantwich. Under the care of the Red Cross, he gradually gathered his strength although the TB had weakened him terribly and he would spend another thirteen months recovering. He was placed on the Disabled Persons Register until he was twenty-one.

Joyce, my childhood friend, got engaged to her future husband Peter and moved to Ellesmere Port and we lost touch for a while. I became friendlier with her sister Barbara, but then she found herself a regular boyfriend as well. I didn't realize it at the time but my loneliness and the feeling that life was happening to everyone else but me made me vulnerable.

At least I had my job, which I loved, although most of the girls at work had busy social lives too. The other juniors especially became like a second family to me. From day one, we were 'the Quaintways Girls' and I became known to all as 'Tilly' Tilston, a nickname which stuck for life.

Quaintways soon became the place to go in Chester and ours was the premier salon. With a food shop, restaurant and nightclub, it felt more like a luxurious social club than a place of work. We even put on little modelling shows after hours for customers with each of us wearing a new outfit chosen from the store. The Quaintways restaurant was very popular, as was the Wall City Jazz Club run by a man called Gordon Vickers, who became a lifelong friend. He booked acts like the clarinettist Monty Sunshine and the Chris Barber Band. When one new group from Liverpool asked if they could play at the club, Gordon told them they could only if they cut their hair. The Beatles refused.

Several of the senior hairdressers who'd been brought into Quaintways from all over the country had famous clients like the singers Alma Cogan, Rosemary Squires, and Dickie Valentine, who'd come to Chester to sing at the Plantation Inn on the Liverpool Road. Through them, the hairdressers were often invited to the Oulton Park race circuit to attend parties with Stirling Moss, Mike Hawthorn and other famous drivers. There was even glamour among some of my fellow juniors too. One called Trish Fields had a fabulous voice and was a part-time singer at the Cavern Club in Liverpool, taking her turn between bands like the Swinging Blue Jeans and those rebellious kids who wouldn't cut their hair.

The older women in the salon seemed so grown up and worldly-wise to me. They dated everyone from sporting heroes to servicemen; they drank, smoked and stayed out late. I used to listen to some of their whispered conversations and wonder what on earth they were giggling about. My mother had never spoken to me about being intimate with a boy and there had never been any sex education at school. Because Peter had been in hospital throughout my teenage years I'd not had a big brother to advise me and I'd never even had a boyfriend, apart from one nice lad who lived across the street and who sometimes took me to the church hall dance. I'd had a silly crush on another boy at school who sometimes let me ride on the crossbar of his bicycle but it had never gone beyond holding hands.

One hairdresser in particular often spoke to me about the airmen she dated from the USAF bases nearby at Sealand, Queensferry and Warrington. 'The Americans are great company,' she'd tell me during breaks. 'They love to dance and they really know how to treat a girl. Why don't I fix you up on a blind date, Tilly?'

I resisted at first, feeling shy and awkward, but the more she spoke about her 'lovely Americans' the more I thought back to the party I'd attended that first Christmas after Dad died. The airmen there had been so charming and kind. Where would be the harm? Eventually, I plucked up the courage to ask Mum if she thought it would be all right.

'OK,' she said as she was getting ready to go out with Harry one night, 'but make sure you're back by ten.'

My friend originally set me up with an airman called Joe but he was sent back to the States so I ended up with someone I'll call 'Jim'. He'd just turned twenty-one and I was not quite sixteen when we first met. He knew how old I was but what he probably didn't realize was that I'd never even been kissed. He took me to the Odeon in Chester to see a film called *Johnny Dark* in which Tony Curtis played an engineer who'd designed a racing car. I don't remember much about the film because I was too excited by the company I was keeping. At six feet two inches tall with smouldering good looks, Jim was quiet, courteous and kind. Better still, he was a singer of country and western songs and he played in the clubs and bars on the American bases. He sang to me on the way home and had a really lovely voice, a bit like Jim Reeves. I was convinced my music-loving father would have approved.

For the next six months I was in a whirl. My lonely days were at an end. Jim was just like a film star, and he was mine. I thought about him night and day and the feeling appeared to be mutual. When we weren't together he'd call me up on the telephone and sing to me down the line, which made my knees buckle. He took me to a dance at one of the bases to meet some of his friends. They were all much older and more sophisticated than me but with Jim on my arm I felt invincible. I wasn't 'Tilly' to Jim, I was his 'Paula' – the name he always used for me – and I suddenly felt so grown up.

He'd meet me in Chester after work and walk me home. More often than not, my mother would be out working or courting Harry so we'd have the place to ourselves. I'd play house – cooking him a meal and making him tea and imagining what life would be like if this was how it always was. I even presented him with my most precious possession – my bronze medal for tap dancing. He said he was thrilled. When he held me in his arms and told me he wanted to marry me, I believed him completely and gave him all that he asked. In my heart, I was still a little girl and he was my first love. I barely knew what I was doing, although I did know it was naughty and that if my mother ever found out she'd be furious. Nobody had ever told me about taking precautions and Jim never said anything, so I carried on obliviously.

All I could think about was that Jim was going to marry me. Excitedly, I blurted out the news to my mother. She was my best friend in the world and I couldn't wait for her to share my joy. Her reaction wasn't at all what I expected. 'You're far too young to think about marriage yet!' she told me, horrified. Although I was disappointed, I was too blind to take any notice.

Then one day she sat me down after work. 'I think you should know: Jim's married already,' she said. I looked up at her in disbelief. 'Harry's sister-in-law works at the base. She found out.'

I was shattered. I couldn't believe what she was telling me, although I knew she'd never lie. A day or two later, my mother summoned Jim to the house to confront him. I had never seen her so angry. All five feet of her stood up to his lanky frame and she dominated the room. I just sat there, crying and trying to take it all in.

His response relieved me enormously. 'Yes, I have a wife, ma'am,' he told her, looking genuinely contrite, 'but I'm getting a divorce.' He pulled out a photograph of a baby daughter he'd also never mentioned. My head was in a spin. I didn't know what to think, but then he told my mother, 'I love Paula, Mrs Tilston, and I want to marry her. I'm going home to arrange the divorce and then I'll send for her.'

Having veered from shock to despair, I was on cloud nine once more.

Mum wasn't at all happy but she knew how strongly I felt about Jim so she reluctantly agreed that I could carry on seeing him until he left for America. I pined for the end of each day when I'd be seeing him after work. Although I dreaded him leaving the country, I couldn't wait to join him and would lie awake at night imagining what our life together would be like across the Atlantic. He told me that we'd be living on a military airbase to begin with and he tried to prepare me for what to expect. He said I'd have to go to a special school to learn about American culture for my citizenship exams. I told the girls in the salon all about it and we chattered excitedly about me moving abroad. Secretly, I was terrified by the idea. I'd never lived anywhere but Chester; I'd not even been to London, and I hadn't ever flown in an aeroplane. But as long as Jim was waiting for me, I knew I could do it – even if it meant leaving everything and everyone that I'd ever known.

I planned our romantic farewell over and over in my mind. I imagined myself tearfully waving him off at the train station or kissing him goodbye at the gates to the airbase. The fairytale ending I'd dreamed of crumbled to dust when he called me late one night to tell me he'd be flying home early the following morning.

'My leave's been cancelled,' he said. 'There'll be no time to say goodbye.' He gave me the forwarding address of his new base and promised to write soon.

I placed the telephone back in its cradle and burst into shuddering tears. At least he had my tap-dancing medal as his talisman but it was all so sudden. I could hardly believe that in a few hours' time my Jim, the love of my life, would be flying away from me.

Three

I'D HAD SUCH AN EMOTIONAL FEW MONTHS THAT I FELT PHYSICALLY AND mentally drained. It seemed that everything that could have happened to me in my life had happened in that very short space of time. Well, almost everything.

When my period was late that month, I honestly didn't think anything about it. I'd not been eating well and I'd hardly been sleeping. I told myself the distress I'd been suffering was bound to have an effect on my body. But as the days passed and nothing happened, I began to grow more fearful, terrified of what this might really mean.

Four months after my sixteenth birthday in February 1955, I finally summoned up the courage to blurt out the news to my mother. The look on her face will remain with me for ever. 'But, Pauline!' she cried. 'What are you telling me? My God, you're just a child yourself. Your body isn't even fully developed yet!'

I sat at the kitchen table, my arms wrapped around me as she scolded me, her voice rising with shock and anger. By the end of that night she was too upset for me and too angry at Jim to fight any more and we were both too exhausted to try. The following morning, she hugged me and took me to the doctor's surgery where I'm certain she hoped he'd tell her I was mistaken. When he confirmed her worst fears, I'm sure she secretly hoped he'd tell me how to get rid of the baby I was carrying, but doctors didn't do that sort of thing back then.

The thought of an abortion never even crossed my mind. This was my baby. I loved its father with all my teenage heart. He was going to marry me and we'd live happily ever after in America. Of course I was going to keep it. I was so shocked when, on the way home from the surgery, Mum turned to me on the bus and said, 'You won't be able to bring the baby home, you know. I'm working. You're working. Peter's in hospital. There's no one to look after it. How can we possibly give this baby the home it deserves?'

I knew she was upset and decided that she just needed time to get used to the idea. As far as I was concerned I had little reason to worry. The minute Jim found out I was pregnant, I was certain he'd hurry through his divorce, send for me, and we'd be wed before the baby was born. Even if there was a delay, it wasn't unheard of for women to become pregnant out of wedlock in Chester. There had been a couple of examples very close to home. A girl across the road from where we lived had a baby by a local boy when she was young and had married the father so they could raise the child together. My next-door neighbour became pregnant in her early twenties by an American long before I'd even met Jim. She didn't marry her airman or move to the States, but she kept her daughter nonetheless.

I wrote to Jim straight away at the address he'd given me, telling him my momentous news. *I'm going to have our baby*, I wrote, choosing my words carefully. *I hope you're as happy as I am.* Every morning in the days and weeks that followed, I watched and waited for the postman to bring me a blue airmail envelope, a postcard, anything ... but nothing came. The daily disappointment made me feel even sicker to my stomach.

After a while, my mother decided to take matters into her own hands. Taking Harry along for moral support, she made an appointment with one of the senior officers at the airbase where Jim had taken me to the dance and demanded to know his whereabouts.

'We have no airman here by that name,' the officer told her blankly. 'We never have had.' Even my indomitable little mother could do nothing against the immovable might of the United States Air Force.

I refused to lose heart and continued to believe that Jim would write any day or, better still, turn up on my mother's doorstep, his cap pushed to the back of his head the way it always was, with that huge grin on his face. There must have been a problem with his wife, I convinced myself. Maybe she was making things difficult? Maybe the USAF was? After all, they'd pretended he didn't even exist.

I'd lie on my bed in my room, playing the number one hit 'Unchained Melody' by Jimmy Young over and over on my little gramophone, hoping that somewhere across the Atlantic Jim might be listening to it too. *Time goes by so slowly and time can do so much. Are you still mine?* The words seemed to have been written specially for us.

The hardest part was going to work at the salon each day, my baby growing secretly inside me. The girls stopped asking if I'd heard from Jim. They could tell from my puffy eyes that I hadn't. They were kind and supportive but they left me alone. There was no more happy chatter about my new life in America or what sort of wedding dress might best suit my beanpole frame. I told no one about the baby and fortunately didn't really suffer from morning sickness so no one suspected. I covered myself up well, despite the fact that I was suddenly not quite so skinny any more.

Then one day, when I was about five months' pregnant and still holding myself in, Doreen 'Dors' Jones, my manageress, told me that the boss of Quaintways, Mr Guifreda, wanted to see me in his office. I'd never been summoned to see him before and I couldn't imagine what he might want. A Sicilian in charge of the restaurant, salon and just about every aspect of the enterprise, he was a kind and friendly man so I wasn't afraid, but I was a little nervous. When Miss Jones came into the office with me, closed the door and stood behind me, I felt my knees begin to tremble.

Mr Guifreda told me to take a seat. 'So, Tilly,' he began. 'Have you anything to tell me?' He gave me a gentle smile.

I looked at him.

I looked up at Miss Jones.

Then I looked down at my hands.

'You're pregnant, aren't you?'

His statement wasn't really a question and I began to cry.

Miss Jones placed a reassuring hand on my shoulder and passed me a handkerchief. Mr Guifreda looked almost as upset as I was. 'Now, now, don't cry,' he soothed, patting my hand. 'We'll take care of you. Everyone will.'

He was true to his word. From that day on, they all did. Within the hour, everyone knew about 'Tilly's baby' or 'the Quaintways' baby' as it was sometimes known. Bowls of nourishing soup were sent to me with the compliments of the chefs in the restaurant. Clearly, they thought I needed fattening up. The other girls in the salon made sure I didn't do too much or strain myself lifting anything. Most of the regular customers soon suspected and started to give me extra tips to buy 'something nice for the baby'. Everyone was so kind and took such special care of me. I couldn't have been in better hands.

* * *

Back home, the atmosphere was far more strained. My mother, who was a very proud woman and worried about the prying eyes of the neighbours, had been summoned to Quaintways by Mr Guifreda, who reassured her that my job would remain open for me. She thanked him but told me not to tell anyone else. Insisting that she was doing what was best for the baby, she contacted social services and the Church of England Children's Society. Between them, they arranged that when I was seven months' pregnant I would go to St Bridget's House of Mercy in Lache Park, beyond Handbridge.

I adored my mother but I pleaded with her to allow me to stay at home. 'Can't I have it here?' I begged. 'Then we can just look after it ourselves.'

'How?' she'd cry, shaking her head. 'Who'll look after it when we're both out at work all day? There's nobody but us here now and neither of us can afford to give up our jobs. You have to be sensible, Pauline. It would be cruel to the baby to do anything but this and they'll take better care of your baby than we could.'

There were no crèches in those days and, even if there had been, we couldn't have afforded one. I earned just over three pounds a week with tips and, although my mother earned a little more, every penny was spoken for. We had few relatives nearby and those we had were working too. Peter knew nothing of my pregnancy and was still at the rehabilitation centre. Nobody could help us.

I was assigned a social worker, a middle-aged Dutch lady called Mrs Cotter, who visited me regularly as the pregnancy progressed. 'You'll stay in the mother and baby home for three months after the birth and then the baby will be put up for adoption,' she told me. 'If suitable parents can't be found, it will be placed in a state nursery until they can.'

I watched the words fall from her mouth but I never really thought they would apply to me. Jim would be back by then, I kept telling myself, or, if for some terrible reason he wasn't, my mother would change her mind at the last minute and let me keep the baby. I was certain of it.

Still in denial, I didn't tell any of the girls at work what was happening. Nor did they ask. All they knew was that I was going away to a special home for the final months of my pregnancy. The worst part was telling Peter. He was finally well enough to come home for a weekend from the rehabilitation centre and Mum, who'd kept it all from him until then, broke the news. He was very upset and worried for me. I guess when he'd last been around I'd been a child. It was a shock for him to accept that I was old enough to have a child of my own. Happily, once he'd calmed down he finally became the big brother I'd always wanted, protective and kind whenever he was home from hospital. We have been close ever since.

As my time drew near the girls at work grew more and more excited. They clubbed together and raised enough money to buy me some maternity clothes. Miss Jones took me shopping to the posh department store Brown's of Chester and helped me choose three beautiful outfits, a pencil skirt that expanded at the top and some smock tops. 'You'll be the best-dressed girl there,' she told me with a hug.

The closer the date came to me going into St Bridget's, the more nervous I grew. I'd heard stories about those sorts of places: former convents where unmarried mothers were regarded as bad girls Up until now I had been treated with nothing but kindness. There had been little stigma to what I had done mainly because everyone knew I was a good girl. The story had gone round that the man who'd 'got me into trouble' was married and had then 'run away', which I guess protected me in many ways.

Having said my farewells to the Quaintways Girls, I packed a small suitcase and went with my mother to St Bridget's, a bus ride away. We hardly said a word on the journey, which was just as well because I could barely swallow. Mum just held my hand tightly the whole way. When we arrived, we found the place was more like a church than an institution. It had cloisters and was deathly quiet. Nuns padded silently by, heads down, in long black robes. I was terrified. We were led down a long corridor to the main office and if I hadn't been so pregnant I think I might have turned and run.

I needn't have worried. Mother Superior was warm and friendly as she welcomed me to St Bridget's and offered to show us both around. She led us into the kitchens first where I was relieved to find several pregnant girls, some much bigger than others, all smiling at me and waving shyly. I'd had no contact with any other pregnant women before and seeing one who looked as if she could have her baby any minute I stopped in my tracks. Oh my God! I thought, staring at her huge tummy. That'll soon be me!

Mother Superior then took us to the nursery, where crib after crib of newborns lay sleeping, closely supervised by nuns. It was like a room full of perfect baby dolls, their tiny hands and feet just like the gorgeous one I had at home. Then we were taken to the laundry where we found more pregnant girls ironing and folding sheets. My mother was impressed with how clean and neat everything was. As we were led along the cloisters towards the chapel I found myself shivering. There's bound to be a ghost here, I thought. I was almost more frightened of the ghosts at St Bridget's in those first few hours than of what might happen to me and my child.

When it was time for Mum to go, I could tell she was as upset as me. We hugged and said our goodbyes and she promised to visit every weekend. I dried my eyes as a nun led me to an upstairs dormitory and my metal-framed bed, one in a room of twelve. I was given a locker and began to unpack my case. Slipping into my new bright red pyjamas which did up to the neck, I felt a little embarrassed as fellow dorm-mates wandered in to introduce themselves and admire my clothes. They seemed terribly nice, though. There was no cattiness as I had feared and everyone was happy to help each other because we were all in the same boat. After a supper that was surprisingly good, we retired to the dorm until lights out when I lay shivering under my blanket as some of the girls told scary stories in the dark. 'There's definitely the ghost of a girl in the laundry,' one announced. 'Oh, yes, and several ghostly nuns who walk the cloisters at night!' piped another. I didn't sleep a wink.

Over the next few days, the other girls became curious about my story and I about theirs. Some, it seemed, had been too promiscuous and were paying the price. Others were the victims of sexual abuse, which horrified me. Two girls had been raped by their fathers. I had only ever known kindness and love from my dear old dad and I couldn't imagine what they had gone through. Strangely, though, they still defended the men who'd abused them. I found that even harder to understand. Most of the girls were relieved to be giving up their babies for adoption but a handful were taking their infants home to be cared for by their relatives, something I was still convinced would happen to me.

The nuns kept us busy, running and managing our own little kingdom. There were strict routines and everything was well organized. We went to chapel every morning and evening but we were never preached to and were mainly left to quiet prayer and contemplation. If we weren't washing, ironing or cooking, we were cleaning the walls and floors, but we didn't really mind and soon got into the swing of things. I liked working in the kitchen best. The cook was a lovely woman who used to tell us to strain the cabbage water and drink it for the extra iron. Her food was good and wholesome. It reminded me of my mother's cooking, and we all gained weight as our babies thrived.

There were six nuns under Mother Superior, each in charge of a dorm. Sister Joan Augustine was in charge of mine but for some reason she didn't take to me. I think it was because I had more visitors than most. My mother came every weekend, often taking me out to the pictures, but Miss Jones and some of the girls from Quaintways would sometimes come too, always fussing me and bringing me nice things. Sister Joan Augustine clearly thought I was rather spoiled, especially as I kept going back and forth to the laundry to wash and iron my new clothes, determined as always to look my best.

When she showed us the cream and grey Silver Cross pram that had been donated to the home as a Christmas present and told us that the first baby born in our dorm would receive it, my heart sang. Looking around the room, I knew that there were two other girls as close to giving birth as me and I prayed I'd be the first. I was due at the end of December but I knew babies sometimes came early and I did all I could to make that happen. I even volunteered for floor-scrubbing duties, thinking of what Sister Joan Augustine had told us when we were on our hands and knees with a scrubbing brush and Vim. 'This helps get the baby's head into position,' she'd insisted.

Beyond the former convent walls, life went on as usual. The American film star James Dean had just been killed in a car crash. Princess Margaret had announced that she wouldn't be marrying Group Captain Peter Townsend. People who could afford televisions were able to watch a new commercial channel called ITV with its advertisements for soap powder between festive programmes. For us, Christmas came and went, and none of our babies showed any signs of arriving. On New Year's Eve, I took part in a little show we put on for each other as we counted in 1956. Even though I was so heavily pregnant, I did a full Fred Astaire tap-dance routine that had been one of my dad's favourites in the hope that it might bring something on. As midnight struck and the most momentous year of my life drew to a close, we were each handed a mug of celebratory cocoa.

I couldn't help but wonder what the New Year would bring. It was less than three years since I'd lost my father and in that time my brother had almost died and my mother had suffered terribly with her hand. It was two months before my seventeenth birthday; I was still so young, physically and emotionally. I had no idea what to expect in the coming days and months and instead of dwelling on how painful the birth might be or how I might cope afterwards, I could only focus on beating the other girls in my dorm to win my prize.

It was the early hours of 2 January and I was lying in bed when my waters suddenly broke, drenching my nightdress and the sheets. My immediate reaction was one of elation. 'This is it! I'm going to get the pram!'

Then the pain began.

Hearing my cries, one of the girls ran to get Sister Joan Augustine, who called an ambulance. She came with me to Chester City Hospital, the place to which my family's fates seemed inextricably entwined. The contractions were getting stronger and stronger and I'd never known pain like it. With only the nun who least liked me for company, I lay on a bed in the labour ward feeling so frightened I thought I might die.

I longed for my mother through wave after wave of contractions, but I tried to be brave. The sisters had explained what would happen during the birth but none of what they'd told us prepared me for the reality. Someone clamped a rubber mask over my face for gas and air but it reminded me of the Mickey Mouse gas mask I'd had during the war and I began to panic. The gas it pumped only made me feel more nauseous. As I retched and writhed, I tried not to engage in eye contact with the doctor and at least six nurses around me. My ankles were tied with bandages to metal poles at the end of the bed. I'd always been such a shy and private person. I had only ever shown myself to one man. Now everyone was seeing everything – and there was so much blood.

'It's a big baby but you're doing really well,' the doctor told me encouragingly. 'Push when I tell you.'

There was no anaesthetic, no epidural. The pain was excruciating and became worse and worse as the hours progressed. Where was my mum? Where was Jim? He should have been there, waiting in the corridor outside for our son or daughter to be born. I wept with pain and bitterness.

At seven in the morning, my eight-pound baby boy finally pushed his way out into this world. He was a little jaundiced and covered in blood but they laid him on my chest straight away. Completely overwhelmed, more exhausted than I had ever felt in my life, I cradled his warm body in my arms.

'Congratulations, Pauline,' one of the nurses said. 'What are you going to call him?'

'Timothy Paul ...' I gasped, barely able to speak.

Unfurling Timothy's perfect little fingers until they curled around one of mine, I looked down at my baby boy and splashed his face with tears of joy and sorrow.

Four

THE FIRST TIME MY MOTHER SET EYES ON TIMOTHY PAUL, HER REACTION was exactly what I'd hoped it would be. 'Oh, he's beautiful!' she cried when she came to visit. 'Here, I bought these for him.' From out of her handbag came a lovely little set of clothes. 'I've been saving in a club. I got them from that shop at the end of the road.'

I could have cried with relief. She'd said her grandson was beautiful and she'd saved for some baby clothes. I knew it: she was going to let me bring him home after all. I didn't dare ask her there and then but the indications were good. Now that I'd had Timothy Paul, now that I'd held him and nursed my beautiful boy, I couldn't possibly give him up.

Mum came to see me when she could after work in the week I remained in hospital with Timothy Paul but she was often delayed. Every night at visiting time, I used to slide down the bed and pretend to be asleep until she got there. I was the youngest in a ward of twenty women and the only one who wasn't married. Through half-closed eyes, I'd spy husbands fussing over their wives and couldn't help but feel sad. I wished with all my sixteen-year-old heart that Jim would stroll into the ward just like the other men, laden with flowers and beaming with pride. I wrote to him again to tell him that he had a son. My mother contacted his base with the same news, but still there was no word.

When she registered my son's birth for me at the council offices, her voice must have wavered as she told the registrar to put down his father as 'US airman' but Timothy Paul's surname as 'Tilston'.

After a week, I was returned to St Bridget's. It was good to be back in what felt like my safe haven and to show off my gorgeous baby to the other girls. Thrilled at having beaten the two who'd had their babies after mine, I couldn't wait to be presented with the beautiful new Silver Cross pram Sister Joan Augustine had promised. That gleaming buggy had been the one goal my childish mind had focused on. It was all my missed Christmas and birthday presents rolled into one. Whatever the future held for me and my baby – and I knew it would be a struggle – I wanted him to have that pram at least.

Sister Joan Augustine told me then that she'd given the pram to someone else: a tall girl called Mary who'd given birth a day after me but who'd come back to St Bridget's earlier. 'Hers was the first baby back from hospital,' she said. Instead she presented me with a shabby little second-hand pram with wobbly wheels and dodgy brakes. I wept buckets over her decision. I immediately hated the horrid pram I was given; I loathed it even more when I came out to where I'd parked Timothy Paul in it one afternoon only to find the wind had blown it down a slope in the garden. One more inch and my precious baby boy might have been tipped over a verge.

My happiest times in those first few months were those spent with my son. As was the routine, all new mothers would wash our babies together and then sit in a row to feed them. Timothy Paul, dressed in the clothes my mother bought for him, clearly loved that moment best because he'd be so contented at my breast that he'd fall asleep and take longer to finish than the rest.

'Tilly, you're always the last,' Sister Joan Augustine would complain. I certainly made a fuss of my baby, and my fussing seemed to upset her routine, but I didn't care. I was growing increasingly attached to Timothy Paul and was determined to squeeze in every extra minute with him that I could. My stubborn streak cut in and I'd insist that he be allowed to finish at his own pace.

Every week I'd be summoned to Mother Superior's office to discuss the future of my baby. 'Now, Pauline, have you decided for adoption or will you be taking your baby home?' she'd ask, peering at me over her spectacles.

Mrs Cotter, my social worker, would often be there, along with Sister Joan Augustine. 'Your mother says neither of you can look after the baby,' my social worker would remind me. 'There are plenty of childless couples who'd give him a better life.'

Sister Joan Augustine would add, 'You must make the decision now before he gets too old.'

I'd sit on my hands and shake my head. 'I just need more time,' I'd tell them. 'You said I'd have three months. After that, we can look at other options. He can go into a nursery somewhere close by maybe? I could visit him every day until I've worked out what to do.'

They were clearly frustrated with me and did their best to persuade me otherwise but I stuck to my guns. Every time my mother came to visit it was the same story. I'd plead with her to help me find a solution but she'd just repeat that it would be cruel to Timothy Paul to try to keep him. 'Adoption is the only option,' she'd say firmly. There seemed to be no way to make her change her mind.

I was dreading the day when our three months would be up. I kept trying to put the date to the back of my mind. I hoped beyond hope that something would happen or that someone would save us. There was still no word from Jim. My mother was sick of me asking if there had been a letter or a call. 'You have to forget about him, Pauline,' she told me testily. 'He'll never send for you now.'

I had Timothy Paul christened in the chapel at St Bridget's, with my mother at my side. 'I name this child …' the vicar said, marking his forehead with the sign of the cross. Bless my tiny son, he didn't even cry. He just lay in my arms looking up at me with that placid expression of his, the one that said he trusted me to take care of him. I could have wept.

Three weeks before my deadline was up, Sister Joan Augustine suddenly announced that I had to stop breastfeeding and wean my baby on to bottles of formula milk. I looked at her in shock. 'B-but he's too little!' I protested.

'He'll be just as happy with a bottle, Tilly. Now, don't make a fuss.'

I wept as I fed him that bottle for the first time. It was a horrible day. This was one step closer to the time when I knew I wouldn't be able to see him every day, to change him and wash him, to cuddle him and feed him myself. He took to the bottle quite well but I never did. The next three weeks were a living agony.

As the date approached when I was due to leave St Bridget's and Timothy Paul would be sent to a nursery, I became increasingly anxious. Mrs Cotter came to see me one morning to tell me what arrangements had been made. 'The state will help you pay the nursery fees but the rest will have to come out of your wages, I'm afraid. We've found him a place. I'll come with you to settle him in tomorrow. We'll have to leave early to make the journey.'

'Journey? Why, where are you sending him?'

'The Ernest Bailey Residential Nursery for Boys. It's in Matlock.'

'Matlock?' I asked, my panic rising. 'Where's that?'

'Derbyshire.'

'But how far away is that?'

'About eighty miles.' Registering the look of shock on my face she added, more softly, 'It was the only place that could take him.'

'E-eighty miles?' I could hardly get my words out. 'That's too far! It'll take me a day to get there and how much will it cost each time?'

Her expression was as stiff as her resolve. This was her job: to figure out what was best for babies like Timothy Paul. He couldn't stay at St Bridget's. He couldn't come home with me. What else could she do? Shattered, I realized that I had no say in the matter. To this day, I don't know if that nursery really was the only one that would take Timothy Paul or whether the authorities chose to make it as difficult as possible for me to keep him. At the time, I must say, the decision felt unnecessarily harsh.

The following morning, I washed and dressed my son, fed him and wrapped him in a shawl. Walking to the railway station with Mrs Cotter, I realized that this was the first time I'd been outside the home with him since I'd brought him back from the hospital three months earlier. If it wasn't for the circumstances I would have been wildly happy: the proud young mum showing off her gorgeous baby boy to anyone who cared to notice. I wanted people to coo and sigh over him as I did. I'd look at other young girls and think they didn't yet know the joys of motherhood: the smell of him, the softness of his skin, the little gurgling noises he made in his mouth, the look of sleepy contentment in his eyes as he suckled at my breast. Then I remembered where I was and why. Sitting in the carriage, cradling him in my arms as I soothed him above the clickety-clack of the train, I stared at a dozing Mrs Cotter in the opposite seat and contemplated jumping off at the next station and running away.

But I was seventeen years old. I had no money; no home of my own. Where would I go? I was a good girl from a warm, loving family. How could I contemplate a life on the run? Tempting as it might seem, it wasn't an option. Instead, I did the only thing I could think of to let my son know how much I wanted him close to me. I told Mrs Cotter that from now on, I would like Timothy Paul to be known simply as 'Paul'.

'Why?' she asked.

'It will make him more personal to me – to my name,' I replied, pushing my forefinger into my son's open palm so that he clamped his own tiny fingers around it.

All the way to Matlock, I had been trying to convince myself that my son would be safe and warm there, fed and well cared for until I could figure out what to do next. When we walked into the imposing stone building, though, I recoiled against the idea of him being there at all. He wasn't a waif or stray. He was mine and he was dearly, besottedly loved.

Shivering, I laid him in a high-sided cot in a room full of similar cots and stepped back. Even though the staff seemed very nice and everybody was ready to welcome him, Paul took one look at my face and screwed his own into a tight ball. Somehow he knew that I was leaving him. I listened to his first howl and watched as he geared himself up for his second. Unable to bear the wrench of our impending separation a moment longer, I fled. I could hear his cries all the way down the street, my little-girl heart jolting with each step that took me further and further away from my son.

Paul was to remain in that nursery for the next two and a half years. As Mrs Cotter had assured me he would, he settled in well and the staff continued to be kind and understanding. I visited him whenever I could but the realities of my situation meant that was only every few months at best. His nursery fees were debited directly from my wages, leaving me with little spare. The train fare was expensive and near impossible on a Sunday. I had to take a day off work each time. The journey left me emotionally drained.

Each time I saw my son I couldn't get over how much he'd grown. He, meanwhile, seemed to be less and less aware of whom I was. After a while, he began to favour one of his young nursery nurses, which cut me to the quick. My mother, who came with me when she could, would walk alongside as I pushed Paul's pram through a local park, clearly loving every minute of being with her grandson. I always hoped that she'd come up with a plan on those visits; that she'd tell me she'd thought of something and we could take him home with us after all, but she never did. She just told me, time and again, that my visits were doing no good. 'You have to let him go, Pauline,' she'd say as I sobbed in her arms all the way home. 'This isn't fair on either of you.'

It was true that leaving him each time was a new wrench, but I just couldn't bring myself to give up my son. Foolishly perhaps, I was still hoping for something to come along and save us. Was it really too much to wish for?

Five

I WAS STANDING AT THE BUS STOP UNDER THE FAMOUS EASTGATE CLOCK IN Chester waiting to go home after a long day working at Quaintways. Having progressed to an improver in the salon by then, I'd been on my feet all day cutting and setting hair.

It was a fine evening and I checked my watch. The bus was late and so was I. Mum expected me home for supper at six. It was shepherd's pie. I was always amazed how she could eke out a pound of mince until the end of each week.

A voice at my elbow startled me. 'Hi there. It's Pauline, isn't it?'

I turned and found myself face to face with a man I knew only as the ex-boyfriend of a girl I worked with at Quaintways called Barbara Hill. He was a steward on the Cunard and White Star shipping lines, one of the young men known at the time as 'the Hollywood waiters' because they were all so well dressed and suntanned. To my surprise, Barbara, who looked like Kim Novak, had dumped him recently for an American airman called Harry.

I smiled shyly. I'd always thought this chap of Barbara's was rather nice. He was certainly very handsome and, although not very tall, he had the strong physique of a sportsman. I learned later that he was a prize-wining boxer among fellow stewards on the ships. It didn't surprise me.

He reminded me of Dirk Bogarde in *Doctor at Sea*. He had the same pleasant smile and gentle way about him.

Having recently dated a steward called Chris I knew that he and the boy at the bus stop had both just returned from a three-month voyage to New Zealand. As I turned to say hello I remembered his name. It was John – John Prescott.

'Hi, John,' I said brightly. 'You're back then?'

'Yes, we docked a few days ago.' He smiled and his suntan made his teeth look really white.

There was an awkward pause.

'I was so sorry to hear about you and Barbara,' I said, shaking my head.

'Oh, thanks, but that didn't matter,' he replied, stoically. 'I had another girlfriend in New Zealand anyway.' He paused. 'Are you still seeing Chris?'

'No. He found another girl. They're getting married.'

'So is Barbara. She's moving to the States.'

'Oh.' I stared down at my shoes, trying not to think what might have been.

'Do you fancy going to the pictures one night, then?'

I looked up. My mind raced ahead of itself. If John knew Barbara and he also knew Chris, whom I'd been introduced to through my cousin, then he probably knew my history and yet he was still asking me out. He was certainly smiling warmly enough.

'Yes, OK,' I replied, on a whim. My bus pulled up just as I spoke, so I opened my handbag and fumbled with my purse. Stepping on to the bottom step, I turned and smiled back at him.

'See you outside the Regal on Saturday night,' he called out as the bus pulled away. 'Seven o'clock?'

I gave him a little wave. His hand came up in a sort of salute and I couldn't help but laugh. All the way home, I hoped that he did know about Paul so that I wouldn't have to tell him. Not that I was ashamed – I was never ashamed of my son – but it was always a little awkward telling someone for the first time. John seemed a nice enough chap, though. I smiled at the thought of an evening in his company. I was eighteen years old. It would do me good to have a boyfriend again.

I'd always liked men in uniform, which probably stemmed back to seeing my dad in khaki during the war. The Cunard and White Star stewards not only had smart uniforms, they were especially sought after by all the girls in Liverpool and Chester for other reasons Having experienced the finest luxury the world's greatest cruise ships had to offer, they knew just how to treat a girl. They earned good money, especially on their longer voyages, and there was something terribly romantic about a man in a navy jacket and black bow tie sending you postcards and messages from around the world.

A few days later, John took me to the Regal to see a film I don't now recall a single thing about. My uncle Wilf, the husband of my father's sister Jane, was probably playing the organ as usual, rising out of the floor on the Wurlitzer, but I don't remember what he played. We sat quite near the front but after a few minutes he suggested we move to the back row. 'You're talking too loudly,' he said, which I'm sure was just a ruse.

I liked John right from the start. He was funny and he made me laugh. 'You remind me of someone famous, now who is it …?' he said.

'Elizabeth Taylor?' I asked hopefully, always flattered when the comparison was made.

'No – Joyce Grenfell!' he replied with a grin.

Chatting over a drink afterwards, I discovered quite a lot about him and what life was like at sea. He told me about one steward on their last voyage who'd kept them awake playing the guitar and singing all the time. His name was Tommy Steele. I learned of John's strong political convictions and his dedication to improving conditions at sea, even if it made him unpopular with his employers.

I was surprised to discover that John's father, a disabled railway signalman from Liverpool known as 'Bert', was a friend of my boss Mr Guifreda. John's mother Phyllis was a Quaintways client. I wondered if I knew her and that – if I did – whether she knew about Paul, too.

I found out soon enough because John took me home to meet her a week or so later. I recognized her straight away. She was a striking, terribly smart lady who was also a professional dressmaker and always wore the most beautiful clothes. I thought she was quite posh. Like my mother, she'd been in service. Like my parents, she and Bert had met by chance, although he'd spotted her on a railway platform instead of across a rooftop. We should have got on like a house on fire because of our common interests but straight away I picked up that Phyllis Prescott wasn't very keen on me. I could guess why. A short time afterwards, my fears were confirmed. Chatting to a neighbour of hers, Phyllis complained, 'My John's taken up with a young girl who's had a baby, you know. I'm sure he could do a lot better.'

'Oh, what's the girl's name?' the neighbour asked suspiciously.

'Pauline Tilston.'

Unbeknown to John's mum, the neighbour was my auntie Jane and she leapt to my defence. 'Pauline Tilston is my brother Ernie's daughter and she was brought up extremely well,' she told her, bristling. 'She's a good girl and John's lucky to have her.'

Despite once being a maid, Phyllis was always a bit of a snob, although she was proud of her social aspirations. She'd happily recount the story that her neighbours in Rotherham called her 'Lady Muck' because she had the cleanest house and the finest clothes. She had a Royal Albert tea service and wore Chanel perfume. It used to embarrass John how his mother would dress – or 'overdress', he'd say. He had a special aversion to her hats, especially the frothy 'jelly bag' ones that sat on top of her hair. 'She came to meet me one time with what looked like a pair of knickers on her head,' he complained. He's never liked hats since.

Having learned flower arranging, cake decorating and dressmaking to the best of her considerable ability, Phyllis entered her family into a national newspaper competition as the 'Most Typical Family in Britain'. Much to her indignation, they came second. Soon afterwards, Bert, who'd lost a leg at Dunkirk, received a grant from the British Legion to buy a new semi-detached house in Upton, which – once again – became the smartest in the street. A staunch socialist, a keen fundraiser for the Labour Party and a huge influence on John politically, Phyllis was a force of nature. Nobody would ever be good enough for her eldest son John. She hadn't dragged her family from Prestatyn via a Rotherham terrace with a lav in the yard and coal dumped in the alleyway for him to take up with a girl who'd had a baby out of wedlock.

Fortunately, John didn't share her view and after a while – perhaps because of Mr Guifreda singing my praises as well – his mother began to soften towards me. She offered to run me up a couple of nice outfits and was perfectly pleasant to me, even when her own marriage was in trouble.

As well as working on the railways, John's father Bert was a magistrate, Labour councillor and loveable rogue who'd had several affairs.

When John was just a lad, he'd spotted his father on the Chester Walls kissing a woman and was so shocked that he ran to the police station to report him. 'I want you to arrest my dad!' he told a sergeant on duty.

'Go home, son, and don't tell your mother,' the sergeant replied, ruffling the hair on his head. John always laughed when he told that story but he felt terribly let down and still does to this day.

Bert was a big man with a big personality; everyone knew him, this gigolo who never paid for anything and only ever took his family on holidays to places like Bridlington and Scarborough to a trade union conference or to bluff his way into the Labour Party conferences and get a free drink. Phyllis didn't seem to mind at first. Coming from a Welsh mining background, she was highly political too, hosting local Labour meetings in her home and delivering pamphlets all around the neighbourhood. In the end, though, politics was all they had in common.

Not long after we'd started dating, John's parents announced that they were getting divorced after twenty-five years of marriage, which was quite something in those days. After years of trying to keep the peace between them, John was the head of the family now and Phyllis came to rely on him ever more. She even asked him to be a witness in the divorce case between her and Bert, but he refused, not wanting to be disloyal to either parent. Maybe because she and I now shared a social stigma, we seemed to get on better after that, even if she was always rather controlling and extremely protective of her son to the end of her days.

My visits to see my son became more and more infrequent owing to my long working hours, my shortage of money and the time I was now spending with John. I found myself speaking of Paul less and less, which felt like a betrayal, but I never stopped thinking of him, and I repeatedly refused to sign him over to the state. Perhaps having cropped my hair for a more sophisticated gamine look gave me the courage to stand firm.

My widowed mother, who was still courting Harry, never stopped working and couldn't have helped me care for Paul even if she'd had the time or the energy. Harry worked full-time too and, even though he was a kind and generous man, wisely never tried to intervene. My brother Peter had emerged from his years in hospital and returned to work at BICC but had since moved to London to work in their overseas sales department. He'd write sometimes and send birthday presents but he'd never even set eyes on his nephew and Paul was never spoken about. I found myself thinking back to my father and wondering if things might have been different if he'd still been alive. Surely Dad would have found a way for us to keep his only grandchild?

Not long after I'd met John, I'd saved up enough money to go to Matlock again but my mother said she couldn't go with me. To be honest, I don't think she had the heart any more. She found it as upsetting as I did. I didn't want to go alone but couldn't think whom else to ask. Then I thought of John. The eldest of five children, John had a brother Ray, sisters Dawn and Vivian, and a little brother called Adrian who was born with a harelip and a cleft palate. I'd seen how kind and thoughtful he was with Adrian. He protected him and played with him so sweetly and that gladdened my heart. Nervously, I told John that I was going to see Paul and asked if he'd come along.

He didn't even flinch. 'We could make an outing of it,' he replied. 'There's some pretty countryside round Matlock.' He'd never once asked me about Paul's father or what had happened between us. He just said he knew all that he needed to know. Part of me would have dearly liked him to have bombarded me with questions. My time with Jim, the lonely pregnancy, being at St Bridget's, Paul's birth and everything that had happened afterwards had been virtually erased from my life. John's family certainly never brought it up. My mother rarely spoke of it and if I raised the subject, it only gave her an opportunity to tell me what I should do next. The girls at work no longer asked after Paul or what my plans for him were.

And so my innocent young son remained the elephant in the room that nobody dared discuss. Yet he was always on my mind and everywhere I looked there seemed to be reminders. John and I would often spend days off at Chester Zoo, and I'd see a mother and son wandering along holding hands and wonder why that couldn't be Paul and me. I'd flick through racks of clothes in the children's department of Brown's and wish I could afford to buy some of them for him. I marked each anniversary privately in my heart: the day I first met Jim; the day I found out I was pregnant; Paul's birthday on 2 January; the date I had to take him to Matlock and then leave.

There were times when I wanted to scream Paul's name from the bottom of my lungs and tell everyone who'd listen how much I loved and missed him and thought about him night and day. 'He's my son and I want to keep him!' I longed to shriek but instead I confined the screaming to inside my head.

Going to see Paul with John would be quite different from going with my mother. Ours was a new relationship and I knew I couldn't blub all the way there and back as I normally did. It was one of the hardest things I've ever had to do: hold myself together when I walked into the nursery and realized that Paul didn't know who I was any more. At two years old, he was wearing clothes I hadn't chosen for him and was playing with friends I'd never met. He was clearly very attached to one particular nursery nurse, and was calling her 'Mummy'. That broke my heart anew.

John must have picked up on how I was feeling because he was marvellous with Paul. He picked him up and cuddled him and cheerily suggested that we take him out for a walk. He bought Paul a lollipop from a sweetshop and didn't flinch when my happy-go-lucky, gorgeous little boy tried to force it into his mouth. He brought his camera and took lots of photographs, which are among my most cherished possessions: images of me and Paul, of John kissing Paul, and a few of Paul on his own, gurgling and laughing happily at these two kind strangers who had come to make a fuss of him for a few hours.

Travelling home on the train, I pressed my head against the cold glass of the window and fought back the tears. John sat next to me saying nothing. I was growing increasingly fond of this kind young man who seemed to accept me for who I was, regardless. I couldn't believe how gentle he'd been with my son. We were a long way off making a commitment to each other; we were both still young, John was away travelling much of the time, and I wasn't in a hurry to rush into anything again the way I had with Jim.

But could I – dare I – even dream that there might be a brighter future for Paul and me after all? That he and John and I might end up together as a family in the sort of happy home I'd grown up in, the kind I'd always dreamed of providing for my son? Turning and resting my head on John's shoulder, I squeezed his hand and let out a sigh.

* * *

Not long after that journey to Matlock, Mr Guifreda called me into his office and asked me to sit down. 'Dors' Jones had left Quaintways by then, to be replaced by Val Pyeman, who was just as nice and who sat in on the meeting too.

'Our managing director has heard of your problems … er, you know, with Paul,' Mr Guifreda told me hesitantly. 'He'd like to help.'

Like Mr Guifreda, the managing director of Lewis's was a real gentleman who cared for his staff and always took an interest in their welfare. I wondered what he could possibly do to help. A pay rise perhaps? A word with social services to get them to move Paul closer to Chester? I hardly dared hope.

'He'd like to adopt Paul,' Mr Guifreda said, as my heart skipped a beat.

'No!' I gave my knee-jerk reaction.

Mr Guifreda pressed on. 'He has three daughters and would love a son. He knows you want what's best for your boy, and he wants you to know that he and his wife would give Paul a marvellous life in the bosom of a loving and wealthy family.'

I shook my head. I didn't know what else to say. My mind was in turmoil. I'd resisted adoption for so long, why would I relent now? And why had the managing director waited all this time to ask? Had John's parents orchestrated this to get my Paul out of the way? After all, Nick Guifreda was a close friend of John's father. Then I had to remind myself that the managing director was a good man. For a moment, I allowed myself to speculate that if he did adopt Paul, he might let me stay in touch. I might even get to see more of him, being that much closer. Realizing that would be impractical and feeling like a rabbit caught in the headlights, I told Mr Guifreda that the answer was still no.

'Think it over. Talk to your mother. Remember,' he added with a smile, 'everyone just wants what's best for Tilly's baby.'

'Me too,' I said, shrugging my shoulders. The trouble was that – confused, isolated, and pressured from all sides – I didn't really know what the best for Paul might be.

I can't now remember how the Derbyshire hospital got in touch with me. I think I must have blanked that particular memory from my mind. But the news they gave me left an indelible mark. Paul was seriously ill. It was meningitis, they believed. I should go to him straight away.

John, who'd taken a job in a butcher's shop between voyages, kindly offered to take the day off and go with me to Matlock. I don't think I can have said a word the whole way there. I sat looking blinkingly out of the train window at the beautiful Peak District countryside thinking how ironic it would be if anything should happen to Paul now, just as I'd found the man I might end up sharing the rest of my life with.

Not that John didn't have his faults. I already knew that any relationship with him would have its highs and lows. He was extremely clever, a man of passion whose fervour for the unions and championing of the underdog I admired, having come from a strong working-class background myself. But with that passion went an inner insecurity and dark moods that I wasn't sure I could spend the rest of my life dealing with.

It was his sulks I dreaded the most: those awful long silences he'd retreat into when he was upset, usually about something quite trivial. Once he was in that mood, he wouldn't listen to a word I had to say. Then I had to remind myself that he always came round in the end, apologizing with flowers and surprises. And I was no longer a silly little girl with a crush. I'd matured a lot. I was more cautious and quite capable of my own moods, too. One night, when I'd made a special dinner for him at my mother's house, he came home so late from a strike march in Liverpool that the meal was ruined.

Pinned to my mother's front door John found a note which read: Darling/Dear (both scrubbed out), then: *John, so glad you're back from your march and you could make it. Well, I've just gone on a march so you can bloody wait for me.* I signed it, *Love, Pauline*, but scribbled out the word *Love* at the last minute. John still has it.

Another time, when he came in late I asked him what he wanted to eat. He replied, 'Just put a couple of eggs on the boil.' I filled a pan with cold water, turned on the heat, waited a few seconds and dropped the eggs in. 'You don't boil eggs like that!' John cried. 'You mustn't put them in until the water's boiled.'

I protested that my mother, who'd been a maid, had always told me that if I boiled them the way he said the eggs would burst. Shaking his head, John said, 'Well, you don't even know how boil an egg!' Within minutes two raw ones were cracked on his head, the yolks dribbling down his face.

Those silly spats all seemed meaningless as I headed towards Paul ill in a hospital bed. Meningitis. What was that exactly? It sounded so serious. What if he didn't recover? The closer we got to the hospital the more my head whirled with all sorts of wild notions.

By the time we reached the children's ward and were directed to the little bed where Paul lay, I was all but convinced that we'd be too late. It was such a relief to see him, even if he didn't seem as delighted to see me. He was sitting up in bed in his little hospital gown and we were even allowed to take him outside in the sunshine for some fresh air.

John had brought his camera along again and took some photos of me holding Paul in my arms.

When we brought him back to the ward, a doctor told us the results of his tests. 'It's not meningitis after all. He has a slight fever and we'll keep him in a couple of days for observation, but don't worry, he'll be fine.' I could have kissed him.

The hardest thing was leaving Paul alone in hospital that night. It was late and John and I both needed to be back in Chester for work the following morning. We had to leave straight away and catch the last train, though we'd still not be home until the early hours. I sat alongside my sleepy toddler and stroked his hair. I kissed his face with my tears as he looked silently up at me with those big blue eyes.

'Come on now,' John said, taking me by the elbow. 'You'll not do Paul any good wearing yourself out.'

Getting to my feet and gathering my things together, I took one last lingering look at my poorly little boy and blew him a kiss. 'Night, night, darling,' I said. 'Mummy will be back soon. I promise.'

Little did I know that it was a promise I would never keep.

Thankfully Paul recovered quite quickly. It was some sort of mild virus, the doctors thought, and would have no lasting effects. I planned to visit him once he was back at the nursery as soon as I could arrange time off work.

Then Mrs Cotter came to call. 'Paul can't go back to the Ernest Bailey Nursery, I'm afraid, Pauline,' she told me. 'They don't keep children for more than two years and he's already been there longer than anyone else. It would be in Paul's best interests if he was placed in foster care now.'

'But I never agreed to that!' I cried.

'This is what everybody thinks would be best for Paul. We've found a lovely couple in Wolverhampton who couldn't have children of their own. They're in their mid-forties. He's a deputy headmaster and she's a school nurse. What Paul needs now is the sort of one-to-one care only they can offer.'

'How long?' I asked.

'Until his next review,' she said. 'In a year.'

My stomach lurched. A year was such a long time in a child's life. He was already growing so fast. Would he even know me after all that time? 'Will I be able to see him?' I asked, afraid of the answer.

She hesitated. 'That wouldn't be advisable. He'd find it too unsettling, especially after his recent illness.'

Both Mrs Cotter and my mother were immovable. They had made the decision for me, it seemed. There was no viable alternative that I could offer Paul. In a year's time, maybe there would be. John had already been so kind. He knew how I felt about keeping Paul and if things developed between us as I hoped they would, then it went unspoken that the boy would end up living with us one day.

OK then, I reasoned, trying desperately to put a brave face on a helpless situation, this buys me a little more time. After all, a lot can happen in a year ...

Six

THE NEXT TWELVE MONTHS WERE PIVOTAL, NOT LEAST BECAUSE JOHN AND I were growing increasingly fond of each other. Ours hadn't been love at first sight as it had for my parents, but over time we came to care deeply for each other and it seemed more and more likely that we'd end up together.

John was still working on the ships, travelling back and forth to New York, mostly on the MV *Britannic*. He also went to Canada, the Middle East and South America on exotically named vessels like the *Franconia*, the *Amazon*, the *Corinthia*, the *Mauretania* and the *Saxonia*. He visited places I'd never even heard of like Auckland, Panama, Barcelona and Larnaca. Using a cine camera he'd bought in the United States he took footage of himself and his mates on the ships and on days off leaping among the giant stones of the Parthenon, on pleasure boats in Istanbul or walking European streets. More handsome than ever with his longer hair and fashionable sideburns, and wearing drainpipe jeans and winkle-picker shoes, he was quite the cosmopolitan man of the world. In New York, he became hooked on jazz and began to bring records back from around the world. I had already been switched on to jazz by my brother, so we now had something new in common. Whenever he returned from a trip, he'd rush home bearing gifts for everyone he knew and loved. He even brought an American washing machine back for his mother once, wheeling it all the way down Fifth Avenue to the ship, and having it rewired for her back in Britain.

Always so thoughtful, he'd arrange all sorts of surprises for me, not all of them entirely within the rules. He and his fellow stewards used to take turns to do 'firewatch' on the *Britannic*, which meant guarding the ship when she was in dock to make sure she came to no harm. A quick bribe to whomever was on duty meant that John could smuggle me on board to spend the evening with him in one of the ship's finest state rooms. It was highly irregular but, my-oh-my; we had a high old time in those luxury cabins.

He surprised me another time by announcing that he was taking me to London for the weekend. We'd see all the sights, he said, and he'd booked us a nice double room at the Strand Palace Hotel. I'd never been to London before and was very excited. I wanted to see Piccadilly Circus and Trafalgar Square and Buckingham Palace where, who knows, I might even spot the Queen. When John told my mother what he was planning, though, she imposed one condition. 'I want to see the hotel receipt,' she said. 'Two separate rooms, John. That's how it will be.' Poor John did as she'd asked which made the whole trip doubly expensive. Not that we ever used the second room. Exactly the same thing happened when he took me to the Isle of Man.

All seemed to be going well for us but not long after my nineteenth birthday I went down with a bad dose of the flu and was confined to bed. To my surprise, John turned up at my mother's house to see me. I decided I must be delirious. Wasn't he supposed to be in New York?

'I'm not here by choice, Paul,' he said. He'd always called me 'Paul', and I loved the endearment.

I dragged myself up on my pillows and stared at him.

'I've been sacked.'

'Why?' I mumbled, my head full of cold.

He grimaced. 'The air conditioning broke down and it was like a furnace below decks. I went to the captain to complain but he called me a troublemaker.'

I knew John had been pushing to get better trade union representation at sea and I knew that his political passions weren't popular with his employers, but beyond that, I didn't really understand. 'Don't worry, love,' I said, relieved his unexpected return wasn't because of anything more serious. 'I'm sure you'll find another passage soon. Anyway, I've still got my job.'

'Um, well, that's another thing,' he told me, looking awkward. 'While you've been here sick in bed, I'm afraid Quaintways has burned down. There was a fire overnight and the place was gutted.'

I couldn't believe what I was hearing. The temptation to slide back down the bed and hide under the sheets was enormous. Fortunately, Mr Guifreda and the managing director decided to keep all of the staff on, transferring us instead to the Lewis's salon in Liverpool for the six months that it would take to rebuild Quaintways. As soon as I was back on my feet I began commuting to Liverpool each morning with the rest of the staff, taking the eight o'clock train for the forty-five minute journey from Chester to Lime Street Station.

John, never a shirker, went back to the butcher's where he was always welcome between voyages. He also did a paper round. Each morning at ten past eight, when he knew my train would be pulling out of Chester, he'd stop on his round and wait in an alleyway between the rows of terraced houses that backed on to the railway line. I, in turn, would sit in the window on that side and wait for a glimpse of the man I knew I'd almost certainly marry. As the rest of the girls giggled and teased, I'd sit on the edge of my seat until the moment I saw him and then we'd wave madly and blow kisses to each other in the few seconds before each disappeared from view. It was such a romantic thing for him to do and made me think of my parents waving to each other across the rooftops.

After work, I'd walk from the station to the street where John worked and sit in a little café opposite sipping coffee. Watching and waiting, I'd stare and stare at the butcher's window until I saw John's hands reach down into the display, pick up a string of sausages and swing it madly from side to side. That was my cue to ask for my bill and it made me laugh every time. He'd be ten more minutes wiping up and putting the meat away before he'd take off his stripy apron and we'd go back to my mother's for tea.

Mum adored John from the moment she met him. Why wouldn't she? He was a hard worker from a good local family who was young and handsome with great style and a wicked sense of humour. Best of all, he wasn't married and never had been. I couldn't help but notice how differently she behaved around him to the way she'd been with Jim. She loved everything about John, from his tidy steward's manners to the meat he brought her, wrapped up in paper and tied with string. Amazing as it seemed to her, this was a man who could not only cook but who loved to entertain, often hosting Australian-style barbecues in his mother's garden with the finest steaks from the butcher's larder or a cruise ship's cold stores. There'd always be music – Sinatra, Glenn Miller, Duke Ellington – and dancing. John was a very good dancer and we loved to show off our moves.

Whenever John did manage to get steward's work again and went off on the ships, he'd bombard me with love letters from abroad. Besotted, I kept every one. He became my uniformed hero who travelled to faraway places and telephoned long distance, or sent romantic billets-doux within hours of arriving in a port. Believe it or not, my John cut his own romantic recordings of tunes like 'Blue Moon' or our special song 'How Deep Is the Ocean?' in special booths in New York and sent them to me on 45 r.p.m. discs.

'Darling, I love you,' the packaging would say. Or he'd write out the words to 'our' song and fold them inside.

How deep is the ocean? How high is the sky?
How many times a day do I think of you?

I thought that was so wonderful.

John was less popular at sea, where he argued with any passengers who whistled or snapped their fingers to attract his attention, in between rallying fellow crew members to complain about conditions. His various captains, who continued to object to his union activities, sacked him repeatedly, often labelling him as 'Not Wanted on Voyage'. Back on land, he had to find work wherever he could. Through Mr Guifreda, he was offered a job in the Quaintways kitchens for a while, which was fun for us both. Then he went back to a place he'd worked in as a commis chef once before, a hotel and restaurant in Warrington called the Patten Arms. I'm surprised they had him back, frankly. He'd been suspended a few years earlier for being too disruptive when he persuaded the rest of the staff to strike over pay. His boss there used to joke that commis chef meant a Communist who cooks.

One night in the summer of 1959, John told me that he was taking me to the Patten Arms for a 'special dinner'. I knew he was going to ask me to marry him; I'd been expecting it for a while. We'd already chosen a lovely antique engagement ring at Walton's jewellers in Chester. It had fifteen diamonds in a marquise cluster and he'd asked them to put it to one side. We'd discussed buying a house and worked out that we should have saved enough for some sort of deposit in two years' time.

The question was where, when and exactly how would my dashing steward pop the question? Would he hide the ring in my dessert? Would he go down on one knee in the restaurant in front of all the other diners and his colleagues? (Unlikely, I thought.) Maybe he'd booked us a room and would ask me in private? I couldn't wait to find out.

I put on my best outfit: a black pencil skirt and a houndstooth jacket with a crisp white collar. I styled my hair, cut short still and not dissimilar to Audrey Hepburn's. I was excited and looking forward to what would probably be one of the most important nights of my life. Looking in the mirror before I left to meet John, I smiled back at my reflection.

We took the train to Warrington but a few miles out of the station John became increasingly nervous. He'd never been very confident in public in spite of what he did for a living. Secretly, he is full of self-doubt and rather shy. He can't walk into a room on his own; he always makes me go in first, and then he only joins me if I have found him a seat facing the wall. Not far from our destination that night he suddenly turned to me and said, 'Listen, Paul, when we get to the restaurant everyone's going to be watching and waiting for the moment I pull out the ring. It'll be embarrassing.'

I waited, wondering what on earth he was going to suggest instead. Maybe this was a trick to whisk me off somewhere else.

'Here,' he said, grabbing my hand and pulling me to my feet, 'come with me.'

Before I knew it, my oh-so-romantic husband-to-be had bundled me down the corridor and pushed me into the cramped train toilet. Pressing me up against the basin to slide the door shut behind us, he kissed me hard on the lips and blurted, 'Marry me?'

I had no time to answer before he whisked out the ring we'd chosen and shoved it unceremoniously on my finger. I was twenty years old. He was twenty-one. I looked at him, glanced down at the ring and burst out laughing.

'John Prescott!' I cried indignantly. 'I see the art of romance isn't dead, then?' He looked crestfallen, so, kissing him back, I grinned. 'Of course I will, you idiot.'

We went on to have a lovely relaxed dinner at the Patten Arms, chiefly because John didn't have to propose in front of anyone. On the way home on the train, he made up for his unromantic proposal by snuggling up to me in our empty carriage.

'John, don't,' I giggled, pushing him away. 'People can see in!'

Jumping up, he unscrewed the light bulb in the ceiling, plunging us into darkness. 'Now they can't,' he said, silencing my laugh with a kiss.

My mother couldn't have been more delighted. After all she and I had been through together, she wanted nothing more than to see me happily married. Rather naughtily, John decided to test his own mother's true feelings for me by telling her that we'd broken up.

'Oh, John, I'm so pleased!' she cried.

'No, Mother. I was just seeing how you'd react,' he told her. 'Now I know how you really feel about Paul.' He never quite forgave her.

Despite her disapproval, his mother put on a good show and kindly offered to host our engagement party in her large garden, usually used for Labour fundraisers. John filmed the whole thing on a state-of-the-art 8-mm cine camera he'd brought back from the States. No one had ever seen such a thing before. All the Quaintways Girls were there, of course, many of whom had also recently got engaged so we were excited about each other's forthcoming weddings. Some of John's 'Brit boys' from the *Britannic* came, as well as friends and colleagues from hotels and the other places he'd worked. It was a lovely do, and his mother even offered to make our bridesmaids' dresses and my going-away outfit, which was very sweet of her. She was a fabulous dressmaker and I was lucky to have her.

Throughout our long engagement John continued to be very active in the National Union of Seamen, which pretty much began to take over his life. Furious at what he called the 'cosy' relationship between the ship owners and the union bosses, which he claimed led to poor pay and conditions, he regularly attended marches and strikes or spoke at rallies addressed by leading union officials. He put so much effort and research into his speeches and would practise them over and over until he – and I – knew them off by heart.

I wasn't that interested in politics, even though my family were always strong Labour people. For John, I was more of a sounding board. Mostly, I made endless mugs of tea and coffee when his union friends came round. I have to admit that sometimes I fell asleep waiting for them to finish their heated late-night debates. What I did come to appreciate, though, was that John had made enemies at the top of the NUS by becoming an unofficial shop steward. I didn't realize how serious that might be at the time; I just loved the maverick side of him that fought so passionately for what he believed in regardless of the consequences.

Knowing that politics was a side of his life that I didn't really understand, despite how much it meant to him, I decided to go to a rally to hear him speak. This particular one was held at the Roodee racecourse in Chester. A huge crowd had gathered, some sitting in the tiered stands, the rest forming a large circle. People stepped up and spoke into a microphone in the middle of the circle if they felt like it or until they were booed off. John, who was far younger than most of the men around him, had to push his way through a huge crowd of hecklers to take his turn. I held my breath as he began falteringly. I knew how nervous he was. After a few minutes, though, he got into his stride and became more and more impassioned, delivering each sentence with conviction and flair. I was so proud of him, I could have burst.

I only wished my father could have been there to see him. Each week, without fail, Dad had paid his union dues out of his hard-earned wages to ensure that his rights and those of his fellow workers were respected by his employers. Now here was the son-in-law-to-be that he could never meet representing all that he believed in and more. The man I was going to marry was someone of principle with strong working-class beliefs. Watching him bringing his speech to a climax at that microphone, I had never been more certain that I was doing the right thing.

The time flew by and before I knew it, Paul's time with his foster parents was drawing to an end. I was still living at home, often working six days a week at Quaintways, what with fashion shows and charity events in the evenings as well. John was abroad a great deal and there was no way we could afford a place of our own yet or contemplate giving up our jobs. My mother and Harry were engaged but hadn't yet married and were both still working so there was no one to help care for my boy even if they'd been willing to. To make matters worse, all the reports I'd had of Paul throughout his first year in foster care in Wolverhampton were that he was thriving and happy.

By the time Mrs Cotter came to see me at the end of 1959 I think in my heart I must have already known what would happen next. There seemed a dreadful inevitability to it all. 'He is devoted to his foster parents,' she told me, 'as they are to him. They are very keen to adopt him and will offer him just the sort of happy home life any little boy would dream of.'

My mother added, 'It would be too cruel to move him again, Pauline. You couldn't do that now that he's so attached to these people.'

'They're his mummy and daddy now,' Mrs Cotter added quietly.

'I'm his mummy!' I snapped, but I knew my protest would be in vain. I held out for a while longer but I knew the decision was all but made. I had run out of options.

When Mrs Cotter returned a few months later with the necessary paperwork and slid it across the table towards me with a pen, my entire body went cold. 'You just need to sign there and there,' she said, marking the lines helpfully with a cross. 'This will start the ball rolling and then the adoption application will be processed through the courts formally.'

I stared down at the documents that would change Paul's life – and mine – and could barely focus on the words. This was it. The day I'd been dreading for three and a half years. The moment when my defences had finally been worn down. John was away; not that he could have helped. I knew he'd have taken Paul on if we'd been married or in our own home, but what could we do in the situation we were in? His parents wouldn't help; they'd done all they could to eradicate what they saw as the shame of my illegitimate son. After three years of battling against the inevitable, I had no one to help me fight this one last round and nothing else to offer him.

If only Paul hadn't got sick with suspected meningitis, I mused sadly. He'd have stayed on in the nursery and I might have had more time. In truth, I'd lost him the minute he was put into care. I should have realized that his foster parents would never want to give up my fabulous little boy once they'd had the joy of him for an entire year.

I had to remind myself what was best for Paul. He was happy with these kind people who would continue to love him and give him a good home. What if my mother and Mrs Cotter and everyone else were right? As his mother, surely it was my duty to give him the best possible life?

'What are the names of the foster parents?' I asked, staring at the piece of paper until my eyes burned.

'I'm afraid I can't tell you, but they're a very nice couple.'

I imagined that they had a lovely big house and a large garden for Paul to play in. They probably had a car. I bet they could drive him to the seaside for his summer holidays or maybe even take him abroad. The foster father was a deputy head so he'd be sure to give Paul a good education. My son would probably learn languages and travel. He might even end up as a teacher, like his adoptive father. His adoptive mother was a school nurse. She'd take care of my son and ensure that he came to no harm. They'd not been able to have children of their own and now, to make their lives complete, I was about to give them my boy.

Picking up the pen, I felt the weight of it in my fingers. Lowering its nib on to the page, I scribbled a few innocent lines of ink that somehow joined together to spell my name: *Pauline Tilston.*

The words may as well have been written in my own blood, so dripping were they with guilt.

Seven

I CRIED ON MY WEDDING DAY. NOT TEARS OF HAPPINESS, BUT THE SORT THAT come from stress and a deep pain that couldn't be eased. My father wasn't there to walk me down the aisle – although my brother Peter made a wonderful substitute. My future parents-in-law, still disapproving, had tried to stop the wedding the night before. When he refused, they told John, 'You've made your bed, now lie in it.' I picked up on the atmosphere between them although John didn't tell me the details until later. Worst of all, my beautiful son, reluctantly given up for adoption, would never be the pageboy I'd always secretly imagined he would be.

To top it all, having slipped on my bridal gown, backcombed my hair and positioned my tiara, my industrial-strength hairspray melted the diamanté, spattering my hair with fragments of silver. 'That's it. I'm not going to the church!' I wailed to my brother. 'Call it off.'

Peter, newly married himself, soothed me as best he could, promising that all would be well the minute I got to the church and saw John waiting at the top of the aisle.

John. My John. That firebrand of a fiancé; the handsome steward who travelled the globe and brought me back exotic gifts. The uniformed waiter who'd courted me under the Eastgate Clock and who asked me to marry him in a toilet because he was too shy to do it in public. The man who, despite knowing my past, had visited my young son with me in the nursery and offered to adopt him as his own. Sadly, that was never to be.

I couldn't remember when I first knew I could spend the rest of my life with John. Was it when he first lifted Paul into his arms and uncomplainingly licked the lollipop my little boy offered to him? I certainly knew then that he'd make a wonderful father. Or maybe I knew when he smuggled me on to the *Britannic* for romantic evenings? Or was it when he waved at me on the train to work each morning?

By the time I got to Upton Church in Chester that wintry Saturday afternoon on 11 November 1961, I was shivering all over and not just with the cold. The wedding had been more than a year in the planning and I'd been involved in everything from choosing the deep pink rosebuds in my bouquet to the style and height of the cake. I'd sold my shares in Lewis's to help pay for my bridal gown, which cost forty pounds although I never told John how much. From Nola Gowns in Chester, the dress was made out of white satin covered with a layer of lace and had a long train. It was exquisite and, to my mind at least, worth every penny. We'd got my mum a lovely dress from Nola Gowns too, and a stylish red hat. I had three bridesmaids – Deborah, the eldest daughter of my childhood friend Joyce; John's younger sister Vivian; and my stepsister Pat, Harry's youngest. John's mother made their outfits, in sky-blue satin. Adrian, John's little brother, was our substitute pageboy, in black velvet waistcoat and pantaloons with a white frilly shirt.

My mum had married Harry by then, in a quiet register office wedding in Chester. Harry had given up the buses and gone into business as a bookmaker with Joyce's father. Their company was called Ashford & Dawson and became one of the largest bookmakers in

Chester. Mum and Harry had kindly helped pay for my wedding, along with a contribution from John's parents, plus our own savings. There was to be a reception for a hundred people at Quaintways, followed by an evening do at St Oswald's church hall for the friends who were working that day. We'd booked fancy cars to take us from the church to the reception and on to the evening event, and John had saved all his duty-free allowances from his voyages to buy the wedding booze. His brother Ray was our best man. After the reception, we were taking the sleeper train from Chester to London to go on our honeymoon to Majorca and Ibiza. John's mum had made me the most gorgeous sapphire-blue velvet dress as a going-away outfit. After that the song 'Blue Velvet' always reminded us of our honeymoon.

Thanks to my brother I reached the church on time, but the tears which had ruined my make-up earlier in the day soon returned. Despite my best intentions, I sobbed my way through my vows. It's all on cine film: me shaking and crying. John's mother said nothing, stylish as ever in her mink stole. My stepfather Harry looked like Clark Gable in the lounge suit he wore in defiance of John's mother's insistence on morning suits. Harry didn't seem to mind at all that he didn't walk me down the aisle, although I know he and my mum would have loved him to.

I was so nervous and full of conflicting emotions that I almost lost sight of what was important. Peter was right. John – my John – made sense of everything that had happened in my life. I loved him and he loved me. I was twenty-two years old, a year younger than my husband-to-be, who looked more handsome than ever in his top hat and tails (even if he was so embarrassed that he made me hide our wedding photos for years). He was so lovely and such a catch. I should have been grinning like the cat that got the cream.

We'd saved hard to buy a lovely little semi-detached house his mother had found us a few doors down from her in a cul-de-sac at Pine Gardens, Upton. It had been beautifully decorated for us by John's new stepfather Ron. After we'd returned from honeymoon, we'd be moving in. I'd have my mum and Harry close by, as well as my aunt Jane, Uncle Wilf and their son John to help me with the children John and I hoped to have together.

On our wedding day, we were surrounded by friends and family who were there to help us celebrate the happiest day of our lives. I had to give up all ideas of what might have been and of how, if the circumstances had been different, my Paul might have been there to share our day. I had to live with my decision; I couldn't keep going over and over what I'd done. There was no way I could ever get Paul back. He was somebody else's little boy now. He didn't even bear my name any more.

By marrying this warm, generous and loving man I was telling the world – and myself – that little 'Tilly' Tilston had finally grown up. I was Mrs John Prescott and I knew from the day I put on John's ring that I'd be a one-man woman. My life seemed all mapped out ahead of me. I'd carry on working as a hairdresser, from home or in a salon, in between having and raising our children. John would continue to work on the ships or maybe eventually for a local trade union. We'd remain in Chester all our lives, probably in the same house, just as both our mothers had stayed in their marital homes their whole lives.

Despite my wedding-day tears, the thought of spending the rest of my life with John really did make me happy. I even managed to laugh when his brother Ray lost the wedding ring and let the cars go home when he couldn't find us because I'd taken my bridesmaids up to the salon. John and I ended up having to walk to the evening reception from the Town Hall Square in all our regalia. Uncle Wilf played Chopin on the organ and I felt like a movie star as we left for our honeymoon on the midnight train from Chester, me all wrapped up in a black astrakhan three-quarter-length swagger coat with a high collar.

We flew to Majorca and I loved everything about it; the light and the seafood and the friendly people. Then we took a boat to San Antonio, Ibiza, which was a small fishing village. The ship we travelled on was like something from a former age, with heavy draped curtains and full silver service. It was really grand but, sadly for John, I'm not a natural sailor and was terribly seasick so I didn't really appreciate it. Reaching dry land, I felt much better and was finally able to enjoy the gorgeous scenery. Having hardly ever left Cheshire, it was quite an eye-opener to visit other countries and see the sparkling blue Mediterranean Sea. With John's expert guidance, I tasted food I never even knew existed, drank strange drinks and swam amongst schools of exotic fish. I took in every new experience he was offering me with childlike wonder. This was my life now. This was what it would be like to be married to such a well-travelled man.

John had made me a pledge on the steps of the church on our wedding day. It was the same promise his father had made to his mother on their wedding day. 'You'll probably have a life of hell but I promise you'll never be bored,' he told me with a smile.

Even then, before life started to get interesting, I knew he was telling me the truth.

We'd only been married a few months when John started going away again on cruise ships, sometimes for four months at a time. Although I'd been accustomed to his long absences before, it was different now. I was in a house by myself and it felt strange not having my new husband around.

My only respite came whenever he was sacked again for causing trouble and would turn up unexpectedly on our doorstep. On one trip the captain tried to get him thrown off the ship in New York but the rest of the men threatened to strike if he did so. John was reinstated until the voyage was over. As the sackings followed one from the other, especially after he became involved in the unofficial National Seamen's Reform Movement, so his political stance began to seriously affect our lives domestically and financially. I was never cross with him for being dismissed. Nor was I worried. John was John and I knew he'd always find work. Secretly, I thought it rather exciting that he held such strong convictions.

Of course, I found his politics a bit of a bore occasionally, especially if it meant he was off to yet another meeting or rally when I'd rather he were home with me. Then there was the catering correspondence course he took at sea, somehow managing to study in between seventy-hour-a-week shifts in a cabin shared with ten other stewards. Whenever he came home there'd be exam papers and books everywhere. It was all or nothing with John. He couldn't play at a thing, especially not if he was passionate about it; but there was a fun side to him as well and I was always spoiled on birthdays and anniversaries, which quickly made me forgive him everything.

Although I was relieved whenever he managed to secure another voyage, I couldn't help but miss him and look forward to him coming home. He'd always bring me lovely gifts, like a New Zealand Tiki love charm in silver and mother of pearl which I wear for good luck on days when I feel I might need it. He brought me a pagoda umbrella from the

Far East and a box of coloured knickers from the United States with the days of the week on them. There were black ones for Saturday and white for Sunday. Each time he went away again, though, I'd face months of coming back to a dark, empty house after work. In the end, the loneliness started to get to me. Although John earned good money on those long trips, we decided to rent out our house and for me to move back in with my mother, Harry, and my stepsister Pat for company, where it was cramped but cosy. However, I'm sure there were times when Mum and Harry must have wanted their own space, especially when John came home and moved in as well.

It was around this time that I also decided to take the plunge and leave Quaintways. From the day I'd started working there aged fifteen I'd been so happy. The rest of the girls were like family; they knew everything about me – good and bad. But I needed a change and thought it would be nice to work somewhere new. A clean slate, I suppose. When a big London company called André Bernard came to Chester and opened a mixed salon with male and female hairdressers, I applied for a job and was thrilled to be offered one. Barbara, Joyce's younger sister, worked on the reception so I knew at least one friendly face.

I hadn't been at the new salon very long when I discovered that John's last leave of absence had some unforeseen consequences. I was pregnant. Feeling the changes in my body as my baby grew inside me brought back poignant memories of my pregnancy with Paul, only this time I didn't have to hide anything. Nor did I have to explain myself at the doctor's surgery. The same GP who'd confirmed to my mother that I was expecting Paul as a sixteen-year-old was in charge of my care once more.

As at Quaintways, the arrangement was that I would work in the salon until seven months, and then – because I'd already given birth to one healthy baby – I'd be allowed to have my second child at home. My teenage experience at the Chester City Hospital had been so traumatic that I simply couldn't face going back there.

The bad news was that John was offered a lucrative four-month voyage to New Zealand on the SS *Rangitata*. If he took it, he wouldn't dock back in Liverpool until six weeks after the birth of his first child, which was due in early April 1963. I'd already gone through one labour without the father being around and I didn't relish the idea of another. But I knew John had to take this job, especially with a baby on the way, so I had to be brave. With my mother's help, I reckoned I could cope.

'Go,' I told him. 'Your son will be waiting to meet you when you get home.' (I don't know why but I always knew I'd be having another boy.) He went reluctantly, but took with him a favourite photograph of me, which he carried in his wallet and proudly showed to all the passengers and crew.

Before he went, we decided on names for the baby. I wanted our son to be called Jonathan with the traditional spelling, but John wanted him called John after him, so we agreed to meet in the middle and call him Johnathan – although I wasn't sure our son would thank us, having to put up with people spelling his name wrong his whole life.

On the night of 5 April 1963, my waters broke and my contractions began. I was at my mother's house and happy that she was close by. It was the midwife, not Mum, however, who was my mainstay. My mother stayed resolutely downstairs with Harry. 'She's boiling water,' the midwife told me whenever I called for her. 'Now push!'

Trying to banish memories of Paul's birth from my mind, I did what I was told and willed this longed-for child of mine into the world. When the midwife finally laid my beautiful baby boy in my arms and I looked down tearfully into his face, I couldn't help but look for a resemblance to Paul. Like him, my second son was a big baby, weighing almost eight pounds. He was twenty-two inches long, with large hands and feet. Gurgling away, kicking out with his legs, he didn't know it yet but his was going to be a life filled with such love and gratitude that I knew he couldn't fail but be happy.

'Hello, Johnathan Paul,' I whispered, giving him the second name I'd insisted on. 'Welcome to the world.'

John arrived home six weeks later and hurried to see me and his son. The first thing that greeted him, dominating the living room of my mother's small house, was a beautiful Silver Cross pram with cream enamel paintwork and a grey cloth hood. My mother and Harry sat in armchairs either side of it, not saying a word.

'What the hell did you have to go and buy that ruddy great thing for?' John asked me. 'And however much did it cost?'

I couldn't begin to tell him why I needed Johnathan to have that particular pram. It would have brought back too many painful memories for me and opened up old wounds for my mother. Even though the Silver Cross was always a bugbear to John – and, I'm sure, to all those who had to step around it or do a three-point turn just to manoeuvre it through the little front porch – that Rolls-Royce of prams made me the proudest mum in the world when I strolled through Chester. If only Sister Joan Augustine and the other girls could see me now, I thought, smiling to myself.

John, the baby and I moved back into our house in Pine Gardens and almost had a normal family life for a while. John had completed his correspondence course and was booked mainly on New York voyages. It wasn't easy when he was away, having to feed and tend to Johnathan through the night as well as dealing with the rolling power cuts of the time. But at least he wasn't on six-month voyages to Australasia, which meant that he did come home more and we were able to enjoy playing house and being the proud parents of our gorgeous boy. Johnathan was a delight. Like Paul, he'd fall asleep when feeding and he was such a contented little baby. I couldn't have asked for more.

This was the perfect family I had always wished for. This was how I had imagined my life to be from the day Timothy Paul was born. I'd lost him and I'd have to live with that loss for the rest of my life, but baby Johnathan filled me with such love and happiness that I sometimes had to pinch myself to make myself believe how lucky I was.

I should have known it wouldn't last.

RUSKIN COLLEGE, OXFORD, WAS NOT SOMEWHERE I'D HEARD OF IN MY twenty-four years. Of course I knew of the famous university, but having left school without any qualifications Oxford was not a place that came up much in conversation. Until now.

John's union activities had, by then, rendered him virtually unemployable. After being accused of leading a mutiny on one vessel he was blacklisted as 'Not for Cunard' and ran out of ships to work on. Deciding to become a full-time union official instead, he then had to struggle against prejudices within his own National Union of Seamen, which saw him as a threat. Probably partly as a ploy to get him out of the way, one of the senior officials told him that Ruskin College had been set up at Oxford to offer education to mature students without qualifications. He said there was a union scholarship available for applicants who wanted to become better trade unionists.

One night soon afterwards, John came home and asked me to sit down. Whenever that happened, I knew something was coming that I probably wasn't going to like much but which I was almost certainly going to have to put up with.

'Listen, love,' he said (another bad sign), 'you know I want to follow up on my political studies and work with the trade unions?'

I nodded, cradling Johnathan in my arms. The baby was unusually grizzly because he was teething.

'Well, there's a possibility I might get a grant to go to Oxford. It's the chance of a lifetime.'

'Oxford?'

'Yes, to study politics and economics at Ruskin College. For two years.'

'Two years?' My mind sped ahead of what he was going to say next. We'd have to move. He'd want us to sell our lovely home. I'd have to live somewhere miles away from Mum and all my friends and be in a strange place with a tiny baby. I could have cried.

'It won't be easy, Paul,' John admitted, sensing my concern. 'There won't be much money and it'll only work if we do this together. If you were to move in with your mum and Harry again, and rent out the house while you go back to work and do a bit of home hairdressing, I think we might be able to manage.'

My first reaction was of relief. I wouldn't have to leave Chester after all. I'd be back with my mother in the house I grew up in. Then I realized that what John was really saying was that he'd be living away from us for two years, leaving me virtually a single parent.

'But when would I see you?' I asked.

'I'd come home whenever I could – weekends mostly, and I'd be back for all the holidays. It'd be better than me being at sea for months at a time. You could come and visit me in the rooms they'd provide for me, too. If you left the baby with your mum, it'd make a nice break.'

Once he started talking about his rooms, I knew he'd probably already decided that this was something he was going to try for. I could have been cross but for the look of fear that briefly flashed in his eyes. Terror, more like. Education was a struggle for John. Ever since he'd failed the eleven plus (and been denied a bicycle for doing so), he'd battled against being labelled stupid. His headmaster warned his mother that he would never 'amount to much'. Writing a love letter to a girl he'd had a crush on, who was going on to grammar school without him, John was devastated when she sent it back to him with his spelling mistakes corrected.

Despite having no qualifications, like me, John had got a job as a hotel porter and had gone on to become an excellent lift boy, waiter, and finally ship's steward; he could easily have stayed proudly in that profession all his life. He'd served countless pink gins and other cocktails to the likes of Sir Anthony Eden, Archbishop Makarios and numerous dignitaries. Eden had even presented John with a boxing trophy. But he had passionate convictions and such a vehement determination to try to make the world a better place, especially for the underdog, that he was prepared to put himself through the mill, even if that ultimately led to failure and humiliation.

He'd pushed and pushed himself to exhaustion to finish and pass his correspondence course. He often felt out of his depth at union rallies and in political debates, spending countless hours on his speeches. He'd refused to give up when the NUS leadership went against him. Now he was considering entering the rarefied environment of the finest university in the world and pitching himself against those for whom learning came far more naturally.

Reaching out to take his hand in mine, I nodded and smiled. 'Don't worry. We'll be fine.'

The first hurdle John had to overcome was to write a two-thousand-word essay on the future of the unions as part of his application. He started it at sea, worked on it at home, and then showed it to someone who said he didn't have 'a hope in hell', so he screwed it up and started all over again. He asked a neighbour of his mother to type his second one up for him before he submitted it. To his surprise and my relief, he was accepted and offered an NUS scholarship for two years. But after he delivered an angry speech against NUS leader Bill Hogarth at an executive meeting the decision to give him a grant was unexpectedly reversed by the General Secretary.

John refused to give up and applied to Cheshire council for an educational grant, wording his application cleverly to say that he wanted to be a teacher rather than a union official. He attached references from a vicar, two MPs, four mayors, two magistrates and several city councillors. This time he was successful. The letter telling him the good news was posted through the letterbox while he was away at sea and I asked his father Bert to let him know by telegram. After another setback when it looked as if he might have missed his slot that year, someone dropped out and so John was all set. Hard as it was to take in, my husband was going to Oxford.

I won't pretend that the next two years were easy for either of us. Crammed into my mother's terraced house again with Harry, Pat and little Johnathan, I was working full-time at the salon and cutting hair in the evenings. Mum helped look after my son whenever I was working but I had to take over each night. It was a lot for a young mum to juggle.

Johnathan's needs took over, and I don't just mean the Silver Cross pram. There were nappies and bottles and toys, endless loads of washing and ironing, not to mention the sleepless nights we all had whenever he wouldn't settle. My stepfather Harry was marvellous and took it all in his stride. He never once complained about his new wife's decision to allow us back home. But there were times, I must admit, when even I longed for the space and quiet of our three-bedroom house in Pine Gardens.

Not that John had it any easier. As the son of a railway signalman from mining stock, he felt intellectually inferior to his fellow students, most of whom had been to grammar or public schools. While he and the other working-class lads had shortish hair and wore suits, the upper-class students wore their hair long, with even longer scarves and military overcoats decorated with Communist Party badges. These were chain-smoking philosophers and devotees of Lenin and Marx. To fit in with them, John dressed more casually and even grew a beard for a while.

He had to work twice as hard to keep up as he struggled with the complexities of his course. One of his first essays was entitled: *Power tends to corrupt and absolute power corrupts absolutely. Discuss.* Another was: *What do you consider should be done to reorganize the structure of the British union movement to make it better fitted to meet modern industrial conditions?* In a blind panic much of the time, he hardly went out and made few friends. He often asked himself, 'What am I doing here?' as he pored over books he didn't understand until the early hours. One of his tutors said he had a mind like 'knitting that the cat has played with'. Arriving for one mock exam he was handed a slide rule which he'd never used before, and he actually ran away, unable to face the humiliation. The invigilator chased after him and his tutor, Raphael Samuel, who'd always believed in him, wrote him a letter telling him not to worry and promising him he could complete the paper in his own time. John still has that note.

I visited him occasionally at his halls of residence in Headington and later central Oxford, leaving the baby with my mother. Coming from 'the wrong side of the tracks', I too felt out of place. I was worried that John's fellow students might think I was thick. As a hairdresser and young mum living with my mother, my world couldn't have been more different to that of the university. Although it was good to see John and make up for lost time, I only visited him on a couple of occasions and was always secretly relieved to come home.

John ploughed on at Ruskin, going back to sea when he could during the summer holidays to bring in a bit of extra money. After two long years, he finally gained his diploma in 1965 and returned to Chester.

We moved back into our house at Pine Gardens again with Johnathan, who was by then two years old. At the end of what had been a difficult time, I looked forward to John getting a salaried job at last. Apart from his student grant and the little extra he'd been able to bring in at sea our only income for the previous two years had been mine. But he was blocked by Hogarth at the NUS again and had to satisfy himself with a lesser position at the General and Municipal Workers Union.

I could tell he wasn't happy, but I never thought that it might mean another huge upheaval in our lives, this time for good. It all came about because his tutor at Ruskin advised him to apply for a place at Hull University to read marine economics and economic history. Owing to a loophole in the NUS rules, he was told that he could work for the union if he was in full-time education. After speaking to Professor John Saville in Hull on John's behalf, Raphael Samuel informed John that a place was waiting for him if he wanted it, supported by Prof. Saville. Going back to university at twenty-seven might have seemed like a backward step but John was assured the degree would stand him in even better stead for a full-time union position. With the persistence of his tutor and with no other work available, he was persuaded to take it.

John succeeded in getting a second grant from Cheshire council and, for the first year, he lived in a student house on the Hull campus, coming home when he could. By the end of that year, it was clear that he wanted me and Johnathan with him. Three years apart from us was taking its toll. Having never lived more than a few miles from my mother, I had no choice but to sell our lovely little home, leave all that I knew, and set off for a new life 150 miles away in the East Riding of Yorkshire.

When I told friends and family that we were moving to Kingston-upon-Hull, they couldn't hide their dismay. Quashing my fears, I made light of the wrench it would be to leave them all and asked if anyone knew what Hull was like.

'Oh, it's a little fishing village,' several replied confidently. 'And it's not *that* far.'

I still found the thought very scary. How would I cope all alone in a remote fishing village with a little one? I'd never lived outside Cheshire my whole life. Would the people accept me? I had to keep reminding myself that this was what John really wanted. I had to give it a go.

Arriving in Hull was quite a shock. It wasn't a tiny fishing village at all. It was a massive seaport with an industrial-scale fishing community. Everywhere you went, you could smell fish. One of the local anthems was an adaptation of a famous wartime song, 'Whale Meat Again'. At first, I felt completely out of my comfort zone. John, however, was convinced we had made the right move. He couldn't have arrived at a better time, politically. It was the start of the Cod Wars in which the Icelanders wanted British fishermen to stop over-fishing the North Atlantic and were cutting trawlers' nets. There were umpteen rallies and marches for John to cut his teeth on as a minor NUS official. Later, when Jim Callaghan deployed the Royal Navy to protect British trawlers, it was my clever husband who was instrumental in bringing abouta compromise, having always claimed that the Icelanders had a fair point. Fed up with the stalemate, he flew to Iceland to negotiate directly with the Prime Minister and with the infamous 'Mad Axeman' trawler captain. It was an unpopular move back home but it worked when the Icelandic government accepted what became known as 'the Prescott deal'.

For me, however, life was less stimulating. There were times in those first few years in the two-up, two-down we bought in the suburb of Cottingham that I was terribly homesick. My mum, who'd always been close by, was more than a hundred miles away and neither she nor I drove a car. John was at 'uni' each day, trying to grapple with the complexities of his new course, and I had little Johnathan to care for. I didn't know a soul to begin with and was very lonely. I never once asked John if we could move back to Chester, though. I'm not a quitter.

If it hadn't been for the friends I made, like my next-door neighbour Josie and her husband Stuart, as well as Sally and Ernie Bamforth who lived two doors down, I don't know what I would have done. Ernie was a builder and he and Sally had the smartest house on the street. Soon after we'd moved in, John came home one day with some friends who'd bought a bottle of champagne to celebrate passing an exam. The trouble was, the bottle was warm and we'd never been able to afford a refrigerator.

'I bet the couple two doors down own a fridge,' John said with more than a touch of sour grapes. 'Go and ask if we can stick it in there to chill it off.'

I knocked on their door and it was opened by a woman who was four feet eleven inches tall and about the same age as me. I introduced myself sheepishly and asked my favour.

'Yes, of course,' she replied, a twinkle in her eye. 'And when it's chilled, I'm sure I have a spare jar of caviar at the back of the fridge for you.' From that moment on, I knew we'd be friends – and almost fifty years on we still are.

John had warned me from the start that moving to Hull would be tough. 'It'll be a long hard slog for us both, but it'll pay off in the end,' he predicted. His course was for three years and, once again, we'd have little income beyond his grant. Even though I'd have liked to have tried for another child straight away, a second baby was out of the question. We simply couldn't afford it. Like my mother before me, I learned how to eke out a pound of mince until the end of the week. I made my own clothes and adopted many of her necessarily frugal ways.

There was no question that I would have to go back to work; I just needed to figure out who would look after Johnathan. My next-door neighbour Josie, who had young children of her own, kindly agreed to look after him until I got home.

Putting on a smart outfit that I'd run up on my sewing machine from a pattern I'd spotted in a magazine, I set out into Hull city centre looking for a job. I hadn't worked in hairdressing for a few years and styles had all changed. The new craze was for big stiff 'saluki' curls that used to take an hour just to put up and which I had no experience of. I traipsed round most of the salons, but many of the managers clearly thought I'd been out of the loop too long. Eventually, Mr Ball, the manager at the salon in Hammonds, the biggest store in Hull and part of House of

Fraser, offered me a job three days a week. He was kind to me and even allowed Josie to drop Johnathan with me for half an hour at the end of the day so that she could get on with taking care of her own kids. When I wasn't in Hammonds, I worked as a home hairdresser, gradually building up a small business with friends and clients coming to my house.

I rarely saw my mum and I missed her dreadfully, even though I knew she was happy for the first time since Dad died. She was enjoying being a bookmaker's wife and travelling all over the country with him to race meetings. She was so busy, she was never able to visit me in those first few years, so the only time I saw her was when we went home for a weekend or during university holidays. Between them, though, she and Harry gave me a love of horse racing which I still have today.

The strangest coincidence was that when Mum did eventually come to Hull and met my neighbour Sally, she took one look at Mum's hand and asked her what had happened.

'I had an accident years ago, at the laundry.'

Sally said, 'Was it the Ideal Laundry in Chester by any chance?'

Mum was amazed. 'How did you know?'

'Because the firm where I worked as a secretary in Hull handled your claim for compensation. I was the one who dealt with it.'

It's a small world. Smaller still, because the person employed to be in charge of all the civic catering at the Hull Guildhall – somewhere John and I were to become very familiar with – turned out to be Mr Guifreda, who'd moved from Chester with his new family after leaving Quaintways. He and John's father Bert had always been good friends and whenever Bert came to stay, they'd go off to the pub together.

Apart from good pals like Sally, life got better for me when I started to make other friends among the wives and girlfriends of John's fellow students. I was the odd one out, of course, being in my mid-twenties when they were still in their teens, but having other women to chat to helped cheer me up. Through them, we learned about the Westfield Country Club in Cottingham, where they all used to go to see top cabaret acts. In any given week, the line-up could include artistes like the Four Freshmen, the pianist Oscar Peterson, the singer Marti Caine, Cannon and Ball, or the entertainer Bruce Forsyth.

Even though John's friends went there regularly, when I asked if we could join too he was indignant. 'I'm not going to belong to a place like that!' he protested. 'It'll be full of bloody Tories.'

It has always mattered deeply to John what others might think of him – hence the fact that I had to hide our wedding photos in case, God forbid, any of his union friends saw him in top hat and tails. Even now, he's uncomfortable breaking away from what he sees as his working-class roots, despite the fact that both his parents openly aspired to better things. I keep telling him that your roots define you and stay with you, whatever you do.

I was really disappointed about not being able to join the country club but then I discovered that Walt Cunningham, leader of the Hull dockers (and someone John respected enormously), was a member. Walt told John, 'It's a great club. Why don't I put your name down?'

I was thrilled. Best of all, by becoming members we got to know Frank and Janet Brown, who ran the Westfield and became two of the mainstays of our lives. Janet was glamorous and bubbly, and wore fabulous clothes, as befitting the owner of a nightclub. It was she who introduced me to fine food and wines, the best places to shop, and who gave me a lifelong taste for champagne. I'd always loved Babycham and used to think I was so sophisticated, sipping it from those special little glasses they served it in. Then I discovered the real thing and, boy, I have never looked back, much to John's embarrassment. He hardly ever drinks – it doesn't really agree with him and he certainly doesn't approve of my expensive tastes. Whenever we fly somewhere together and the stewardess comes round, he says, 'Don't you dare ask for champagne!' but I do anyway.

As I always say to him, why should champagne just be for the Tories and not for the working class too? Bob Edwards, a Labour MP and journalist friend, once told me, 'Always remember, Pauline, nothing is too good for the workers.' I agreed with him 100 per cent.

Nine

IN MARCH 1966, A YEAR AFTER STARTING HIS DEGREE, JOHN HEARD THAT there was going to be a by-election in Southport, Lancashire. It was a traditionally strong Tory seat but he still thought he might stand a chance. This chance improved when the NUS – who'd blocked him for so long – finally agreed to back him as the Labour candidate.

I was shocked when John first told me what he planned to do. I'd never imagined that his politics would dominate our lives in that way. I just thought he'd become a senior union official; I had no idea that his aspirations included becoming a Member of Parliament. More scarily, if John was going to be an MP that meant I was going to be an MP's wife. Me: little Tilly Tilston, Chester hairdresser. Although daunting, I must admit I was secretly quite excited by the idea. I was always up for a challenge and I knew I could manage it if I had to. I remember asking my mother, 'Gosh, Mum, do you think I could do it?'

Without a moment's hesitation, my mother – the former housemaid – gave me her stock answer: 'You're as good as anyone else and better than most.'

In preparation for the campaign, we travelled as a family to Southport, a pretty Victorian seaside resort, and checked into a boarding house for a month. Johnathan was almost three and he loved every minute of it. There was an old-fashioned dumb waiter between floors which went down to the kitchen on pulleys and he used to travel down in it to watch the chefs cook. Just before dinner was ready, the lift would come up and out Johnathan would pop. It was his little routine.

The campaign trail was new and exciting to me as we toured unfamiliar neighbourhoods, knocking on doors, handing out leaflets and shaking countless hands. I made John the largest red satin rosette you've ever seen to wear on his lapel and on the back I wrote a little love note so that he'd see it every time he switched it to a new jacket. We didn't always get the warmest welcome in Southport, being Labourites in a largely Tory constituency, but people were always very polite. Johnathan was usually the centre of attention, of course, and John proudly showed him – and me – off to potential voters. We have much of our time on the trail on cine film, thanks to my husband the amateur film-maker.

I was very aware of how well turned out I needed to be as a candidate's wife, but we had little spare cash so John's mother came to my rescue and made me a few classic dresses and jackets so that I didn't let her son down. I tried to make sure there was always something in Labour red on my outfit, or to carry a red handbag. And, of course, I had my own homemade rosette – though never as big as John's. It was in the days when I wore my thick black hair long and usually pulled to a bunch at one side. Pale blue eye shadow was the fashion of the day and I tried to create the appearance of a young, trendy wife standing next to my John, with his red kipper ties and bushy sideburns.

Phyllis joined us whenever she could and was enormously proud of her son. In her mink stole or full-length musquash fur coat, she would have made a wonderful MP's wife herself, especially with her long history of politicking. Fortunately, I didn't have to do much – just stand at John's side being supportive while making sure that our boisterous blond toddler with his Beatle haircut behaved himself. It was before the days when the wives were taken off to attend their own engagements, thank goodness. I wouldn't have been comfortable with that sort of responsibility back then.

John had to keep up with his studies, writing essays and reading books, so after a long day shaking hands he'd settle down in our hotel bedroom and do his homework. I don't know where he got the stamina. Sadly, in spite of all his hard work and increasing the Labour vote by a considerable margin, when the final vote came in he was eleven thousand votes behind the Tory candidate. It was worth going for, though. We'd had such fun trying and it proved to be one of our happiest times as a young family. Better still, I think we both got a taste for what political life might be like.

For the next two years John continued to juggle union business and his studies, travelling all over the country during the official seamen's strike and then staying up all night to study for his exams.

Exhausted, he arrived to take one paper after a rally but walked out without writing a word. Thankfully, his tutor let him resit the exam and he passed. When he finally graduated with a third in his BSc in economics and economic history, I was so proud. No one knew better than me what he had put himself through to achieve that piece of paper. His mother travelled from Chester for his graduation ceremony and insisted on having a photograph taken of John wearing his black graduate's gown and mortar board. Oh, how he hated that! Phyllis displayed that photo prominently in her house for the rest of her days. John shoved our copy to the back of a drawer somewhere.

Despite the opposition of his nemesis, Bill Hogarth, John became a full-time union official with the NUS, and we finally had two incomes. I was left alone with Johnathan a lot of the time again though, as much of my husband's working week was now spent in London writing pamphlets on safety at sea and helping to draft union submissions to the government-appointed body set up to investigate the seamen's strike. In the capital, he found himself mixing with like-minded unionists and politicians. It was a pivotal time for him, even if he suspected he was being investigated by Special Branch as an activist.

Johnathan started at the Cottingham Village School and Josie carried on taking care of him for me whenever I was at work. I'd get him up each morning, washed and fed, and then she'd take him to school. I'd take the train into Hull and then she'd bring him to the salon just before it closed, or I'd pick him up from her house after work. Then, when I got in, I'd cook supper and catch up with all the household chores like washing and cleaning before a client might call in for a cut and set or a perm.

There was still no time or money for a second child, although John and I were fairly relaxed about that by then and decided that whatever happened would happen. Although I missed Johnathan all day once he started at school, I had lots to do to keep me busy, running a house, working, and being a wife and mother. I couldn't help but wonder, of course, what Paul's first day at school had been like and where he was in the education system by then. Was he a bright boy? Did he fit in? Was he happy? I had to push those thoughts from my mind each time they barged in or I'd have driven myself crazy.

* * *

Even though John was young and qualified and had so much to offer the union, he continued to be blocked by Hogarth, who warned him that he would never make it to the top. So when he heard that the long-standing Labour MP Harry Pursey would be retiring in Hull East at the next general election, which was expected in 1970, he came rushing home to tell me the news.

'I think I might be in the right place at the right time,' he said. 'The NUS will probably support me for selection if it gets me out of their hair. Being an MP would probably be my best chance now at improving conditions at sea.'

There have always been Labour MPs in Hull. I hope there always will be. His opposing candidates included the local Labour Party agent Councillor Harry Woodford (who went on to be John's agent for forty years). As John suspected, his friends in the NUS promised their backing – which was key – and he was duly selected. It was a great day for us all. He only had to wait eighteen months before a general election was called by Harold Wilson and John's chance of finally going to Westminster loomed. His chief rival was a Tory called Norman Lamont whom John referred to as 'that merchant banker from London'.

By this time, I was pregnant with our second child, which was due in June 1970, on roughly the same date as the election. I'd already told my employers at Hammonds and the girls at work were excited for me, but I wasn't quite sure how I'd juggle caring for Johnathan and working until I was seven months' pregnant with being on the campaign trail as well.

John was thrilled; not least because he was convinced that my pregnancy would give us what he called 'the Kennedy touch'. Jacqueline

Kennedy, the youngest First Lady in American history, had given birth to their first child John Junior just two weeks after JFK won the presidential campaign nine years earlier. My John worked out the timings: my due date was 27 June, nine days after polling day, 18 June.

'This is going to be an election baby!' he declared. 'Don't tell anyone it's due on the twenty-seventh. Tell them it's the eighteenth.'

'But, John, that's not true!' I protested.

'It might be,' he countered. 'You were early with Johnathan; this baby could well come then.'

I thought, What the heck, and told him I'd do my best, but that it was rather out of my hands. Mainly, I was just delighted that this time he'd be around for the birth and would make a fuss of me.

In the earlier stages of my pregnancy, before my tummy began to swell, the newspapers described us as one of the most glamorous young couples in politics. I didn't feel very glamorous. The house was cluttered with boxes of political flyers, leaflets, banners and posters, as well as Johnathan's toys and clothes, piles of washing, ironing, and the things I was collecting for the baby. The beautiful Silver Cross pram had gone to Mr Guifreda and his second wife and baby, so I had to make do with a second-hand lightweight version that was far more practical – if less nostalgic.

John and I toured the constituency in the evenings and at weekends in his old black Rover, which had terrible suspension. It was plastered with posters proclaiming slogans such as: *Now Britain's Great, Let's Make It Great to Live In*, or *Back to Work with Labour*. An enormous loudhailer was strapped rather haphazardly to the roof. It was only John's second car and replaced a fibreglass sports car with a broken gear stick whose bonnet had flown off. We'd drive between all the rows of little houses, stopping and starting, knocking on doors, handing out leaflets. It was a lot of hard work but John always made it seem like an adventure with his cine camera and buoyant mood and I wouldn't have missed it for the world.

Knowing that we needed a bigger house and with John deciding he should live in his potential constituency, we sold our little house in Cottingham and found a property in an area called Sutton Park, Hull. I was sad to leave Sally and Ernie, Josie and Stuart, and all the neighbours and the friends we'd made, but I did love our modern open-plan house and we soon made friends amongst our new neighbours, who were always very kind to me. So, as well as everything else that was going on with the campaign and my pregnancy, I had to pack up our belongings and organize a move. In preparation, John made me sell or get rid of anything we didn't really need. Sadly, that included my wedding dress.

'I'm fed up with lugging this thing around,' he announced as he came upon it in the spare bedroom, wrapped in tissue paper in its big box. 'It's got to go.'

'Go where?' I asked.

'To the dump. With all the other rubbish.'

Heavily pregnant and extremely hormonal, I sat in the front seat of John's car fighting back the tears as I watched him heave my exquisite Nola wedding gown out of the boot and hurl it on to the top of a rubbish tip. How foolish was I?

As the election loomed, John decided to take the question of the 'election baby' into his own hands. Helping me into the front seat of his car, he drove me full pelt up and down our road, crashing over every bump to try to induce me. I'd have thought our laughter alone might have done the trick, but it didn't.

By election night it was clear that nothing was going to happen despite our best efforts, so I waddled into the count; I was absolutely enormous. Norman Lamont took one look at me, his face a picture of mock surprise, and said, 'Oh, Pauline, I thought you would have been in hospital by now.' I could tell he suspected John might not been entirely honest about my due date.

The Hull *Daily Mail* echoed Norman's thoughts. One report said:

> Perhaps the most excited supporter of Mr Prescott was his raven-haired wife Pauline. Smart and erect in a striking red frock, no one would have guessed she was within a few hours of giving birth to her second child. All yesterday, this birth had been expected hourly. But the baby did not arrive and Mrs Prescott was able to realize her dearest wish, to watch her husband declared the East Hull victor.

Yes, John won the count that remarkable night, even though Harold Wilson ended up losing control of the country to Ted Heath. Phyllis and Bert Prescott came across from Chester to stand by John's side as he was declared a Member of Parliament, a dream come true for them both. Phyllis had always treasured a letter John wrote to her from sea, while he was doing his correspondence course. *Though I have a lot of time to catch up on*, he wrote, *I will make the grade in the future. One day, be assured, you will have something to be proud of me*, Mum. On that night, in that place and at that time, Phyllis thought her first-born son could never do anything else that would make her prouder. Little did she know what was in store.

* * *

Four days after the count and shortly after we'd moved house, I went into labour in the early hours of 22 June. John had been half right; I was early, just not quite early enough. As the contractions began my mind couldn't help but flash back to Paul's birth and the bittersweet memory of that night at Chester City Hospital. Once more, I was reminded of the son I had lost; the boy who'd now be fourteen years old. *Fourteen.* Where was he? How was he? What did he look like? Was he happy? Even as I was suffering the pain as my latest child began to push his way into the world, I longed to know.

Towards the final stages of labour, I breathlessly asked the midwife where John was. 'Tidying his office,' she replied. I seemed destined to have my babies on my own. Still, he was by my side within minutes of the arrival of our second beautiful son, my third boy. At 3 a.m. that happy day, David Peter Prescott was born. We named him David for the Welsh connection John and I shared, and Peter after my lovely brother.

Less than two hours later, newspaper photographers were in our home taking pictures of the new MP for Hull East, his wife and young children amid boxes we hadn't yet unpacked. When a local reporter asked my reaction to my husband's election, I got rather carried away and completely forgot John's warning to be careful whenever I spoke to the press.

'I'm so proud because John was only a waiter when I met him!' I replied happily, giving them a quotation that would haunt me for years.

My time in the political spotlight had just begun.

Ten

WE HAD NEVER REALLY DISCUSSED IT, BUT I THINK I'D ALWAYS ASSUMED that if John became an MP the children and I would relocate to London with him and start our new life together. Having survived the move to Hull and ended up loving it, I was quite excited about this new adventure. Of course, the idea of living in such a big city scared me a little but as long as we were all together I knew we could cope with anything.

My husband, however, had other ideas. 'Now listen, love ...' he said.

What now? I thought

'... I'm a great believer that an MP should live in the constituency that he represents.'

I stared at him open-mouthed, trying to take in what he was telling me. 'What you mean', I corrected him, 'is that I live in the constituency that you represent.'

He nodded. 'It's just the way it has to be I'm afraid, Paul.'

'But it's not always like that,' I protested. 'Glenys Kinnock lives with Neil in London. In fact, several of the other wives do. It doesn't reflect badly on their husbands so why should it reflect badly on you?'

The last thing I wanted to do was raise two small children single-handedly all week while my husband was two hundred miles away, working in London. I'd already had a taste of that kind of separation. But I had to accept John's decision. I knew of old that there was no arguing with him, despite how strongly I felt. It was yet another matter of high principle to him and I had always been so impressed by his principles. I could hardly rock the boat now, so I did what was necessary: I agreed to stay in Hull.

There were more disagreements to come. John – who claims to be an atheist and once wrote in a school notebook that he didn't believe in God – refused to have our boys christened. He insisted that, as with politics, they should make up their own minds about religion when they were old enough. He called it the 'socialist alternative'. My mum, who'd been at my side when Paul was christened at St Bridget's, was especially unhappy about John's decision. His mother was too. I tried to argue against it but John was adamant.

'I was sent off to Sunday school each week with my brother and sisters to give my parents a few hours' break,' he told me. 'I hated it. If our boys want to become Christians then it will be their choice when they have grown up. And I'll tell you something, Paul; if they do then they'll be better Christians than most.'

I didn't like it but I didn't fight him on that one. As he forced me to admit, I didn't go to church so why did I care? I argued that I believe myself to be a good Christian but that it's how you carry on in your life that counts, not how often you go to church. John insisted that being christened was part of that same philosophy, so, once again, I had to back down. It's not that I was a doormat or downtrodden and I certainly haven't always shared John's views. I'm just a traditional wife who believes in a more traditional role, even if that sometimes means living with decisions I may not always like.

More important than any political point-scoring between husband and wife, I believe passionately in the importance of a mother's presence in the lives of young children and I am glad that I was always there for Johnathan and David; even more so after I had to give up Paul. Raising my boys was never a chore for me. I loved every minute of being a mum. It isn't for everybody, but it was for me. Each to their own.

That's not to say I haven't had strong opinions or that I haven't always expressed them. John isn't a chauvinist, either, although I'm sure the women's libbers think so. He always treats a person the same whether they're male or female and gives as good as he gets if someone comes on strong. He's actually very courteous – apart from to women drivers! So there he is: a mass of contradictions, like most men.

When it came to winning arguments, it was more that John always explained things so very well. I couldn't be fighting him all the time, even if my views differed. That wouldn't have worked. Compromises could often be found – like the naming of Johnathan, for example. More often than not with John, I had to accept that I might not always like certain things but we had to agree and be a team or he couldn't do what he was doing. His being an MP was very important to us both. If I was going to support him in this political journey of his, which I'd always backed, then I had to make certain allowances.

Nor have I ever been someone who is confrontational. My nanny Ada always told me to count to ten whenever I was upset about something and that advice stayed with me. John, on the other hand, is someone who loses his temper and shouts, especially if someone's late. He can't abide bad time-keeping. I suppose he's a bit of a bully, in the nicest possible way. The thing that really annoyed me about him was that he would get so agitated whenever I did try to interrupt and make a point.

Then he'd go off in one of the sulks I'd dreaded having to live with from when I first knew him. Fortunately, they don't last long. I always say that he can go up the stairs in one mood and come down in another. A typical Gemini. I usually wait until he's back down again and then quietly get my point across.

I did go against him once, over something I felt passionately about. When Johnathan reached secondary-school age, I fully expected him to go to one that was in walking distance from where we lived. But the local education authority decided that there was no room there and found him a place at an estate school five miles away, in a working-class area of north Hull. I was furious and took a stance. Ever since I'd had to give up Paul, I had been over-protective of my boys. I was not about to lie down and let my Johnathan take a ten-mile round bus trip each day – especially not when I'd agreed to remain in the constituency with them.

'Do something!' I told John.

He looked horrified. 'I can't. I'm the MP. They can't make an exception just for me. It wouldn't be proper.'

'Right then,' I announced, 'if you won't do something, then I will. I'll go before the committee and I'll explain to them how unfair this is and what it means for our son. I didn't agree to live here for our boy to be bussed out to another constituency!'

Sadly, the committee refused to see me. As John predicted, they claimed they couldn't make an exception in our case. I was livid. I'd never driven (mainly because I've been a passenger with John Prescott for too long), and I had no one at home to help me with David. I couldn't take Johnathan to school each day, so he had no choice but to catch the bus, coming home well after dark in the winter. For the whole of his secondary-school education, I never relaxed until he walked in through the front door.

John, meanwhile, had his own stresses to deal with in London. Having taken office at the age of thirty-two as one of the youngest MPs in the country, this grandson of a coal miner found himself in the bewildering surroundings of the House of Commons. It wasn't completely new to him, of course. He'd sat in the public gallery listening to debates about shipping acts and taken part in committees on numerous occasions, but this was his first time on the shop floor.

His mother went to see him in Westminster and cried as she watched him take his place on the back benches. She kept a copy of the menu from the Members' Dining Room where he took her to lunch afterwards, writing on it: *The proudest day of my life*. John's first few weeks were mystifying as he found his way around, moved into an office shared with three other new MPs, and prepared to make his maiden speech. Although Michael Heseltine praised him for it, some of his other fellow politicians were far from welcoming.

'I'll have a gin and tonic, Giovanni, and one for my friend!' a Tory MP called Nicholas Soames would call, once he discovered John had been a waiter.

'At least I'm here because of my brains, not because of my father's balls,' John would later retort.

They'd laugh at the way he spoke and taunt him about his grammar, his accent, and any mistakes he made in his speeches. Someone dubbed him 'the Mouth of the Humber'. The trouble with John is that he talks very fast, which was something he picked up during strike meetings and political rallies. If he didn't someone would always jump in and heckle.

His brain races ahead of his mouth. Writing out his speeches and practising them helps, but having to speak off the cuff is much harder. He recognizes his public speaking as a weakness and works jolly hard to put it right. Unfortunately, others spotted this weakness too and picked on him because of it, which I never thought was terribly fair. Someone even collated his worst gaffes in a book.

To his credit, John mainly took the ribbing in good sport. When he was involved in an accident in the back of a London taxi and bumped his head years later, he was taken to University College Hospital for an MRI scan. Fortunately, no harm had been done. Joan, John's long-suffering chief of staff, asked him afterwards, 'Did they find any syntax?'

John shook his head sadly. 'Not a trace,' he replied.

Another time, a journalist who'd been researching John's background told him he'd read every speech he'd ever made in twenty-five years in the House. 'Did any of it make any sense?' asked my self-effacing husband. As he always said, it was wrong to assume just because he didn't speak fluently that he didn't think fluently either. Nothing could be further from the truth – just look at what he's achieved. Within his first few years in the House, he campaigned against the policy of ships flying flags of convenience to bypass safety laws and avoid tax. He was instrumental in getting a divers' charter passed to protect divers working on the new North Sea gas rigs. He became the youngest Labour front-bench spokesman on shipping and campaigned for inquiries after several maritime disasters.

Another thing he had to contend with was snobbery – something he's battled against all his life. At one dinner he was invited to, he met Lord Caradon and told him, 'We've met before.' The former governor of

Cyprus didn't remember so John enlightened him: 'I remember you dining on the captain's table on the *Britannic* … I was your waiter.'

'Really,' said the lord, before turning back to the man on the other side.

On a wall in our house is a painting of the main chamber of the House of Commons, depicting Prime Minister Margaret Thatcher at the despatch box. The painting was taken from a photograph, which John has hung nearby. The chief difference between the two framed images is that in the photograph John is on the front bench as a Labour spokesman but in the painting he's been moved to the second row in a demotion nobody has ever been able to fully explain. The discrepancy between reality and fantasy irks him to this day. Experiences like that reinforced all John had ever felt about the class system, having spent much of his life serving the wealthy upper classes in restaurants, hotels and on the ships. It also made him ever more determined to prove all the snobs wrong.

Ever since I'd been quoted on his election that 'he was only a waiter when I met him', I had decided to keep a low profile. It was much easier for me to do that living in Hull. Constituency wives are largely anonymous to the British media who tend to focus instead on those wives who live in London with their husbands.

Not that I wasn't as busy as any London spouse or didn't have my work cut out. In those days, people used to ring their MP's house to ask all sorts of questions, like the names of their local councillors or when the next surgery would be held. I sometimes felt like a switchboard operator. When the boys were young, the telephone rang non-stop and I'd have lists upstairs and down to give people the information they wanted. That was part of my constituency role and I didn't mind. John's agent Harry Woodford and his wife Dora did more than their fair share and became dear and supportive friends. No candidate could have had a more loyal and dedicated agent than Harry. John's constituency agent for two decades was a little bundle of dynamite called Rita Johnson; she is now sadly missed. We couldn't have achieved what we did without their support and that of the Labour councillors and other friends in east Hull.

What I tried not to do (apart from the issue over Johnathan's schooling) was get involved in local council meetings that might throw up controversial issue or be a political ambush for me. I didn't want to be seen siding with people I might know socially or through the boys' schools. I'd seen other wives embarrass their husbands in public and I never wanted that to happen to me. Only once did I step out of line, years later, at one of the Labour conferences. I was chatting to two journalists at a cocktail party who'd asked me how John was going to vote in the London mayoral election. I told them I wasn't sure, which was true. Then, for some reason I added, 'I'd like to see Glenda Jackson win. I think she's absolutely wonderful; the way she works a crowd. People really warm to her.' To my horror, the journalists printed a story that John wanted Glenda Jackson to be mayor of London. It was the only time I voiced my opinion and it backfired. I never did it again.

Then, of course, there were all the Labour Party fundraisers to help organize or attend, and the campaign trails to go on with the children in tow. Fortunately, I didn't have to make him a new rosette each time because he considered the first I'd made his good-luck charm and, although tatty, it stood the test of time. One night, after a fundraising barbecue at his mother's house, John and I were on our way back to Hull and extremely tired. It was the early hours of the morning and Johnathan was asleep in the back, while David was on my knee in the front seat. John's brother Ray was shadowing us in his car in the next lane, which was just as well because a car in front of us suddenly slewed across the road and we hit it head on. Fortunately, we were wearing seat belts so all I suffered was a bump on the head and the children were unharmed. The car was a write-off and we were extremely shaken but grateful that no one was seriously hurt.

Later, one of the Chester newspapers tried to make out that John might have been drinking, which was blatantly untrue. He's never been a drinker and was breathalysed at the scene and found to be alcohol free but it was, for us both, an early example of how a horrible situation can be made even worse by the media if they so choose.

John worked incredibly hard and was probably one of the busiest MPs in the House. When he came home, usually on a Friday night, he was often exhausted. He would be the first to admit that he was never a model father like Gordon Brown or Tony Blair, who were very hands on. He was good with the boys and played with them when he could but he'd never kiss or hug them. That is not his way. He grew up with the idea that if you kiss you're a sissy.

Not being very demonstrative, he didn't want family photographs around and never put a photo of us in his office, even when the boys were young. I'd go into some of his colleagues' offices and say, 'Hey, look at all these family snapshots! Why can't you have some of ours in your office?'

'It means nothing; it's just a status symbol,' he'd reply, reminding me of one friend whose office was like a shrine and yet he and his wife divorced. I had to accept that; I knew it didn't mean he wasn't proud of us.

The boys missed him when he was in London and we all had to cope with not having him around for school and social events, sports days and parents' evenings. He was rarely there to have supper with them, bathe them or tuck them in at night. Once when John was away I saw David go to the fridge and pull out a stick of celery. Intrigued, I followed him back into the living room. John was on the television taking part in some debate in the House. My youngest son, knowing his father liked celery, was trying to feed him through the TV screen.

John missed the boys as much as they missed him, I think, although he'd never actually say so. 'Use the cine camera. Film everything,' he'd tell me whenever he knew he'd miss some important event like the boys' sports championships. Johnathan represented Hull in sprinting and David was good at rugby. (They must have inherited those genes from my family!) Then, when he came home, their father would sit and watch the films, reliving the occasions he'd missed, usually complete with a hilarious running commentary from young David. We have so much footage of the boys growing up that they only have to watch it to know they've had a good childhood. And I made sure to make up for the absence of their father, physically and often emotionally, with plenty of extra kisses and cuddles.

As the boys grew older, they'd often be teased at school for having an MP as a father. This was especially bad during an election when just about every household in the area had a leaflet shoved through its letter-box featuring a posed photograph of John, me, and the boys. 'What does MP stand for?' the other children would cry. 'Mucky Pig!' came the usual reply. Being the son of an MP was a bit like being the child of a police officer. The boys knew that they had to be careful and never be caught doing anything that might shame or embarrass their father – from taking drugs to being seen drinking too much. The name Prescott is easily recognizable and they'd invariably be asked if they were related, which happens even now. I think they'd say it closed more doors than it opened.

Our whole week would be geared up to the moment John came home. Everything had to stop then so that he could walk through the front door and unwind. All the shopping, cleaning and ironing had to be done during the week, as did any socializing. I'd acquired many close friends among the other MPs or trade union wives – women like Diane Meale, Margaret Caborn, Ann McCartney and Pat Bickerstaffe – all of whom had remained in their constituencies and who understood what my life was like. Friday would be the day I did my hair and make-up, put on a nice outfit, and prepared something special for dinner. The moment John walked through the door, the focus would be on him and what he needed. I was never resentful – this was his time. On Saturdays, we'd potter in the garden or go out in the car somewhere fun with the boys, and then on Sundays we'd have a lazy day with a lamb roast, a dish I inherited from my mother and a favourite with all the men in my house.

Then off John would go again, for another week in London or wherever his work took him. He'd had use of a flat in Maritime House in Clapham, south-west London, when he was with the NUS, but when he became an MP he shared a flat with the MP Dennis Skinner. The media dubbed Dennis 'the Beast of Bolsover' but he is actually the most lovely, sensitive man – although he'd hate me to say it. He and John have been friends for years and I was glad John had some company when he was so far away from home, if only to accompany him to Ronnie Scott's on the rare nights he took off. Poor Dennis was now the one being kept awake all night by John practising his speeches, but he got his own back by watching sport on TV, something John was never interested in. I called them 'the Odd Couple'.

If I was lucky, John might have some constituency matters to attend to or a local surgery to run, so I'd have him home for a few extra days. That always felt like such a treat. Occasionally I would be invited to London to accompany him to an important social occasion and my mum and Auntie Ivy would happily volunteer to come to Hull to spend time together and babysit for the boys.

The most memorable early invitation we received was to a dinner at Downing Street as the guests of Harold and Mary Wilson, just before he left office. John was a new Labour MP and was among several who'd been invited along with their wives. The first thought that entered my head was, Gosh, what do I wear? Flicking through a Vogue catalogue, I spotted a pattern I liked and decided to run up my own dress. John would have let me buy something new, but I really liked the look of this one. If I say so myself, the resulting outfit was a triumph in pale lilac – a gorgeous one-piece in heavy silk jersey. There was only one seam up the back which came to the waist and was then sewn into an elasticated band so that it slipped over my head. The front section lay over my bust and the back formed a lovely big cape. It was fabulous. I wore a long string of pearls and high stilettos and felt rather good.

We sat at this enormous candlelit dining table under sparkling chandeliers while uniformed butlers came round with silver platters of food from which you had to serve yourself. The plates and the silver were exquisite. I was terrified I was going to drop something on my lap. I was so nervous, in fact, that I hardly ate anything even though I was famished. I couldn't chew; I couldn't swallow. I just spent my time chatting to the person next to me. I don't even recall whom it was – another new MP, I think.

It was a fabulous experience and fortunately I've never been nervous of whom might be sitting next to me at a dinner, just the event itself. After years of being a hairdresser, I've never found chatting to people a problem and I could always keep the conversation going It went with the job. As I love meeting people, if there was ever an awkward pause I found that I could easily draw the other person out to talk about themselves and their families. That was always common ground.

Harold Wilson sat next to John at the head of the table, puffing away on his pipe. The two men were deep in conversation and John didn't seem fazed in the slightest. Mary Wilson sat a few seats away from me and I liked her very much. She was quiet and kindly looking. She didn't say much (other than that she liked my dress) and I could tell that being the Prime Minister's wife didn't come naturally to her.

I was still a hairdresser then and found myself in a rather unique position when I returned to the salon after my trip to London. Applying perming solution to someone's hair, trimming it or rolling it into curlers, a customer might enquire, 'Did you have a nice weekend, Pauline? Do anything special?'

'Well, er, actually ...' I'd begin.

Not long afterwards, I was back at Downing Street, this time for afternoon tea with the next Prime Minister's wife, Audrey Callaghan. She was different again; a politician and campaigner in her own right and much more at ease in her surroundings. It gave me cause to think, not for the first time, how difficult it is for a private woman to be thrust unwittingly on to the world stage and how tough-skinned you have to be to survive it.

John began to receive invitations to events like royal garden parties and state dinners, which I'd have loved to have attended, but he always refused to go, much to my annoyance. Not only did being at Buckingham Palace go against his political principles, but what he really didn't like was having to wear what he thought of as a uniform because he'd always worn dinner jackets or white ties on the ships. He might have taken me to a few more parties if he'd been allowed to wear a regular suit. At one dinner he couldn't get out of, he did just that but decided to stay in the background in the hope that no one would notice. Someone did. It was Prince Charles, who asked him, 'What are you skulking back here for? Come and meet some people.' Always so sensitive to how others were feeling, I think Charles must have been aware of my husband's awkwardness. Another time, some years later, when Charles and John were at a meeting, they were served tea and John had nowhere to put his cup. Sliding down his seat, he rested it on his stomach, which provided a perfect table. A few days later, someone spoke to Charles about John and he said, 'Yes, I saw him recently. Interesting fellow. I've never met a limbo tea drinker before.'

When I heard that the Queen was making a royal visit to Hull as part of her Jubilee tour, I was over the moon. As one of the city's MPs, John would have to be in the welcoming party – along with me. To meet the Queen was a dream come true for the girl from Chester who'd watched the Coronation and wondered if I'd ever see her in the flesh. A staunch royalist like my mother (and in contrast to my husband), I always thought the royal family did a wonderful job and that it was damn hard work. They spent their lives in the eyes of the media, especially the women, and the little taste I'd had of that made me appreciate how tough that was.

John knew he couldn't get out of it this time. Being John, though, he foolishly announced in advance that he wouldn't bow to the Queen when he met her. His statement caused a great deal of controversy but as a socialist he felt he couldn't, in all conscience, do it. I didn't agree with him but I admired him for sticking to his guns.

Our boy David, however, felt quite differently. Aged seven he wrote out a lovely message in stencil, which he put it in an envelope marked: *To the Queen. From David.* Then he asked me, 'Mummy, when you meet the Queen, can you give this to her?'

I flinched. 'Oh, I don't know, darling. I probably won't be able to.' Watching his face fall, I added, 'But I will try.'

The Queen arrived early in the morning of that special June day. Her schedule was gruelling: opening a new hotel, shops and offices in the marina, several walkabouts, a lunch, a dinner and an evening reception. We were waiting in the main square in Hull when her huge car pulled up and out stepped a tiny little figure in a lovely lilac dress. I must say she did look tired. She is clever, though. You have to be up very early in the morning to get one over on the Queen. Having read or heard that John had said he wouldn't bow to her, she probably thought, Right, Prescott, I'll get you. Stepping towards him, her head down, she spoke in a very low voice.

'Are there three MPs in Hull?' she virtually whispered.

John had to lower his head to hear what she said. 'Pardon, ma'am?'

At that point, a hundred camera lenses clicked and whirred and the photograph that appeared everywhere was of my John bowing to the Queen. She got him! I had to laugh.

Maybe because of her success, she seemed to come to life after that. The people of Hull certainly made her welcome. They lined the streets, waving their Union Flags wildly. One group sang 'Rose of England' as she did a walkabout with the mayor. I was one of the lucky ladies charged with walking behind her to gather the dozens of flowers she was handed. I knew Mum would be watching on the television news and resisted the temptation to give her a little wave.

In the evening, we were invited to a reception on board the Royal Yacht *Britannia*, moored in the harbour. It was all very informal and the Queen wandered around chatting to people. Clutching David's envelope in my hand, I finally said to John, 'I must at least try to get it to her. I promised him I would.'

John was mortified. 'Paul, you can't!' Seeing my look of determination, he snapped, 'Well, if you're going to try, can you at least do it in the other stateroom?'

'OK then, I will,' I retorted, sounding braver than I felt. Secretly, I hoped I might be able to pass David's letter to a lady-in-waiting. Approaching the Queen in the adjacent room, I heard her say to someone that she had an appalling cold and hadn't been feeling well all day. Despite her ball gown, long white gloves and tiara, she seemed very approachable. She smiled and came towards me. I curtsied deeply and smiled back.

'How are you?' she asked.

'Very well, thank you, ma'am,' I replied. 'I'm so sorry to hear you have a cold.' She thanked me, so I summoned up my courage and held out David's envelope. 'May I leave this letter with you? My little boy wrote it specially.'

'Oh, how nice,' she said, looking at my young son's scrawl. 'What's his name?'

'David.' She nodded. I hesitated. 'I'll just put it on the table over there,' I said, pointing to a corner of the room.

'No, don't do that, it'll get lost,' she said and, to my surprise, she took the envelope from me. I thanked her and curtsied again before she wandered off to chat to the next person. John couldn't believe his eyes when she walked into the room where he was, clutching David's tatty little envelope in her immaculately gloved hand.

Within a week David received a reply. It was a letter from Buckingham Palace, with a special stamp on it. In it, a secretary to the Queen thanked him for his message. He was over the moon. John caught him a few days after that, sitting at the kitchen table, writing a note in his best handwriting. *Dear Queen, it's David again ...*' it began.

John raised his eyes to the heavens. 'Great!' he cried. 'Now we have two royalists in the family.'

Eleven

IN 1972 JOHN WAS APPOINTED TO THE COUNCIL OF EUROPE, AN ENORMOUS honour. In the space of the next two years, he also became delegate to the European Parliament, leader of its Labour Group, and Parliamentary Private Secretary to the Secretary of State for Trade.

These were leading roles he somehow managed concurrently along with doing the job of MP and playing for the House of Commons football team, as well as being a husband to me and the father to two young boys. He'd always been busy and deeply dedicated to whatever he was working on, but – as a wife – I did begin to worry that he had taken on too much. He was exhausted whenever he came home. I could tell he was under a lot of strain.

Any concerns I had that his new European job would mean that we'd get to spend even less time together as a family, though, were allayed when John began taking us with him on some of his trips. 'Pack the car,' he'd say, 'we're off to Paris.' (Or Strasbourg, Brussels or Rome.) I loved every minute. While John worked until the small hours, I'd take the children out sightseeing or go shopping with some of the other wives. It was such a treat even though John often had to stretch our finances to have us with him.

My role as John's wife was becoming increasingly high profile in other ways. I was now expected to attend every Labour Party conference as well as many of his union meetings, especially if he was addressing a crowd. I continued to be the sounding board for his speeches, which he'd rehearse over and over again. I'd be lying in bed in the early hours of the morning and still hear him practising. By the time he stepped up to the podium I'd know the text so well that, I told him, if he ever couldn't deliver his speech I could do it for him. I'd only relax when he threw the floor open to questions because that was when he was at his best. That's when his passion would come out – the same passion I first witnessed at the Roodee racecourse and which never failed to inspire me.

Every general election, of course, I also went on the campaign trail. Being a young mum home alone without help, I took the children along too. Fortunately, the boys loved electioneering. Our son David would sit between us in the car, his mouth pressed to the tannoy, crying: 'Vote Yabour! Vote for my daddy!' (He never could say Labour.) Little old ladies would come rushing out of their houses to give him sweets.

David was interested in politics from the earliest age. On one trip with John, he spotted Barbara Castle, Secretary of State for Health, just as we were about to board a campaign bus. At that point, Barbara had a remarkable record as a Cabinet minister under Harold Wilson and had risen to be his First Secretary of State, before becoming an MEP.

'There's that lady!' David cried excitedly. Before I could stop him, he ran over to say hello. 'It's Mrs Castle, isn't it?' he asked. 'Can I sit next to you?'

'I'd like that.'

'I've never sat by anyone famous before,' he added earnestly.

'But your daddy's famous too,' she said, laughing.

'Yes,' David replied glumly, 'but only in Hull.'

Barbara Castle reminded me of my little mum. She was neat and trim and always beautifully turned out. She was as tough as any man yet feminine with loads of style. I remember being most impressed with her when she stayed with us once. She was shattered, having just flown in from Europe after a heavy week. She arrived at ten o'clock at night, exhausted. Imagine my surprise then, to find her walking around the garden with our dog, Fred the basset hound, at five in the morning.

I had always taken great care with my appearance and had my own definite sense of style, but now that John was in the public eye, I made sure never to let my standards slip. Increasingly, I looked to people like Barbara, as well as other political wives and female politicians I most admired. My major influences were Betty Boothroyd (then on the Council of Europe with John but later the first lady Speaker of the House), and the MPs' wives Susan Crosland and Caroline Benn, who used to wow everyone when they took to the dance floor at the end of each party conference. Sandra Howard, wife of Michael, was another one to watch. She'd been a favourite of the girls in the salon when she was a fashion model adorning the pages of the glossy magazines I used to devour at Quaintways. I always thought she was the typical English rose.

Betty Boothroyd had become a good friend to both John and me, and I loved her no-nonsense Yorkshire style. I especially admired the fact that she had achieved a childhood ambition of mine: to be in a dance troupe. As a member of the famous Tiller Girls, Betty had wowed men for years before knocking them dead in the House. When she became Speaker years later, she invited us to her official residence with some friends and showed us a step or two. Wow! And she has such nice trim ankles. Coming home from Europe with John once, Betty took me to one side in the airport duty-free shop. 'Listen, kid,' she said (she always called me 'kid'), 'this sorts the men from the boys. The boys buy cologne, the men buy perfume.' It was sound advice.

In 1980, partly as a ruse by Jim Callaghan to get John out of the country because he was ruffling too many feathers, my husband was offered a post as a European Commissioner. The job carried a salary of around four hundred thousand pounds over five years. When John first told me, my reaction wasn't quite what he might have expected.

'Does this mean I can buy a Brueghel print I've spotted on the chipboard in W. H. Smith?' I asked. 'It's called *Country Fair* and it'll be perfect for the study. It's seven pounds.'

John laughed. 'Listen, love, if I take this job, we can buy the original.'

I laughed too, although personally I'd have gone for a Renoir.

For a brief moment, I fantasized about being wealthy. Our lives could have taken such a different turn. Oh, and to live in Brussels – although, knowing John, he'd have told me to stay on in Hull. In the end, it didn't matter because he turned down the post, knowing that it would mean the end of his parliamentary life when he felt he still had so much left to do. He said the move to Europe would be like 'cutting his own throat'. It was the same with all the directorships and after-dinner speaking he's been offered over the years and passed on either because they'd clash with his principles or not leave him enough time for politics. Needless to say, I ended up with only the Brueghel print, which I still proudly own.

So, John stayed on his MP's salary, which he used to secure us a mortgage on a castellated Victorian property at Sutton, on the outskirts of Hull. We first spotted the £28,000 house in an estate agent's window but when we went to view it John thought it far too grand with all its gargoyles and turrets. His mother disagreed. 'Nonsense,' she replied.

'It's perfect for an MP of your stature.' All I could think was, How am I going to clean all this?

Wandering around the garden, Phyllis saw a splendid magnolia and told me, 'When I die, I'd like to be buried under a magnolia tree.'

When Bert came to visit the house later, I showed him the garden and told him what his ex-wife had said. Quick as a flash, he quipped, 'That could be arranged.'

A former Salvation Army commune, the house eventually made a beautiful family home for us in which to raise our boys. More than thirty years later, we're still here, so Phyllis wasn't wrong, even if the property she helped us choose did become known locally as 'Prescott's Castle', a name that has stuck ever since.

As John continued to rise through the political ranks, I found myself hosting all sorts of illustrious guests in our new home, including Tony Benn, Michael Foot and John Smith. Later Tony Blair, and Gordon and Sarah Brown came and stayed as well. For me, our new home was a delight. It reminded me of the red-brick Georgian house in Queen's Park, Chester, that my mother used to work in as a cleaner after my father died. I used to wander through those lofty rooms when I was a little girl, trying to imagine what it would be like to own a house like that. Now, here I was, twenty-five years later, mistress of my own castle.

Mum and Auntie Ivy were even more impressed. As former housemaids, they'd both lived and worked in grand old houses for much of their lives and now 'our Pauline' was living in one. They were such fun to have to stay. They spoilt me terribly and I loved every minute of it. Like two peas in a pod as they grew older and began to look more and more alike, they'd have a little tot of whisky in the afternoon before taking turns at the ironing board. Like them, I've never had help around the house – I still do all the cleaning and ironing myself – but whenever they came to visit, we'd sit at the dining-room table together and polish the silver and brass just like the old days. They were such happy times.

Not everything was going our way, though. In the spring of 1981, just before the official opening of the Humber Bridge by the Queen, John left the house in the early hours to give some Dutch MPs a private tour of the bridge. He was to meet Austin Mitchell, Euro MP for Grimsby. Crossing the bridge at some speed, John's driver hit a concrete block lying in his path and lost control. John was just about to put on his seat belt when – wham!

Austin rang me at 7 a.m., about an hour after John had left home.

'Don't panic, Pauline, but there's been an accident. John's hurt. He's in the hospital.'

My heart did a somersault. 'Where?'

'The Royal Infirmary. He's in intensive care.'

By the time I got there in a taxi, the doctors were able to brief me on his injuries. 'He's broken his back, but it's a clean break,' one told me as I reeled in shock. Broken his back? Would he be paralysed then?

'The next forty-eight hours will be critical,' the doctor added. 'But this kind of break is better than a fracture and the good news is he has full sensation in his limbs.'

When I first walked into intensive care, I was afraid of what I might find. I was right to be scared; John looked dreadful. His skin was grey and he was wired up to all sorts of monitors and drips. For a day or two we didn't know if there would be permanent damage. The boys came to see him, as did friends and political colleagues, so he tried to put a brave face on things. He hated being in there, and we all hated waiting for news, but once the doctors assured us that he should make a full recovery, we relaxed. He was moved to a room on his own where he could carry on working from his bed, despite my protests. I visited every day and then, when he came home, I had the unenviable task of trying to persuade him to convalesce for several weeks. Getting John Prescott to relax isn't easy, believe me. A pipe-and-slippers man he is not.

It took years for his back to recover and he still has to be careful. He lost an inch in height and will have problems for the rest of his life. He has stooped slightly ever since and blames the accident for the weight he started to gain afterwards because he could no longer exercise as before. John had always been so fit: the boxer, the swimmer, the man who never sat still. Like most politicians, he worked jolly hard but had quick powers of recovery, chiefly thanks to his fitness. Once he lost that, then his habit of always eating on the hoof (usually takeaways, sandwiches and fast food) began to take its toll on him.

My husband is one of those people who will come in from work and go straight to the fridge. I've always been quite careful about what I have in the house, but I also know that I can't mollycoddle him and that if he has a problem then he has to come to terms with it himself. In my fridge there are all the naughty chocolaty bits that I love, plus lots of healthier options like fruit. I'll say to him, 'It's all there, John: good and bad. It's up to you.' I was never with him during the week anyway and I knew he often ate badly but that was his choice.

What surprised me the most about his later weight gain was that he never seemed to eat enormous amounts. I ate more than him, although he does bolt his meals and always clears his plate. Throughout our marriage he has asked me why I take so long to eat and then leave food on my plate. 'My father used to say the people in China are starving for that.'

I tell him, 'Well, John, they're welcome to it but I don't want it.' I pointed out that he didn't need to eat every mouthful, not if he was already full. Eventually he saw that I was right and he will now leave things if he's had enough.

I really never worried about what he ate because he'd always burned it off with nervous energy. Even when he started to get a little stockier, I knew he was still healthy, and he never stopped going to the gym. Genetics played a part too, I reminded myself. Once he broke his back, though, everything changed. Having been so active, it was tough on him to lose his fitness. I was just so grateful that the break wasn't more serious and he didn't come home in a wheelchair. Then the media started poking fun at him in cartoons and being cruel about his weight. Even though John joked publicly that he was 'fat for purpose', it was something he took deeply to heart, although it was a long time before I realized just how deeply.

It was my mother who first noticed that something was wrong. She was staying with us once and noticed that he kept disappearing to the loo after meals. 'Keep an eye on him, Pauline,' she told me as she helped me clear the dinner plates. 'I think he's making himself sick.'

I was so shocked. I couldn't believe what she was telling me at first and assured her that there was nothing like that going on. Then I began to watch him too and, sure enough, the signs were all there; I just hadn't noticed them before. He started to be very secretive about food. He'd tell me not to put much on his plate but then I'd find him snacking in the kitchen. Food began mysteriously disappearing from the fridge. The more I watched his habits, the more convinced I became that he was secretly picking at his favourite things, maybe even stashing them, and then making himself sick.

I read up on eating disorders and found out that there was a condition called bulimia, in which people binge and purge, binge and purge. This was before Lady Diana famously owned up to suffering from the condition and long before newspapers like the *Daily Mail* ran regular features on the subject. Sufferers show signs of bloating around the throat. They lose the enamel from their teeth because of all the acid in the reflux, and they can do serious damage to their kidneys. Once I knew all I needed to know, I confronted John about it at home one weekend, telling him that I thought he had bulimia.

'What the hell's that?' he asked.

When I explained, he denied it at first.

'Listen, love,' I said, 'there's no use pretending. Mum picked up on it and now I have. I know what you're doing and you can damage all sorts of organs if you carry on. I've read up on it.'

It took a few months for him to finally admit that he had an eating disorder but when he did, he confessed that it had been going on about fifteen years. He didn't know it had a name, he just knew that if he vomited up what he'd just eaten he wouldn't put on so much weight. In the previous few years he'd been given more and more responsibility in the various shadow departments he'd been shunted between: Regional Affairs, Transport, Employment and Energy. Each new role required him to read his way into the job, do tremendous amounts of research, get to know his staff and help devise policy. He'd also put himself up for the deputy leadership election against Roy Hattersley and Neil Kinnock and lost. The pressures on him were enormous.

Whereas I would lose my appetite whenever I was worried or stressed, John was secretly binging on burgers, fish and chips, biscuits, trifles, chocolate, everything. It was comfort eating, I suppose; his way of making up for the feelings of being overwhelmed by work in what were often sixteen-hour days. He finally accepted that he had to do something about it when Lady Diana admitted she had a problem too and that it was much more common than people realized. Up until then John didn't think men could suffer from it as well and he felt such shame. Once he'd admitted it, though, he was able to face up to what he had to do about it.

In February 1991, I made him go and see a doctor at the House of Commons and for a while he had some therapy, but that wasn't really for him – not least because he was the only male patient in a room full of women. When they suggested acupuncture or 'nails in his hands', as he described it, he decided to sort it out for himself. Although he has had his lapses, he now claims to have been bulimia-free for several years.

Around the same time, I also noticed that he was drinking an awful lot of fluids and going to the loo too often in the night. I made him get a blood sugar test and the doctors discovered he was diabetic just like his father Bert. So, as well as being mindful of his eating disorder, he has to be very careful with his diet. John being John decided to go public about his diabetes and set up a new government initiative to help sufferers, which has gone from strength to strength. Different foods can really give him mood swings, bread especially. He can become quite cantankerous on bread. I also have to hide all the chocolate in the house or he becomes my very own Victor Meldrew. As a child, John had played Grumpy in a school production of *Snow White and the Seven Dwarves*. I always say he's been playing it ever since. The boys even bought him a mug which reads 'Grumpy Old Man'. He laughed about it and said thanks, but I notice he hides it in the back of the cupboard.

For John, living with an eating disorder will be a lifetime struggle. He is still working at it. He says he isn't making himself sick any more and I believe him. I could always tell when he was, because he was swollen under the jaw and he isn't now. He is certainly much better about his diet these days and he has lost two stone in recent years. In the end, I think he scared himself. He began to worry that all the acid he was regurgitating might give him cancer and he gradually became more disciplined. Now that he is past the worst of it, he puts the whole thing down to stress and exhaustion. It was the job, he claims, that made him do it. Being a workaholic isn't dissimilar from being addicted to anything else, I guess. It's just another addiction; another way of getting through the day.

My mother could always look on the bright side of life. She told me, 'It could have been worse, Pauline. John could have become an alcoholic and that would have been much more expensive.'

My mum had been so very happy with Harry that when she eventually lost him after a bout of pneumonia, she was devastated but consoled herself with her memories. 'I had fourteen years with your father and fourteen years with Harry,' she said. 'I couldn't have hoped for two more wonderful husbands.'

She was still living in the same house she'd bought with my dad and was to remain there for the rest of her life. As she always said, 'I want to die in my own bed.' The house was spotless and no one in Chester had a cleaner front step. But she was lonely after Harry died, and especially missed their fun times together at the races, so I started travelling to

Chester more often to take her to town for a special day out. We'd always start with some light refreshment in the Library Room of the Grosvenor Hotel, not far from the Eastgate Clock where John first asked me out.

The Grosvenor holds a special place in my heart because it is where I still go with some of my oldest and dearest friends. Gordon Vickers, who ran the Wall City Jazz Club, comes along and Margaret Fell, who used to be one of my Quaintways clients. She brings her daughter Melanie and whenever she can make it my cousin Rita, who lives in Canada, joins us. We have our reunions in Arkle's Bar, named after a famous horse, before we head off to the races.

John took me to the Grosvenor Hotel quite recently. He hadn't been for years. We were in Chester and he suddenly suggested we have afternoon tea. We wandered in and found a table and the waiter came up to serve us. He took John's order for a pot of Darjeeling, then turned to me and said, 'Your usual champagne, madam?' John was quite taken aback.

My mum, who never drove, would order us a taxi into Chester when she could no longer climb on to the buses. She ordered taxis everywhere – it was her little treat – and the local drivers adored her. When we'd get to the hotel, a waiter would come up to take her order for tea.

'We have Earl Grey, Lady Grey, English Breakfast, Lapsang Souchong, China tea, Darjeeling, Indian, green tea and an assortment of herbal infusions,' he'd say, taking her around the world.

My little mum would wait until he'd finished and say, 'Do you have Yorkshire tea, please?'

'No, madam,' the reply would come, 'I'm afraid we don't serve that.'

'Oh,' she'd say a little sniffily. 'Then English breakfast tea will be fine.'

Mum and I always had such a laugh, mainly because she was a young woman trapped in an old woman's body. I'd take her to the Ladies and they'd have piles of gorgeous thick paper hand towels with 'Grosvenor House' embossed on them. 'These are lovely, Mum,' I'd say, feeling the quality, 'and great for travelling. Here, open your handbag!' We'd come out of the loo giggling like a couple of schoolgirls, our handbags stuffed with towels.

She was so organized and still so frugal, even though she no longer had to be. She'd always managed, even if she only had tuppence half-penny, and she never owed anyone a penny. Bright as a button, she had put up with such a lot in her life and everybody loved her. She'd tell a story with that Cheshire accent of hers and then turn round and ask, 'Do you get my drift?'

Once a week, Mum would get her hair done by her longstanding hairdresser 'lovely Rita' at a place she often mistakenly referred to as 'The Hair of House and Beauty'. When she wasn't out shopping with Freda, Gordon Vickers's sister-in-law, who was like a daughter to her, or Maureen, who did her cleaning and took her to medical appointments, she'd be home watching television and catching up on the telephone. We used to speak at least twice a day, morning and night. As she got older and began to suffer from arthritis and bad hips, she was cared for by her guardian angels and Freda's husband Stan, who did all her gardening and odd jobs. I don't know what we would have done without them.

Mum loved a 'flutter', as she put it, and we'd place bets each year on several races but always the Grand National. John's father Bert, a great racing fan as well, would take our bets half an hour before the off. I was with her one Grand National day and Mum said to me, 'Quick. Ring John's dad. It's almost time for the start.' We'd studied the form and I fancied a horse called Johnnie Likes Jazz because my John does so love his jazz. I was torn between that one and a horse called Party Politics but time was running out. Mum was standing beside me when I dialled the number and, after dithering a little, I asked Bert to put my money on Johnnie Likes Jazz.

As usual, Mum started interrupting, something she did whenever anybody was on the phone. This time she said, 'Don't be rude, Pauline. Ask him how he is!' There wasn't really time before the race so I finished placing my bet and put down the telephone only to have her scold me as if I was a little girl. 'You didn't ask him how he was.'

Imagine her delight when the horse that won that day was called How's Your Father? I said, 'Mother, you've done it again.'

I remember asking her once, 'Gosh, Mum, whatever will I do without you?'

She looked across at me and gave me that smile I'd known all my life. 'Even I can't go on for ever,' she told me.

Twelve

JOHN'S RISE UP THE GREASY POLE CONTINUED APACE AND HE HELD A number of posts in the Shadow Cabinet under the leadership of Neil Kinnock and later John Smith, both in opposition to Margaret Thatcher.

I met Mrs T. once. She presented a Wilkinson Sword award to John for a sponsored swim he did for charity, and David and I were invited along. John always said that he admired her for the courage of her convictions and for carrying out the policies she believed in, even though they were everything he detested. I certainly didn't agree with much of what she did and found her rather contrived, but she always looked extremely smart in spite of her busy life and I had to admire her for that.

I was on the sidelines again, this time in the early 1980s, when John did something rather unusual for an MP. He'd learned how to be a deep-sea diver so that he could personally experience some of the conditions his NUS members had to endure on the oil rigs and elsewhere. The children and I used to go along to a lake in Hull and watch as he was helped into a diving suit that resembled something from *Twenty Thousand Leagues Under the Sea*. It even had a brass helmet, which was screwed down before he was lowered into the water attached to a lifeline. Once, something went wrong and we could hear him via his intercom crying, 'Bring me up! Bring me up!' I had the children with me and it was terrifying until he finally emerged from the water, breathless but OK.

Because of his experiences, John was invited to be the first MP to dive the wreck of the Tudor warship the *Mary Rose*. I was a little more nervous about that. After all, John was a father of two boys and diving wrecks is notoriously dangerous. But he was so excited to be going to the Solent and swimming over the bows of Henry VIII's finest vessel, which had lain at the bottom of the Channel for more than four hundred years, that I had to support him. David and I watched as he put on his wetsuit and jumped into the sea. Supervised by members of the advisory committee for historic wreck sites, John explored the wreck with maritime archaeologist Dr Margaret Rule, who'd led the expedition to salvage the vessel. The experience proved to be one of the most memorable of his life. We certainly cheered when he came up. Later, Dr Rule presented him with a beautiful painting of the *Mary Rose*, which still hangs in our house.

In 1983, John donned a wetsuit again to swim two miles up the Thames from Battersea Bridge to Westminster Bridge before walking to Downing Street to protest against nuclear dumping at sea. Appearing on the sofa at TV-am with Nick Owen and Anne Diamond just before his swim, he spoke with his usual passion about the environmental matters close to his heart. 'Britain continues to accept the nuclear waste of other countries and dump it into our seas,' he said. 'I'm not prepared to tolerate it.'

As the dutiful wife that I was, I waved him off in his wetsuit and watched him start swimming against the current in the freezing, polluted water. He was flanked by Greenpeace boats waving banners of support, plus TV crews and cameramen in several other boats. I took a taxi to Westminster Bridge to greet him when he finished an hour later. Dripping wet, he emerged flushed and cold but smiling for the waiting cameras. I posed happily until the photographers asked me to kiss him. Not much fancying a mouthful of the Thames and thinking that John resembled the Creature from the Black Lagoon, I told them, 'No, you kiss him!'

John still travelled a great deal but every now and again, I'd go with him. On one working trip to Florida with the Council of Europe, he and I were taken on Peter Pan's Flight at Disney World's Fantasyland in Orlando. All we could think of was how much the boys would love it as we flew out of the window of the Darlings' townhouse and soared over a remarkable scale model of Big Ben, on our way to Neverland. We made a promise to take Johnathan and David back one day, which we did a few years later and had one of our best family holidays together. That Florida holiday certainly beat a choppy boat trip on Loch Ness, which I'd had to endure the previous year. When John picked me some heather because I was seasick and scared, I hit him with it and then burst into tears – remembering my father picking heather for my mother in Scotland when I was a little girl.

A few years later John took us all back to America, this time to Washington, which was hugely exciting for the boys. We stayed at the famous Watergate Hotel and the boys and I were given a special tour of the White House, including a visit to the Oval Office while John was in meetings all day. Then we went to New York and took Johnathan and David to the Empire State Building and the Statue of Liberty; they loved every minute.

I was just getting ready to set off on that trip from Hull when I checked the house one last time and found the kitchen window swinging wide open. I thought, I didn't leave that open. Someone must have broken in! Even though I was alone in the house, I was so furious that I flew around the place looking for the intruder to see if he was still there. I don't know what I would have done if I'd confronted him – thrown something at him, probably. Luckily for me, he'd gone. The police thought he had probably been scared off when he heard me. They said that what I'd done was 'a silly thing to do'. I suppose it was, but I was so angry I wasn't thinking straight. Needless to say, we now have even better security.

It was on a visit to Washington that we first met Senator Edward Kennedy, which was an enormous privilege. John was so impressed, he asked him to sign our visitors' book, which he took along with him as a sort of unofficial autograph book. We were fortunate enough to meet Senator Kennedy a few times after that: when he came to Britain to receive his honorary knighthood and at a dinner with the Belfast politician John Hume. A charming man, the last surviving Kennedy brother was sitting just across from me and I heard him talk about his family. 'They're all well,' he said with a smile. 'I'm looking after the Kennedy stables now; especially with the young ones coming up.' I couldn't help but think of all he had gone through: the assassination of two brothers and the ups and downs of political and family life. Yet somehow he managed to maintain such a cheery disposition in the face of it all, even his own failing health. He was an inspiration to us all.

Another friend of ours from those early trips to Washington was the Connecticut Senator Chris Dodd who was in the Council of Europe with John. He was close to the Kennedys and later became Bill

Clinton's campaign manager. I liked Chris enormously and am delighted that he is now such a key part of the Senate and the Obama administration. I can remember years ago looking at him and John standing side by side, both of them bright young politicians with their political futures still ahead of them. 'Just think, Chris,' I told him, 'one of these days you could become President and John could be Prime Minister!' They laughed it off but John went on to become Deputy Prime Minister, standing in for the PM on numerous occasions, and Chris ran for the Democratic Presidential nomination in 2007. I wasn't so wide of the mark, was I?

Once, when Chris was campaigning to be re-elected to the Senate, we went with him on the campaign trail in his home state, which was a very different experience to our own. His constituency was vast and hundreds of miles had to be covered so we often flew in jets to the various events he was expected to attend. The whole experience was like a five-star version of what we'd always known as campaigning in Hull. There was no knocking on doors in rows of terraced houses, no bleak polling stations or visits to factories. American politics in a wealthy state involved lavish fundraisers at luxurious country clubs, and posh dinners and events at private mansions.

Not that the pace was any slower than ours. After a day or two on the trail, with early starts and late nights coupled with our jet lag, we were exhausted, so Chris took us to the house of one of his staff for an afternoon nap before the next fundraiser. John and I were shown to a spare bedroom and slept for over an hour. When we woke up, the house was empty. The political entourage had all left, forgetting about their sleeping British guests. We had no idea where we were other than Connecticut, and no idea how to reach Chris and his staff.

Just then, the man of the house came home, walked in, took one look at us and said, 'Who the hell are you?'

We had to explain rather hastily before he called the police. Eventually, we were reunited with Chris's team and the campaigning went on.

Following Neil Kinnock's resignation in 1992, John was deeply engrossed in political matters closer to home. John Smith had been appointed Labour leader and began to rely on my John more and more. They were the same age, became MPs in the same year, and had 'grown up' together in the House, although John Smith had ploughed ahead to become Secretary of State for Trade under Jim Callaghan.

When John Smith decided to abolish the controversial trade union block vote at the Labour Party conferences and even though Margaret Beckett was his deputy, it was my John whom he asked to make the closing speech. If he didn't get the vote, he confided in John, he'd resign as leader. His career rested heavily on my husband's shoulders.

I was in the audience and sat holding my breath as John gave his impassioned delivery on the 'one member, one vote' policy that was widely believed to have secured his own political career as well. He'd only had half an hour to prepare – a far cry from the hours and hours he normally spent writing, rewriting and rehearsing. Emotional and spontaneous, it was the best speech he'd ever given. Standing before conference, he jabbed his finger at the sceptical audience and told them, 'There's no doubt this man, our leader, put his head on the block when he said he believes, he fervently believes, in a relationship and a strong one with the trade unions and the Labour Party. He's put his head there; now's the time to vote; give us a bit of trust and let's have this vote supported.' He was absolutely wonderful and I had never been more proud.

I remember turning to Alastair Campbell, who was standing next to me, and saying, 'If he doesn't make another speech that will do it for me. That was the pinnacle.'

Alastair, then the political editor of the *Today* newspaper, laughed and shook his head. 'Believe you me, Pauline,' he said, 'John Prescott will be making many more speeches after that.'

Later, John bumped into his father, who attended every conference. He hoped that his dad might congratulate him, but Bert said only, 'Where's your first reception?' John was really hurt by that. I congratulated him later privately, though. 'You did it so well because you spoke from the heart,' I told him with a kiss. I think that really meant a lot to him.

On the night of 11 May 1994, John helped to host a £500-a-head fundraiser at the Park Lane Hotel in London. It was a star-studded affair which for some reason I couldn't attend but he did ring me around midnight to tell me how it went.

'It was a great night,' he told me. 'John was in really good form, laughing and joking with everyone.' The following morning, John Smith dropped dead of a heart attack in his London flat. He was fifty-five years old. The news came as such a terrible shock. I could hardly believe it when I heard. My John cried when he was told by his staff – one of the few times I have ever known him do so. He had lost a close friend and a political ally. John can get very emotional, but he isn't easily moved to tears. I guess his friend's death must have made him think of his own mortality too.

The subsequent memorial service at Westminster Abbey was one of the most touching I have ever attended and an event that united all political parties. Everyone had such great hopes for the gentle Scotsman most expected to be the next Prime Minister. The Archbishop of Canterbury said he'd had 'the name of everyman' and called him a 'man of the people'. He was certainly one of the nicest people you could hope to meet, with a beautiful family. I was lucky enough to have met him and his wife Elizabeth many times. He is missed to this day.

John Smith's death left a huge void, not only emotionally but also politically. It took me several days to appreciate that my husband was now among the most highly qualified to fill that void. His two main contenders for the role of leader of the Labour Party were the deputy leader Margaret Beckett, and a young man by the name of Tony Blair, then Shadow Home Secretary. John called Tony 'Bambi' because he was so young and innocent-looking. Tony was supported by his close friend and mentor Gordon Brown, who had also been waiting in the wings.

The country was deeply disillusioned with John Major and the Tories and I realized quite quickly that if my John did win the ballot, he might actually go on to become Britain's first Labour Prime Minister in eighteen years. I'd had some big adjustments to make in my life. Having had Paul at sixteen, I'd married a waiter and left all that I'd known and loved in Chester. I'd moved to Hull, had two more children, given up hairdressing and, before I knew it, I'd become an MP's wife. I'd grown accustomed to being a mostly single parent, running a home on my own and managing the lives of two energetic boys. I'd travelled widely; I'd met the Queen; I'd done a thousand things 'Tilly' Tilston from Boughton Heath never dreamed she'd do. Now, because of an unforeseeable and tragic event, I might suddenly be on the way to becoming the wife of the leader of the Labour Party, and – who knew – eventually maybe even the Prime Minister's wife? Me? First Lady of

Britain? The very thought of it made me quiver to the tips of my black patent shoes.

John has always believed in me, which is a wonderful attribute in a husband. 'You're a very stylish lady,' he tells me, 'any man would be proud to have you by his side ... when you're not wearing a hat.' I have no doubt that he would have made a very good Prime Minister, given the chance. His style would have been different to any before or since, certainly, and, boy, wouldn't it have been extraordinary to have stood beside him on the steps of Number Ten?

The question back then was whether I wanted it, for me or for the boys, who were both young men by then. Johnathan was just starting his own property business and David was working in Fleet Street. Every aspect of our lives would change. They would come under scrutiny as well and, as for me, I wouldn't even be able to go shopping on my own or have lunch with a girlfriend without a bodyguard. Life would be so different.

Right back from when I'd met Mrs Wilson and Mrs Callaghan, I'd appreciated that the media lens zooms in on Prime Ministers' spouses and doesn't allow them to have a life of their own. Norma Major was picked on and so was Denis Thatcher. It was just like what happened with Lady Diana and Fergie, although they each found their own way eventually. What sort of time would the media give me? If you step into the spotlight you have to be prepared for the glare of publicity and, although I had a tough little streak, I wasn't sure if I could cope with all that the spotlight might show. Once I start to wonder what people might be thinking and saying about me, I get nervous of them being picky. Worse still, what if the newspapers started digging into my past and found out about Paul? What would that mean for John's career, and for the boys? My goodness, Johnathan and David didn't even know Paul existed. What would they think of me?

I remembered my mother's age-old advice: 'Head high. Shoulders back. You're as good as anyone else and better than most.' If I'd had to do it I would have done, and, wow, would she have been proud. It certainly would have been a challenge and an honour and I'm sure I could have managed it in my own way. But the truth was that I preferred to be one step down from the top rung. In his heart, I think John did too. He might have enjoyed playing the role for a short while just so he could say he'd done it, but I don't think he really ever wanted to be Prime Minister.

Luckily for us both, it never happened. Tony Blair won the leadership election and I completely understand why. Not only was he very young at a time when everyone wanted somebody youthful and healthy after John Smith's death, he was absolutely charming; a true gentleman and always extremely courteous, which is something I admire in a man. He was also politically astute in making John his elected deputy leader, cleverly recognizing the value in a 'New Labour' government of having someone as his DPM who was deemed 'old Labour'.

John, to his credit, backed Tony all the way. He told voters, 'We represent different parts of the party – each of us represents the parts the other can't reach.' There were no sour grapes; no regrets. As far as John and I were concerned, the best man had been picked for the job, for the party, and for the country – and his name was Tony Blair.

At the glitzy London celebration of Tony's success and the announcement of John's role at the Festival Hall, Cherie Blair and I waited in the wings for the moment we'd be allowed up on the platform together to congratulate our husbands. It had all been stage-managed in advance but the nearer the time came when the world's cameras would focus on us, the more nervous I became. Nor, even though she was a barrister, did Cherie behave like someone accustomed to the public eye. I think she was as nervous as I was, and as our time came and we set off for the stage together we rather stupidly held hands. It felt the natural thing to do.

Tony's father Leo was there too – someone I came to adore. He was a Yorkshire Tory councillor, a barrister and retired lecturer. Fostered as a child, Leo hit it off with me from the outset. When I saw what a success he'd made of his life despite his inauspicious beginnings, I couldn't help but hope for the best for my Paul.

As Cherie and I stood on that platform alongside our husbands, overwhelmed by the cheering applause and dazzled by the flashing cameras, I think we both wondered what on earth we had let ourselves in for. People have tried to suggest over the years that we didn't really get along but the truth was that I admired Cherie, who combined her role as a hands-on mum with holding down a high-powered job extremely well. It wasn't an easy position to be in, even though it was a very privileged one. As I was a constituency wife with my own friends at the other end of the country, we were never going to be close and, anyway, she was busy with her boys and her work. We came from completely different backgrounds and I don't think we had much in common apart from our husbands' shared passion for politics.

Aware that I would be standing alongside her and that comparisons would almost certainly be made, I chose my outfit very carefully that day: a lovely white suit with navy-blue edging by Bruce Oldfield at Mansfield. Bruce Oldfield had long been a favourite of mine. A Yorkshireman, he'd been raised in a children's home and I secretly admired his rags-to-riches story. What I loved about that particular Chanel-style suit was that it was simple but elegant. I felt really smart and, having done my hair and make-up, I was quietly confident.

To my horror, a double-page spread appeared in the *Daily Mail* the following day headlined *A Tale of Two Wives*. The article compared me to Cherie and said: *Mrs Prescott walked on stage after her husband's victory to plant a lipsticked kiss upon his cheek, each step of her high heels crushing the myth that the wives of Labour MPs have to be drab. Compared with Cherie Blair and Margaret Beckett, she looked like Bet Lynch arriving by mistake at a session of the Open University*. It was horrid. I'd had such a wonderful day but then they'd shot me down and almost ruined it for me. I remember reading it and saying, 'Well, for crying out loud!' I began to worry that I might have embarrassed John somehow on what should have been the best day of his life. Then I realized that some reporters only build you up to knock you down. I decided after that never to speak to the press unless it was on my own terms.

Thirteen

ON THE AFTERNOON OF POLLING DAY, 1 MAY 1997, JOHN LEFT OUR HOME IN Hull to go on a remarkable journey. He and I had voted at our local polling station early that morning and then went off to rally support in the constituency. Soon after lunch, my husband boarded a helicopter and was flown to Sedgefield in County Durham, the constituency home of Tony Blair, for a private meeting that would change our lives.

In the living room of Tony and Cherie's four-bedroom detached Victorian house, 'Myrobella', John was promised that if Labour were to be elected (as everyone hoped) he'd be given the role of Deputy Prime Minister, a position that any Prime Minister can create at his own discretion. It was the British equivalent of the American vice-presidency, and an enormous honour conferred on my John. There had only ever been seven deputy prime ministers before and they included Clement Attlee, Anthony Eden, Willie Whitelaw and Michael Heseltine. John was in historic company.

What an incredible accolade that was for a man who'd started off scrubbing pans. As well as being 'DPM' (as the position is always abbreviated), John would be put in charge of a new 'superdepartment', combining several together. Armed with this momentous news, he flew back to Hull and waited with me and the boys at the Guildhall for the election results. When the final count came through at two o'clock in the morning it was the most thrilling moment. Labour had surged to power on a landslide with the charismatic Tony Blair as its new figurehead.

My John had been a huge part of this incredible political change sweeping the country, which led to the first Labour election victory since 1974, with its largest number of seats ever. I felt humbled to have had a ringside seat at that moment in history. Hearing that the Conservatives now held their fewest parliamentary seats since 1906 really was the icing on the cake.

The night didn't stop there. Whisked off and into a motorcade, police sirens wailing, John, the boys and I were driven to Humberside airport where the boys joked about which plane was ours. The Labour Party chartered a private jet to fly us to London to meet up with the Blairs and the Browns, the Kinnocks, Alastair Campbell (now Director of Communications) and Peter Mandelson (who'd been given his first job in the party thanks to my husband).

We boarded the plane and then most of us got quite tiddly. John didn't drink a thing. He was absolutely shattered after two gruelling months on the campaign trail. His battle bus, the Prescott Express, had covered ten thousand miles in the previous six weeks and as soon as he settled into his seat on the plane he began to nod off.

I didn't feel like sleeping one little bit. Dancing in the aisle of that luxurious plane while our boys and John's staff sang 'Come Fly with Me', I nibbled at smoked-salmon sandwiches and posed for the cine camera. 'I could get used to this!' I cried merrily. 'I'm Pauline, fly me.'

What I didn't think I could get used to, though, was the presence of the bodyguards who had joined us for the first time and who went on to become an integral part of our lives. Settling into my seat opposite a dozing John, I looked across at the burly men who'd been assigned to him and noticed that they were both drifting off as well. Winking at John, I whispered, 'I'm going to attack you now.' He half smiled and went back to sleep.

One of the security men, eyes closed, muttered under his breath, 'Just you try,' and he smiled too.

Those men – and one woman, Leanne, a gorgeous blonde – were to become part of our family. Along with John's drivers, they changed shifts each week, alternating with each other. They'd walk into our home each Friday night ahead of John and hand me a bag of his dirty washing, then sit down and relax while I made them a cup of tea and refreshments. Even though they were always on duty with their loaded guns in their holsters, they'd stay for meals and join us for barbecues in the garden. One of them, Harry, whom all the girls loved because he was so good-looking, was a special friend to us both. Whenever I had too much luggage and maybe a hat box that John would definitely blow up about if he spotted it, Harry would say, 'Don't worry, Pauline, we'll put that in the back of our car. He'll never know.' Harry's mum was apparently quite a fan of mine and she would send me little cards and notes. We still exchange Christmas cards.

Our security guards were with us that historic May morning when our plane landed at Heathrow airport in the early hours. They accompanied us as we were whisked off in a fast car to where everyone else was waiting at the Royal Festival Hall. The world's media were there too, to herald in the 'new dawn' Tony had promised and the New Labour government he'd led to victory. None of us had slept. We hadn't even eaten; but it didn't matter. We were high on victory.

It was a bittersweet moment for John as we watched Tony and Cherie pose for photographs. The thought of what might have been must have entered his head, although personally I was happy with the way things had turned out for the boys' sakes, if not ours. Leaving the Festival Hall, we took off on a tour of London in the Labour Party battle bus. Later on we did something a bit naughty. We drove round to the Conservative Party campaign headquarters in Smith Square to witness the staff dismantling it and heading home. 'Out, out, at last you're out!' people on the bus chanted as the Tory faithful watched dolefully from the windows. It wasn't a nice thing to do and we were gloating slightly but I'm sure they would have done the same thing had the tables been turned.

The next few months were a whirlwind but John managed to retain what I called the 'Prescott sense of humour' throughout. I always said it wasn't humour, it was sarcasm. During an official photo shoot for him and Tony and Gordon Brown, who'd been appointed Chancellor, one shot included me with the country's three most powerful men. Just as the photo was about to be taken, the photographer asked John to smile. He replied grumpily, 'Oh God, does this mean I'm one of the beautiful people now?' I couldn't help but laugh.

In the space of a few days, John had been appointed Secretary of State for Environment, Transport and the Regions. Given a choice of buildings to work from, he chose the Environment department as his HQ. Then, the best bit ever: he was officially announced as the Deputy Prime Minister of the United Kingdom. My former waiter of a husband was now the Queen's Second Minister. I felt fit to burst.

I could hardly believe the journey John had brought me on from the days when we were first courting. Was this man the same one who'd been too shy to ask me to marry him in public? The young newspaper delivery boy who had waited in an alleyway to blow me kisses? The uniformed steward who'd smuggled me on board the *Britannic* for romantic trysts? Who would have guessed that by impulsively agreeing to go to the pictures with a man I barely knew one Saturday night in 1957, I'd become the wife of one of the most powerful men in the country?

When John heard that as Deputy Leader of the Opposition he had to be sworn in as a member of Her Majesty's Most Honourable Privy Council and would gain the title of 'Right Honourable', he thought it was a joke. When he realized it was part of the traditions of government and that it would also mean bowing to the Queen and kissing her hand he said, 'Oh, no, I don't want all that stuff.' As far as he was concerned, he'd bowed to the Queen once too often already.

The departing Prime Minister John Major insisted that the ceremony would be in private and that this was 'the only honour worth having'. Tony Blair told him that, like it or not, it went with the job. I was thrilled for John, even though I had no idea what the Privy Council really did. When I looked it up and found out that being one of the three hundred or so members meant that he would become one of the Queen's closest political advisers, bound by ancient laws and rules of secrecy dating back to the days of William the Conqueror, I was even more impressed. My only disappointment came when I learned that I wouldn't be allowed to attend the private induction ceremony at Buckingham Palace that July afternoon in 1997. Oh, and I'd had the perfect hat!

John, grumbling all the while, was relieved that no one else was allowed in to see him hopping from stool to stool, as is the strange tradition, and brushing the Queen's hand with his lips. He then had to swear to be 'a true and faithful Servant unto the Queen's Majesty'. Tony, watching to one side, was amused by it all and gave a passable John Prescott impression of him saying, 'By heck, bloody hell, I'm not having this nonsense!'

The day after John was affirmed as a Privy Counsellor, it was back to business for him. I think he'd rather everyone forget the whole episode. But in three homes across the north of England, Phyllis Prescott, my mother and I were carefully snipping out the twelve-line item from the Court Circular in all the broadsheet newspapers announcing our John's membership of this august body.

John was given a separate office at Admiralty House in Whitehall for him and his new DPM's team. He also had his office at the House of Commons, headed by his chief of staff Joan Hammel, a very able lady who'd previously been in charge of Neil Kinnock's office and is to this day a good friend. Rosie Winterton had run his office before that but she had become MP for Doncaster. Joan Hammel was assisted by one of John's Environment Department civil servants, Della Armstrong, who was to become an integral part of our lives.

As DPM, John was required to live in London. His job entitled him to a grace-and-favour home in Admiralty House so he invited me down to London to help him choose which one. The first time I saw the three-storey building's grand neoclassical entrance with its columns and porticos, I said, 'Oh dear, John, that's a long way to come down and put out the milk bottles.'

The housekeeper showed us the ground-floor flat first, which she told us had a resident ghost of Lady Hamilton. John looked at the painting of Nelson's mistress and said, 'She looks like Margaret Beckett,' which was strange because Margaret Beckett eventually took that flat. Then the housekeeper showed us the top-floor rooms which Lord Mayhew had used. His family lived there permanently. They weren't quite right either.

'There's another flat, isn't there?' John asked.

The housekeeper hesitated. 'Yes, but that's usually reserved for the Defence Minister,' she replied.

'Can we see it please?' he asked, knowing that the role of Deputy Prime Minister outranked that of Defence Minister.

When we walked into the second-floor flat we knew that was the one. There was a lovely reception area, then a long corridor with an amazing ceiling leading to a large lounge. It had three bedrooms and a dining room from which you could look out along the Mall. The master bedroom looked out over Horse Guards Parade. Winston Churchill had lived in the flat at one time when he was with the Admiralty. Michael Portillo had the use of it immediately before us and the place was cluttered with heavy antique furniture, not enhanced by poor lighting. It made it feel dark and dismal, more like a museum than a home, but some of the furniture was lovely and I could immediately see the potential, despite the higgledy-piggledy rooms.

'Right, I can sort this out a treat,' I told John. 'What a challenge.' The biggest challenge would be to do it up within the strict budget the department allowed so, with that in mind, I started making plans.

Having made our decision to take the flat, we went back to see it again the next day so that we could measure up and decide which rooms should be decorated first. To our surprise, the place had been stripped bare. John was hopping mad. After making a few enquiries, he found out that a senior civil servant from the Defence Department had ordered that the government-owned furniture be removed and placed in storage. Maybe he was a bit put out that John had pulled rank and pinched a prime flat from the Defence Minister.

Fortunately, John was able to get a few things returned, including the long dining table, and we refurbished the rest with a few pieces from his own departmental stores. John managed to get his own back on the civil servant some years later when the man in question came to work for him. Ushering him into his new office, John watched the civil servant's face fall as he walked into a room stripped bare but for a telephone.

I had told John that I wanted his Admiralty House place to be a proper home for him and somewhere nice for people to visit. He even allowed me to put a few family photos around. I couldn't do all that I wanted, obviously, but I did try to make the best of a bad job. In the master bedroom, which was rather oddly decorated – everything was in floral apricot, including the curtains, wallpaper and even the drapes over the bed – I had the old wallpaper stripped off and the walls emulsioned in a pale apricot. The carpet, which was a grubby cream, needed to be replaced and I said to John, 'I think we should get a fleck on the new one,' but we went for a plain apricot one instead. Although it looked fabulous for a year it was the wrong decision in the end as it showed every mark.

In the corridor there was a heavy paper which I had removed and then the walls painted in various shades of cream and beige to enhance the architectural angles and the features. Everything I did needed approval from English Heritage, and they complimented me on my choice of decor. It looked completely different when it was done; the place seemed to breathe again. One of John's staff told me that we would be entitled to choose some pictures for the flat from the government Art Collection archives in Soho. 'They own hundreds of paintings and prints stacked up down there that nobody ever gets to see,' I was told. 'You can help yourself.'

The staff were so kind, showing me all these incredible and important paintings and prints collected over the years by previous governments. I stood in front of these enormous great panels they wheeled out one after the other, full of the most amazing art by some of Britain's finest artists. I was allowed to take my pick. Me? Who'd been delighted with a Brueghel print from W. H. Smith?

Having thought long and hard about what I wanted, I selected prints for the central corridor to honour our friends and John's staff. Della came from Lancashire so I chose some wonderful Lancashire scenes for her. Alan Meale, MP, represented Mansfield, so I picked something just for him. I found several prints depicting Chester for John and me.

'Just for a laugh,' I told the archive curators, 'can you show me the biggest painting you have?' They brought this vast canvas out and I took one look at the landscape in oils and cried, 'That's it! That's the one for the lounge.' We had that painting in the flat for ten years. The sun would settle on it and light it beautifully. After we left and Gordon Brown became Prime Minister, John said to me, 'You'll never guess which painting Gordon chose for his private quarters in Downing Street: the big one you picked.'

I was immensely proud of what I achieved in redesigning John's flat in Admiralty House. I loved bringing all the elements together to make it a real home from home. Even the housekeeper complimented me. And wow, what a home it was. The wealthiest of people could not afford to buy that property with its views over Horse Guards Parade with ringside seats for the Trooping of the Colour and the Queen's Birthday parade. When everything was decorated, refurbished and the paintings hung, I said to my mum excitedly, 'Wait until you see the flat!'

She looked at me rather witheringly and said, 'Pauline, it's an *apartment*, not a flat.'

With such a place to stay, I began to go to London much more than I ever had before. Our boys were both in London by then so I enjoyed visiting them and John, rather than being on my own in Hull. With my husband's new job came a constant stream of events he was invited to, so if I felt like a night out I had quite a choice. John still hated going to functions and would tell me, 'I'm not in this job to play around.' I'm sure he kept invitations from me, either because he didn't want to go or, more likely, because he didn't want to have to get all dressed up. It was a shame because we must have been invited to a lot of places I'd have given my best hat to visit. Not that I'm complaining. Meeting Tony Bennett after a concert he gave at Leeds Castle in Kent and then staying at the castle overnight made up for almost everything. Then there were the official state functions at Westminster, which never failed to move me.

The trouble is, John hates me wearing hats – a throwback to his mother and her jelly-bag hats, I'm sure – so if I'm wearing one to something like the State Opening of Parliament, he'll always make me walk in alone first rather than have any attention drawn to him. The ones he dislikes most from what he calls my 'Berlin Wall' of hats are the large-brimmed ones that he says are only any good if it's raining, because he can walk under them. He'd rather not go to an event with me wearing something like that than risk being photographed alongside me. On a day out at Brighton Races with senior members of the Cabinet, I wore a black Frederick Fox hat which I'd trimmed myself with a strip of faux ocelot fabric. Looking through his binoculars as he urged on the horse he'd placed a bet on, he suddenly claimed my hat was obscuring his view and squashed it down with his hands, almost ruining it. 'John! Don't!' I cried and whacked him on the side of his head with my race card.

On another occasion he had to be back in London for an important late-night vote after my nephew's wedding in Portsmouth and there was a mix-up with the official car. 'It's not coming, Paul, and I must get back so we'll take the train to Victoria and then jump on the Tube,' he told me. In high heels, a tight skirt and a fancy hat, I wasn't best pleased as I toddled behind him to the station. 'Take that bloody hat off,' he told me as we stepped into the carriage of the busy Underground train to Westminster.

'No!' I declared, even though I felt like an idiot so dressed up on the crowded Tube train full of holidaymakers and families. Putting on my dark glasses to shut all the other passengers out, I sat defiantly in full wedding regalia, determined that John wouldn't dictate to me. Seeing my jaw set, he knew he couldn't win so he did the only thing he could think of in the circumstances – he moved to another carriage.

If my mother wasn't fazed by Admiralty House, then I knew that Dorneywood – the country home John was granted use of in Buckinghamshire – would blow her bed socks off.

He was originally offered Chevening in Kent, the official home of the Foreign Secretary (once again, the rank of DPM took precedence), and we went to look at it together. It was the most incredible house but completely overwhelming with more than a hundred rooms set in I don't know how many thousand acres. It was enormous, with a sweeping gravel drive and formal gardens, and reminded me of Versailles. We were shown around and taken into one room where the men used to retire to play billiards and to smoke. Queen Victoria, a frequent visitor, would often lock the men in the room apparently to force them and their cigar smoke out into the garden. Chevening also had a lake and a maze, and numerous outbuildings and cottages. It was a very nice place to visit but we knew it was far too big for us.

Alan Meale, whom we call 'Mr Fixit' because he's one of those people who seem to know everything, said he knew just the place we needed. 'It's not Chevening you want,' he said. 'It's Dorneywood, which is usually set aside for the Chancellor. Ken Clarke used it and it's small compared to Chevening.'

John learned that although Gordon Brown agreed Dorneywood was available to them both, he had no plans to use it as his country home as he would rather spend weekends visiting Scotland,so we drove to Buckinghamshire to take a look around. I fell instantly in love with this Queen Anne-style property, which is managed by a trust. It was built in the 1920s and has nine bedrooms and four reception rooms, a swimming pool and a lovely secret garden. John was delighted to learn that Lord Eden once lived there. He wondered what the man to whom he'd once served pink gins would think of him living in his old house.

Having gratefully accepted Dorneywood as John's official country residence, we visited at least once a month during the ten years we had use of it. More if we could manage it. This time, I didn't have to do a thing. The place was perfect as it was, fully furnished, beautifully decorated and held in trust for the nation. All we had to do was pay for our food and drink. Life was very 'proper' there: if we wanted anything, we rang a bell and Ian the butler appeared within minutes. My mum and

Auntie Ivy couldn't get over that. Those two elegant little old ladies would sit at the beautifully polished dining table and take turns to ring the cut-crystal bell. We took as many of our friends and family there as we could, including John's 'Brit boys'. Johnathan, David and their friends often came too and we used it as a place to unwind rather than for political functions – although John did treat his staff to working days out there every now and again. As at our apartment in Admiralty House, we were to become Dorneywood's longest-serving residents and, I like to think, its happiest.

I never failed to be impressed by the places I was able to go and the people I was able to meet. Every invitation that John's job brought us made me count my blessings. One of my favourites was the State Opening of Parliament, which I attended each year without fail. Who else gets to look down on the Queen from the Special Gallery? I would see the diamonds in her tiara sparkling in the bright television lights and remember noticing the same thing as a little girl when I held my breath in Joyce's lounge as I watched the crown placed upon her head during the televised Coronation. Now I was there in person, seeing it with my own eyes. I sometimes had to pinch myself. Cherie Blair would sit alongside me and, to begin with, she never wore a hat as I always did. Later, she began to. The newspapers published one photograph of us giggling together, and they all speculated as to what we were laughing about. What we'd spotted that so amused us was an elderly lord of the realm sitting upright but fast asleep on the back benches, mouth open and snoring gently as one of the world's most historic pageants unfolded before him.

Dorneywood was really the icing on the cake, though. Each weekend we were able to spend there, enjoying the pool or the secret garden, was cherished and appreciated. I wished we could have stayed at Dorneywood for ever. Every New Year's Eve we threw a party for our closest friends, plus the boys and their friends, making the most of those incredible surroundings. After dinner, we'd retire to the Music Room and have friends like Laurie Holloway sit at the grand piano, playing Fats Waller as a nod to my father while his American wife, the late great Marion Montgomery, sang for us. What a privilege. I'd first met Marion through Frank and Janet Brown when she did a series of shows at the Westfield Country Club years earlier and we became firm friends. John and I would go and see her frequently when she was appearing at Ronnie Scott's or Pizza on the Park. Sadly, she eventually succumbed to the breast cancer she'd fought so bravely for many years but her funeral near their home in Bray, Buckinghamshire, was a glittering musical celebration of her life, with family friends like Michael Parkinson and Rolf Harris wishing her farewell.

When she was still with us, Marion was the life and soul of our New Year's Eve parties, singing and encouraging others to join in– even my tone-deaf husband. Although typically of John, the one occasion he did step up to the piano and attempt one of my father's favourite Fats Waller songs, 'I'm Gonna Sit Right Down and Write Myself a Letter', he got so cross with himself for messing up the lyrics halfway through that he insisted Laurie go back to the beginning so he could get it right. We were all laughing our heads off, but he took it so seriously and became quite grumpy, so I pulled him to the middle of the room for a dance, knowing this was one thing we could both shine at.

Charades was a favourite game, and I have footage of John somewhere miming movements to illustrate the Charles Aznavour song 'Feelings' that are best left to the imagination. 'All right,' I told him, 'that's enough of that, thank you,' but I had to laugh. And Laurie's camped-up interpretation of the film *The African Queen* has to be one of the funniest things I've ever seen. We'd sing and play games until midnight when we'd all go out on to the terrace to watch a magnificent fireworks display. They were such happy times.

I was always so sad that my dad had missed all this. He never met John, never saw his grandsons, and never got to roll back the carpet at Dorneywood and dance to 'Ain't Misbehavin''. Boy, would he have had fun. At least we were able to treat Mum and Ivy to visits there whenever they were well enough to make it. While they relaxed, Ivy's daughter Anne and I would go shopping in nearby Marlow, with one of our security men in tow. I didn't need security, but rules were rules.

John's mother Phyllis loved coming to Dorneywood and was in her element wandering around those elegant rooms in her little mink jacket. The house was beyond anything she'd ever dreamed for her son. We also took John's father Bert there in a wheelchair just before he died and he especially loved it. When we showed him around the house and gardens, he was overcome with emotion and pride. The man who'd lived through the war and lost a leg fighting for his country wrote in the visitor's book, *If there is a heaven on earth, this is it.*

Bert was a highly political man who used to come to all the conferences – and all the receptions afterwards, announcing himself as 'John Prescott' and ordering a double brandy. He'd followed his son's career with interest and yet he was sometimes tricky to deal with. Not long before he died though, he was interviewed on camera for a programme and announced, 'I've never said this to John, but I'm extremely proud.' That meant the world to John.

* * *

It was in John's first year as DPM that Princess Diana was killed. We were having a short holiday in a villa in Cyprus with our friends Harry Sophoclides and his wife Diana when David, who was working for the *People* newspaper, rang at six in the morning to tell us the news. We just couldn't take it in. When I rang Mum a couple of hours later, she said, 'What? Our Diana?' She summed up what people thought of the Princess of Wales.

Naturally, John was expected to attend her funeral at Westminster Abbey and I was invited with him. That was such an incredibly moving occasion. We were seated right at the front with all the other British politicians and watched the young princes walk in behind the princess's coffin with their father; we were so close, we could smell the lilies. I could hardly believe who was seated all around us, from distinguished royals and world leaders to film stars, musicians and people from ordinary walks of life, all of whose lives Diana had touched. So many tears were shed, especially when Elton John sat at the piano and sang his personalized rendition of 'Candle in the Wind' with the words, 'Goodbye, England's rose ...' To me the most poignant thing was that Diana was a mother, not just a national figurehead. Those two young men had lost their mum, and in such an unexpected way. I thought then of my own boys, and of Paul, who was probably watching the service on television somewhere, unaware that his own mother was sitting in the audience.

When the thousands gathered outside the abbey began to clap during Earl Spencer's speech, the applause rippled through the building like a wave until we all found ourselves clapping, my anti-royalist husband included. Tony Blair, as the newly elected Prime Minister, had to give a long and complicated reading and did it extremely well. I'm sure it must have been one of many occasions when John was relieved it was Tony, not him, in the spotlight as millions of people watched around the world.

After the funeral, we attended a lunch at Downing Street for foreign dignitaries who'd travelled great distances to pay their respects, including Hillary Clinton and Queen Noor of Jordan, the widow of King Hussein. If the reason for us all being there hadn't been so sad, it would have been a day to enjoy. Cherie introduced me to Hillary; she seemed a very strong woman, the kind to be admired. (I met Bill Clinton some time later; he is extremely handsome and charismatic with a real twinkle in his eye. I liked him enormously.)

I am sad to say that I never got to meet Diana, but I have since met Prince Charles on a number of occasions. He and his wife Camilla have been very kind to John and to me over the years. John worked quite closely with Charles when he was in charge of planning, and we have been fortunate enough to have had lunch at Clarence House with them both. My mum, of course, wanted to know every detail so she could tell all her friends and neighbours. A staunch royalist, as far as she was concerned Charles was not only going to make a wonderful king one day, he was all right because he was a fan of Spike Milligan and the Goons, whom she and my dad used to listen to on the wireless when I was a child.

There was a moment, I must admit, eating sole *bonne femme* in the elegant dining room of Clarence House overlooking the Mall, that I really did have to pinch myself. Was I really there? Had I travelled all the way from my mum and dad's red-brick terrace in Boughton Heath, via Quaintways in Chester and a two-up, two-down in a suburb of Hull, to be having lunch with our future king and his bride-to-be?

Looking around me, I felt like jumping up and launching into the Shirley MacLaine routine from the film *Sweet Charity*. You know, when she sings:

If they could see me now, that little gang of mine!
I'm eating fancy chow and drinking fancy wine …
What a set up, holy cow!
They'd never believe it if my friends could see me now!

Fourteen

JOHN'S FIRST TRIP ABROAD AS DEPUTY PRIME MINISTER WAS TO AMSTERDAM. This was the first time he'd travelled with his new team and the entourage that went with it. Unusually, I was invited along. The plane journey wasn't long but it was tedious as John spent the entire time working. The only consolation was that I managed to grab a glass of fizz, which cheered me up no end.

As the plane landed and taxied to the terminal, I looked out of the window and saw a fleet of limousines lined up on the tarmac.

'Oh, look, John!' I cried. 'There must be a VIP on the plane. I wonder who it is.'

John didn't say a word.

Looking around in Business Class I couldn't spot anyone famous and was a little disappointed, but as we stepped off the plane I saw the line-up of European dignitaries waiting at the bottom of the steps and the penny finally dropped. They were waiting for my John!

Later, I went on quite a few official trips with him although I never went to China, a place he began to visit often. 'I'll go there when they move it closer,' I told him. I did go to Japan, though, as part of an official visit he was making, because I'd been invited to launch a new container ship, bringing to four the number of vessels I'd launched. I guess people asked me because of John's new role and his long-standing maritime connections.

As always when we arrived on official business, we were escorted to our hotel and treated extremely well. The Japanese held a reception for us the night before and introduced us to everyone, including their wives, to try to put me at my ease. Then they took us to the shipyard and briefed me on what I'd have to do. I was really rather overawed. What if it went wrong? What if the bottle of champagne didn't break? Wasn't that supposed to signify bad luck? Each country had its own way of launching ships and I was relieved to discover that the Japanese didn't use champagne at all. Then I found out what they did instead. They presented me with a little hatchet to whack down on a thin piece of string held tightly between two points, which was attached to a thicker piece of string, which linked to a rope that disappeared beneath the podium.

'You must hit the string dead in the middle,' my adviser warned me with a smile. 'Once it breaks, it sets off the whole mechanism and the ship slides down the ramps.' No pressure then.

When it came to the big moment at the Mitsubishi Kobe Shipyard, there were thousands of people watching and I was amazed I could even hold the hatchet my hands were shaking so much. Fortunately, all went well and the MV Hatsu Ethic slid effortlessly down the slipway. I'd done it.

That evening, the Japanese hosted a special ceremony for us that they call the *kagami-biraki* or the sake-barrel ceremony, which is meant to bring good fortune. We were asked to stand in a circle around a big barrel of sake with the lid floating on the top. Half a dozen of us were each given aprons and a big mallet and told that when the master of ceremonies raised his hand we should bring our mallets down on to the lid together, 'breaking it' so that we could dip in our cups. I got a bit carried away. While the man in charge was still talking, I suddenly banged my mallet down on the lid, splashing everybody. 'I can't believe you've done that!' John said, laughing.

The Japanese gave me a beautiful diamond and sapphire brooch, which I still have. Under strict Cabinet Office rules, all presents valued at more than £125 become the property of the state unless the recipient buys them. At my request, John bought the brooch for me and after that I asked ship owners to donate money to the NSPCC instead of buying me a gift. All in all, I raised more than ten thousand pounds for the NSPCC through my various launches.

From Japan we flew to Mumbai in India, which was an amazing experience too. The hotel we stayed in overlooked the Arabian Sea. John was downstairs in meetings all day so I took a long soak in a bathroom whose walls were floor-to-ceiling windows looking down on to the beach. As I lay there I could see that there was some sort of religious ceremony going on. Families were flocking to the beach, the young girls all in frilly dresses, and then they ran fully clothed into the sea. As I watched, people lit camp fires and exotic music wafted up from below. When I got dressed, I thought I might wander down on to the beach to experience the happy family gatherings closer up. But when I opened the door of my room I found myself face to face with a dozen armed guards, who told me I couldn't go anywhere as it wasn't safe. It was quite daunting. I'd never had to deal with that level of security before.

Fortunately, Harry, our handsome bodyguard, accompanied us on that trip so I had at least one friendly face around me. On our last night we were all sitting by the pool having drinks when I noticed a crowd of young Americans edging nearer and staring at us. 'Harry,' I said, under my breath, 'I think those people must have spotted John. They seem to be closing in on him.'

Harry took a quick look and went straight over to see them. 'Is there a problem here?' he asked with a polite smile.

The Americans seemed embarrassed. 'Oh, no, sir, sorry,' one told him, 'we didn't mean to stare. We were just wondering: isn't that Elizabeth Taylor sitting over there?'

John's face said it all. I just know he wanted to call out, 'No, it's Joyce Grenfell!'

Leaving India the next day our entourage was marched through Mumbai airport at 5 a.m. by a throng of security guards. Everyone was tired, including me, and I was dragging back slightly. The men in the party were walking so fast ahead of me, with John heavily protected in the middle, that I couldn't keep up. I turned to look in the window of a shop and when I turned back they'd disappeared. There was no sign of any of them anywhere. I really panicked then. Looking right and left, I realized I was the only Westerner there. The others had forgotten all about me, John included. I was furious. Eventually one of the security guards came back and found me, sent by John's head of staff Joan, who'd suddenly realized I wasn't with them.

When I finally reached the plane and settled into my seat next to John, I said, 'Didn't you even miss me?'

'No,' he replied, flatly. 'That'll teach you to keep up.'

To make matters worse, the stewardesses made such a fuss of John on the plane and virtually ignored me. One stood to attention and asked him, 'Would you like something to drink, your excellency?'

'What did she call you?' I cried.

John looked quite pleased with himself until I ordered two glasses of champagne – both of them for me. That soon wiped the smile off his face.

Before my Japanese ship launch, I'd been lucky enough to set three other ships on their way: the *Gosport Maersk*, the *Stena Britannica* and the P&O container ship the *Nedlloyd Tasman*. I also officially reopened the Queen Elizabeth II Terminal at Southampton. (Recently I opened a new Boots chemist in Sutton, Hull, so there's really no end to my talents!)

When I went to Southampton to launch the *Gosport Maersk*, my first, I asked John if he thought I'd be expected to say anything. 'No,' he said, 'you've seen them do it on the telly often enough. They just say "I name this ship" and that's the end of it. All you have to do is make sure you get the name right.' Sally and Ernie, my old neighbours from Cottingham, came with me for moral support because I was so nervous, and my nerves certainly didn't improve any when I spotted the red carpet, the gathered dignitaries and the television crews all waiting

At a cocktail reception half an hour before the launch, one of the officials asked me for a copy of my speech. 'My speech?' I asked, swallowing hard. 'Oh, er, I wasn't planning on making one.'

I could see the disappointment in her face so I went off into a corner and, pacing up and down, quickly tried to think of something to say. A few minutes later I was led towards the platform. John had written the name of the vessel on a piece of paper for me so that I wouldn't forget it but I'd forgotten my reading glasses and couldn't see a thing. Then, just as I reached the podium, the Band of the Royal Marines began to play one of their distinctive marching tunes; I think it was 'Anchors Aweigh'.

Suddenly, I was flooded with memories of my father marching home from Scapa Flow in 1945. Shaking like a leaf, it was all I could do to avoid bursting into tears, never mind launch a ship. I was really shaken that despite the fact that Dad had been dead fifty years his loss could still affect me so deeply. Pulling myself together, I decided that if I was going to make a fool of myself, then what better way to do it than to the music of the Royal Marines?

Standing before the crowd, I cleared my throat and said, a little tremulously at first, 'It is a great honour to have been asked to launch this ship – and what a fine tradition it is that only a woman can launch her.' Getting into my stride, I added, 'It does feel rather good to have my husband standing behind me – I could get used to it. I believe you refer to a ship as a "she". That being the case, I not only have sons I now have a daughter.' That went down well and everyone clapped so I started to relax and enjoy the experience.

'This lady will certainly turn heads wherever she sails,' I continued. 'She is magnificent and, being British, she proudly flies the red ensign which pleases my husband greatly.' Releasing the bottle of champagne and smashing it successfully into her side, I cried, 'May God bless her and all who sail in her.'

What a waste!

It is often difficult to know what to wear on such occasions and I choose my outfit carefully each time. I've always loved clothes, ever since the days when I made matching umbrella covers for each of my outfits or adorned a plain suit with a bunch of silk flowers. Those days are long gone now; I'm too busy running around after John to run something up on the sewing machine – not that I couldn't if I wanted to.

John allowed me a certain amount of money every year to spend on clothes so that when I had to accompany him or appear in public as the wife of the DPM, I'd feel confident that I was dressed correctly. Over the years, I've come to know what suits me and I tend to go for the classical, elegantly cut suits with jackets and skirts that flatter my shape. I like trousers too. Good quality clothes aren't cheap but they do last and they dry clean beautifully. Most of my suits are timeless and some have been wheeled out time and again over the last twenty-five years. I just accessorize differently each time with shoes, bags and hats.

Despite some of the tabloid newspapers rather unkindly suggesting that I must buy my clothes from the high-street chains, most of my special outfits bought new each season for conferences and important public events are designer. I don't like a lot of fuss to my clothes, nor do I want them to date. I'm very fond of a French designer called Claude Bassant whose clothes I first came across on that trip to Amsterdam. I also have a particular fondness for Jaeger, which I can buy off the peg, and I do have a few exclusives that I know that no one else has. I like to buy British if I can and I'll always try to find an outfit locally first before looking further afield.

My friend Janet put me in touch with a designer from Liverpool called Helen Anderson, who was at art school with John Lennon and who lived not far from my mum in Chester. She's given up fashion now for her primary passion of art but she was fabulous. Whenever I wear something she's made I know I'll feel good. There is one black cocktail dress with little bugle beads and a tight skirt that I hope I'll always be able to get into. When Helen Anderson stopped designing, Janet took me to a great dress shop she goes to in Leeds owned by another Helen, an octogenarian named Helen Sykes. Ladies travel miles to visit her, including me and the novelist Barbara Taylor Bradford. A Frenchwoman who married a Yorkshireman, Helen has an innate sense of style and can pick just the right thing for me. The outfits I buy from her aren't made specifically for me but by the time she and her team have finished everything fits beautifully and hugs in all the right places. She stocks most of the designers I love, although sadly not Valentino, who is probably my all-time favourite designer and – sadder still – out of my league.

I'd have loved to have worked in the fashion industry and helped women decide what suits them. So many get it wrong. They hear that a certain style is in and then they wear it regardless of their shape, size or age. One of the events I always made the journey to London for was Fashion Week and I loved to see all the designers and check out the new styles. The first time I went I was with Paul Boateng, MP, and his wife Janet. I was lucky enough to meet Vidal Sassoon whom I'd admired since my hairdressing days. Hilary Alexander, the fashion critic, introduced herself to me with her spectacles perched on the end of her nose and told me how much she loved my suit.

'It's a Nolan Miller,' I told her proudly. 'He used to design all the costumes for *Dynasty* and still makes clothes for Elizabeth Taylor and Joan Collins.' Hilary made a note.

When it comes to colours, I love the classic combination of black and white or black and cream but I also like the jewel shades: emerald green, sapphire blue and the fuchsia colour that rubies can sometimes be. I'm not a beige person, that's for sure. I don't mind spending money on good clothes if I know I'm going to get a lot of wear out of them. One of my most expensive suits was a fitted one in hyacinth blue, beaded with Swarovski crystals, which I bought for Johnathan's wedding. Six years later I wore it to Buckingham Palace which, to my mind, gave it a great carbon footprint.

I will never buy something that doesn't feel really comfortable to wear, no matter how much I like it. That rule doesn't always apply when it comes to shoes, though, and I must admit that I have far too many of what one of my daughters-in-law describes as car-to-bar shoes, which aren't at all sensible but which look like works of art in their own right. Never mind my wall of hats; my shoe rack should have its own postcode.

Mary Jordan shut her hat shop in Chester long before I was able to afford to buy one of her wonderful creations. Even as a grown woman, I'd press my nose up against her window and gaze at all the brightly coloured hats, which looked like flowers in a beautiful garden. Now I tend to shop for hats at Harvey Nichols in Leeds or, when I'm in London, I go to Harrods, which is my favourite store. Actually, my perfect London day starts with a light lunch in Patisserie Valerie in Knightsbridge, followed by a stroll to Jaeger or Russell & Bromley, before meeting Janet and Frank in Harrods. Remember, nothing's too good for the workers!

When I'm home in Hull, my perfect day is spent once a week with my friend Sally in our local market town of Beverley. We call it our 'Thelma and Louise' day. We start with lunch in Pizza Express, then we hit the shops. Once, during a lunch, I spotted a couple of grey-haired elderly ladies wandering into the restaurant arm in arm. 'Oh, look, Sal,' I said, giggling. 'That'll be us in ten years.'

'Do leave off, Pauline,' Sally said.

To our amazement, the impeccably dressed ladies not only ordered a whole bottle of wine, they finished the entire thing off. Good for them.

Shopping with Sally is always a hoot, especially when we have more 'senior moments'. I was in our favourite shoe shop once, a place called

Ciel, and chose a particularly beautiful pair. One of the assistants took me to one side and said, 'But, Pauline, you bought those last month!' Sally's husband Ernie dreads the moment we walk back into their home, laden with shopping bags. It has got to the point now where Sally hides hers in the boot of her car and creeps out in the dead of night to retrieve them when Ernie's asleep.

I usually try to buy John something nice too, especially if I've treated myself. He's always liked clothes and is very aware of what looks good on him. Ever since the days when he had to wear a uniform every day, he's looked smart. He gets most of his outfits from James Wright Tailors in Hull. I help him choose his suits and ties and pick which one goes with which suit, but he does the rest. He even packs his own suitcase whenever he goes away. The first thing he does when he gets home is unpack, putting everything away neatly, before slipping into his casual clothes. It must be the steward in him.

John is at his most relaxed when he comes home for the weekend. Too relaxed, sometimes. He'll come into the living room, switch the television on and sit down in front of it cradling his mug of coffee. He'll flick straight to the history or biography channels – he loves programmes about the war, or his hero Cromwell. Those programmes are all very interesting but some of them can be a bit depressing. I much prefer Fashion TV, which I always put on when I'm doing the ironing. I also like the True Movies channel or any screen adaptation of a Danielle Steel novel, although I watch news programmes too.

I'll always sit down with him, happy to have him home, but within half an hour he'll be fast asleep. If there is one thing I could change about John, it would be his snoring. It is unbelievable; it could lift a roof off. He is known for it. He had to be woken up during a service at Durham Cathedral once because everyone could hear him. He started snoring during a Cabinet meeting another time and when he snapped out of it, Tony asked him, 'Not boring you, am I?'

Joan, John's chief of staff, often had to nudge him to stop him snoring in public. She did it once on a plane and he asked, 'Why did you wake me?'

She replied, 'Because I thought you'd be embarrassed.'

He closed his eyes and growled, 'How can I be embarrassed when I'm asleep?'

John also has sleep apnoea when he's very tired, which means that for a few seconds he stops breathing altogether. I've given up worrying about it now. These days I'll be lying next to him and when he falls silent I pray, 'Please don't start breathing again for a bit longer, I might get some sleep.'

When he drops off in front of the telly, I really don't mind. What I do object to is him falling asleep with his hand gripped firmly on the remote control. Desperate to change channels, I creep across the room and try to get it from under his fingers. Do I pull it out quickly like the tablecloth under the tea service, or do I try to prize it out slowly? It never matters because the minute I click over to another channel, he wakes up and announces: 'I was watching that!'

That drives me mad.

'How can you watch that and be in such a deep sleep you're snoring?' I'll ask.

Then he gets the hump and says, 'I'll watch it in the other room then.' The other room isn't always heated so that's quite a sacrifice.

'No, John, I don't want you to do that,' I say, guilt-ridden because he's only ever home for a few days and I've caused a scene. I guess it's just that when he's away so much I get used to my own routines and my own way of doing things.

Fortunately, Della, who runs John's office at the Commons, likes the same sort of things I like on the telly so whenever she comes to stay when John is off somewhere on the battle bus, she and I have a lovely time. I adore Della; she's kept everything together in John's office over the years, along with Joan Hammel. I don't know what we would have done without them.

Della is a Lancashire girl who was a civil servant in John's department and who enjoyed working with him so much that she left the Civil Service to work for him in the House of Commons. She's great fun, and makes me laugh whenever she is at my side. I tell all my friends everyone should have a Della, but not 'my Della'. On several occasions, she was staying with me when John called in to update us on his campaign trail. One evening he rang to tell me he was doing a big speech that was to be broadcast on television later. 'Make sure you watch it,' he told me.

I asked him what time and wrote it down. Then I cooked a nice meal, lit the candles and we had supper. 'Let's watch a Barbara Taylor Bradford,' I suggested to Della, so we curled up and were soon totally engrossed, loving every minute of it. Three-quarters of the way through, the telephone rang. It was John.

'So, what did you think of my speech?' he asked.

I held my hand over the phone and looked at Della. 'Oh bugger!' I said as she quickly cottoned on. Removing my hand, I smiled into the receiver. 'John, it was really wonderful. Well done! Della, it was one of John's best speeches yet, wasn't it?'

By the time I put down the phone we were in creases.

Fifteen

THE FIRST CONFERENCE AFTER THE LABOUR PARTY VICTORY WAS QUITE something. The sense of triumph in the conference hall was palpable. After so many years in the political wilderness, it was thrilling to be in power.

The worst thing about the conferences, though, was how everyone piled into our hotel room. Staff, trade union leaders and my sons all used the lounge of our suite as a makeshift office to help put John's speeches together with the speech writers. They often stayed up all night. People used to walk through our bedroom at four in the morning just to use the loo, forgetting that I'd be in bed trying to get some sleep. There was no privacy.

As usual, John would end the conference with a speech designed to wind the proceedings up. He was nervous enough about that but this year he also had to make a keynote address as DPM. Tony Blair always liked to speak on the Tuesday, so John's big speech would come on the Wednesday. He was an absolute nightmare to live with until then – so stressed, so determined to do his best. I'd ask him, 'Why do you put yourself through this? You don't need to. It's all in your head. You should throw your notes away. Look at that great speech you made off the cuff for John Smith.' Nothing I said could soothe him.

The first time we went to Blackpool, we were given a lovely suite in the hotel – identical to the Blairs' on the same floor. It was beautiful but when I walked in I said, 'Oh, no. The lighting's appalling.' I swear men design the lighting in these places. It was so dim and depressing; it wouldn't do at all. Proper lighting can make the world of difference to a room, especially with the clever use of table lamps. You need a good light to get ready and a good light to work by. It's not all about *feng shui* or what may be in vogue at the time. It's about practicalities.

We had loads of staff coming to the suite to work and I knew they'd need better light so I called the manager. 'Have you any more table lamps?' I asked with a smile.

'Certainly, Mrs Prescott,' he said, and within a few minutes several large lamps arrived at our door. When I turned them on, though, the bulbs were far too dull. There was nothing for it, so I hurried from the hotel, found a hardware store and bought a dozen or so 150-watt bulbs. Before anyone complains about our carbon footprint I'd like to point out that I turned off the main lights so that we just had the table lamps on. The girls were thrilled and said they could see much better. 'What a difference!' cried one.

Then Anji Hunter, Tony's head of staff, walked in. 'Wow!' she said, looking around, 'your suite's so much better than ours!' I was happy and relieved to tell her that it was exactly the same; it was just the lighting that was different.

It was at another conference a couple of years later that my determination to look my best ended up inadvertently causing John some unwanted controversy.

September in Bournemouth can be terribly windy. We were checked into the Highcliff Hotel on the front and, as usual, my dear husband was in a fluster about his speech. He'd been up all night with his staff, hammering out the finer details, and I'd had little sleep in the adjacent room.

John always insisted that I walk into conference several minutes before him so, like it or not, I had to go in first – usually on my own, sometimes with Cherie or one of his staff – and take my seat, which signalled to everyone that John wasn't far behind. Having to do that at a national event like the annual Labour Party conference was quite a different kettle of fish to just walking into a restaurant or a room on my own. All eyes would suddenly be upon me. I'd have to sit facing a bank of photographers who'd been hanging around for hours and were desperate to take pictures of anything, if only to test the light. Hundreds of lenses would swivel to face me and start clicking away. Those lenses would remain trained on me until John, Tony and the rest of the team arrived and quite often I was left sitting there for what felt like an age. It was most disconcerting and I was painfully aware that, for that half-hour or so, I really had to look my best.

Nor was there any time to prepare myself for the fray. Once inside the hall, I'd usually be rushed into the office to say hello to the staff before maybe having two minutes to go to the loo and touch up my lipstick before I'd be pushed out in front of all those cameras. There was no time to do major repair work if my hair or make-up had been ruined by wind or rain. The conference hall was never very far from whichever hotel we were staying in, but it's often difficult to walk there in high heels and if the weather was bad you were in trouble.

This particular year, John was already running late. Then he looked outside and said, 'It's pretty windy. We'll jump in the car.' If he'd have been on his own, I'm sure he'd have walked, but he suggested it out of courtesy to me. I was grateful for the suggestion because the minute I came down the hotel steps I was really battered about and the waiting photographers were clicking away. The journey to the conference hall was three hundred yards and when we got there, the car stopped and we stepped out and walked in. At the Tory party conferences, almost all of the wives do that: step out of their hotels, get into their husbands' cars and glide to the venue looking impeccable. Nobody says anything. But when it came to John, being a socialist Minister of Transport, the press decided to have a go. And have a go they did. The headlines the next day were unbelievable. Instead of focusing on the triumph of the conference or John's terrific speech, they homed in on the fact that he'd used his car for such a short journey. I suppose they felt he was fair game and it was too good an opportunity to miss.

To make matters worse, when they asked John why he'd done it, he was his usual honest self. 'Because of the security reasons for one thing and, second, my wife doesn't like to have her hair blown about. Have you got another silly question?' Some people decided it was rather ungallant of him to blame me. The poor man couldn't win.

It was another case of having a go at someone they saw as easy prey. He was already under fire for having the use of two Jaguar cars, although I never really understood what the problem was with that. He loves Jags; he always has, for their quality and build, plus the fact that they are a British icon. We'd had a second-hand one from our earliest days of electioneering; we'd strap a loud hailer to the roof and plaster posters over the doors and windows. We'd used our old Jags for family holidays and weekend outings. They'd been washed and polished by the boys for extra pocket money and driven us to and from visits to Chester to see friends and family.

John was initially offered a Rover as his official government car but asked for a Jag XJ8 instead, which only the Prime Minister was normally allowed. The response was no. John complained that Michael Heseltine, deputy leader of the Tories, had a Jag so why couldn't he? The answer was that Heseltine, a man of considerable independent means, had bought his own. I knew John should have considered some of those lucrative directorships and European jobs he'd always declined over the years. John dug his heels in and, after three months, it was finally agreed by the powers-that-be that he could have his Jag. He was delighted. It was his first ever new car and the one perk of the job he'd really wanted.

The press, of course, not only latched on to the fact that he'd asked for a better car but that he was now 'Two Jags' because he also had a Jaguar at home, an old second-hand XJ6 sports version that he'd paid about five thousand pounds for years earlier. John tries not to get annoyed about the fact that few other ministers would come under such intense scrutiny over their cars, but he doesn't always manage it. With the Prescott sense of humour, he tells people that he later had to get a bigger second-hand Jag as well because the sporty little one doesn't take more than one hat box.

The year after he was given so much grief in the media about being driven to the conference hall, we were back in Bournemouth and I was horrified to see that it was very windy again. I realized that we couldn't possibly use the car again after last time so I'd have to make the best of a bad job. Thankfully, the manager of the hotel assured me all would be well. 'We are much closer to the conference hall this year,' he said, 'and an extension has been built as a direct link.' I smiled and thanked him, enormously relieved.

When I learned later that the media had dubbed the link, 'Pauline Prescott's Wind Tunnel', I had to laugh.

My hair became an issue again, but not one of my making, a year after Labour were elected when John and I were invited to the Brit Awards at the Docklands Arena in London. He doesn't normally accept those kinds of invitations but if he thinks it's something I might like, he will. I was thrilled. I'd always watched the Brits on television each year and was really looking forward to being there in person.

The organizers gave us a table near the front and I must admit to being a bit starstruck, looking around at all the rock stars and personalities. Richard Branson was at the next table with a large group and it's always interesting to see people like that. Cherie Blair had broughther boys and was sitting a little further back. We were halfway through our dinner when I suddenly became aware that someone was standing behind me. Turning, I saw that it was a man and a woman talking; I remember thinking it a bit odd that they were standing right over us when we didn't even know them.

Then a huddle of press photographers gathered in front of us as if they sensed something was going to happen. I don't know if John noticed, but I did and I can remember wishing our Special Branch security guards were close at hand.

All of a sudden, the man standing behind me jumped up on to our table wearing a leather kilt and big boots. Kicking over glasses and upsetting plates, he cried, 'This is for the Liverpool dockers! See how this feels!' He reached down and picked up a bucket of iced water as big as a dustbin and full of bottles and threw it at John and me, drenching us completely in freezing cold water. I screamed as bottles and glasses went flying. I had a lovely black designer suit on and my hair was ruined even though – when I realized what he was about to do – I turned at the last minute so I got most of the water down my back.

Shocked and angry, I jumped up to dab myself down. John was on his feet too, his face like thunder. He pulled the kilted man off the table, punched him hard in the ribs and dragged him to the floor. He was about to hit him again when security arrived and dragged our attacker away. We learned later that he was a singer from a so-called anarchist band called Chumbawamba who probably needed the publicity.

Once the drama was over and the photographers had got what they wanted – a picture of John's face contorted in anger – John sat down again. I was still on my feet squeezing water from my hair and clothes. 'John!' I cried, 'I need to go and get dried off.' I looked and felt like a drowned rat.

'Sit down, Paul,' he commanded under his breath. 'Don't move. We're not giving them the pleasure.'

So for half an hour at least, while Fleetwood Mac continued playing their set on the stage in front of us, we sat in our seats, soaked through to our underwear, trying to pretend nothing had happened. So much for our glitzy night out. The only nice thing that happened was that Fleetwood Mac took us to their dressing room afterwards to dry off, and the Liverpool dockers, who'd been involved in a two-year industrial dispute that ended a few weeks earlier with a lock-out, rang John the next day to tell him it was nothing to do with them. Better still, the following day a tabloid reporter threw a bucket of water over the singer who'd soaked us just as he was boarding a plane to China. He had to sit in his wet clothes the whole way. Shame.

I'm proud of so much that John has achieved, from the congestion charge to the Channel Tunnel, but I think the success of which I am most proud is when he helped persuade 176 countries to sign the Kyoto Protocol on climate change in 1997. To have got such a controversial environmental issue on the world agenda at that time was nothing short of a miracle.

The Kyoto accord didn't come easily. John didn't sleep for forty-eight hours and kept the other delegates up all night until they signed. He had Tony Blair lobbying just about every prime minister or president in the world on the telephone until they cracked. I love how he bullied them into it. I almost felt sorry for the delegates because I, of all people, know how persuasive he can be! He said afterwards it was just like the all-night trade union negotiations of old; diplomacy by exhaustion.

Talking of diplomacy, John's other great success was mediating between Tony Blair and Gordon Brown, which wasn't always an easy path for him – or me – to tread. What started off as 'the Big Three' in charge of Labour Party policy – Tony, Gordon and John – quickly morphed into 'the Big Four' with Alastair Campbell, and Peter Mandelson sometimes trying to nudge John out. Within that new grouping, one would complain about being excluded and another would moan that the rest were talking to the others behind his back. John was kept out of the loop so often that he threatened to resign. The backbiting and sulking that went on between them all sometimes made me think they were back in the school playground instead of trying to run the country. John was the piggy-in-the-middle, telling them to stop bickering and get on with the job.

I was quite often party to the endless telephone calls to our home at weekends; mostly they were from Tony and Gordon as each used John as a sounding board for their separate grievances. Even in London they used to come to the flat to complain to him about each other. Sunday mornings were the worst. Phone call after phone call interrupted our breakfast.

On one occasion, I was emptying the dishwasher when John took yet another call.

'Be quiet, can't you?' he hissed. 'It's Tony on the phone!'

'I don't give a toss who it is,' I told John indignantly, looking up from the cutlery tray. 'Would you mind taking them out of my kitchen?'

John's 'partner in crime' at Kyoto had been the American vice-president Al Gore, whom John liked enormously. The two men seemed unlikely companions, but got on extremely well. I think Al understood what it was like to be a sounding board and was himself often caught up in tricky situations with his boss. Despite criticism from the press that he could be boring, Al was actually extremely charismatic in person, as is Gordon Brown, believe it or not. With Al at least, people began to see his worth, especially on environmental matters.

When Tony Blair invited Al to Chequers for the weekend, John and I were asked along for lunch. It was the first time we'd both been invited to the Prime Minister's country home. It also happened to be the week of my sixtieth birthday, so it was a double celebration, which had begun with a few days at Dorneywood with friends and family.

I made John ask Tony what we should wear.

'Oh, nothing special,' Tony replied. 'I'll probably be in chinos.'

'What the hell are they?' asked John.

Tony explained and added, 'Tell Pauline she can dress casual.'

John retorted, 'My wife has never dressed casual in her life.'

Chequers was an amazing place to visit and John and I had a lovely day. It was a house full of the memories and ghosts of remarkable lives. I was no longer frightened of ghosts as I had been as a little girl at St Bridget's but even if I had been, I think the noble spirits of Chequers wouldn't have scared me. Tony Blair showed us around like the proud owner and, for once, John was speechless. One of his heroes is Oliver Cromwell and there we were in Cromwell's grandson's former house, looking at all sorts of memorabilia, including the great man's swords hanging above the fireplace, which John was allowed to hold.

During lunch in the grand dining room, John suddenly asked Al Gore about Bill Clinton's affair with Monica Lewinsky and what effect it had on the President and the Democratic Party. I was tucking into my meal when I piped up, 'What amazes me is why he did it in the White House.'

As John's jaw dropped, Al Gore looked at me, laughed, and said, 'Why, Pauline? Where else could he have done it?'

It was a good point. President Clinton didn't have a country retreat like Chequers to take his mistress to. But even if he had had a bolthole, what difference did it make where they had been when he committed adultery? He'd still been unfaithful to his wife and, although I liked the President when I met him, I was deeply disappointed that he'd behaved in such a predictable way. At the same time I admired Hillary enormously for keeping her dignity. As I told John many times, if I ever found myself in that situation I'd never be able to forgive him.

Sixteen

FOR MY SIXTIETH BIRTHDAY IN 1999, MY SON DAVID – BY THEN WORKING AS a journalist at GMTV – put together a wonderful video tribute for me, featuring family, friends, and political allies past and present.

Sitting on the famous GMTV sofa, he announced that I'd married a 'cocky little short-ass who worked on the ships'. Johnathan added that, thanks to me, John had 'dumped his Man at Hepworth's look' for a new smart-suited image. David added that I'd always be a 'First Lady' to him and his brother. What more could a mum ask for?

Others who were interviewed for my birthday tape included Tony Blair, Alastair Campbell, Rodney Bickerstaffe, Marion Montgomery and my own dear mum. There were clips of me urging on a horse at the Brighton Races in the hat John almost squashed and launching a ship. I was filmed walking into the State Opening of Parliament looking like an excited schoolgirl. Several photos showed me on the podium with John, Tony and Cherie at various Labour Party conferences, travelling the world as the wife of an MEP, and with my oh-so-proud mum at Dorneywood. Watching the video even now makes me emotional, for it so perfectly sums up the remarkable life I'd led to that point as the wife of a brilliant man.

There was, of course, one key person missing from the video tributes. In all the years that had passed, throughout John's incredible career and my life as a proud daughter, sister, mother and wife, hardly a day had gone by when I didn't think about my son Paul. From the moment I'd had to give him up, I'd peered into the faces of passers-by – little boys at first, then teenagers, then grown men – thinking: 'Is that you? Are you my Paul?'

Every 2 January, his birthday, I'd retreat into my own private thoughts and wonder how he was celebrating it. Each important step in the lives of Johnathan and David – the day they spoke their first words, the moment they were able to ride their first bikes and the times they brought home their first girlfriends – made me think of what I was missing with Paul. There were reminders everywhere, even in my favourite television programme *Dynasty* in the eighties when the Joan Collins character Alexis Carrington was reunited with the son she gave up for adoption. I'd watched anxiously and wondered if that could ever happen to me.

Where was Paul? What was he doing? Had he become a teacher like his adoptive father? Was he married? With children? Did I have grandchildren? Did he ever watch families reunited on *Surprise, Surprise* with Cilla Black as I did and think bittersweet thoughts? Did he know how much I missed him?

A few years earlier, Clare Short, one of John's fellow Cabinet ministers, had been successfully reunited with Toby, the son she gave up for adoption more than thirty years before. To her surprise, she discovered that Toby was a Tory-voting City gent and that she was a grandmother. Having lunch with John in the House of Commons one day, I spotted Clare sitting with her newfound son at a table. Before John could stop me, I'd gone over to introduce myself, shake Toby's hand and wish them all the best. On the long walk back to my table, I kept thinking, Lucky Clare. If only that could be me.

Since that fateful day when I'd signed the papers handing Paul over to his foster parents for ever, his name was rarely mentioned – not by my mother, not by John and, eventually, not by me. That was the past, my mother would say. 'You must move on, Pauline.' If ever I tried to bring the subject of Paul up with her, she ended the conversation. My closest girlfriends in Hull like Sally and Janet knew nothing of my first-born son and it went unspoken that John and I would never tell Johnathan and David about their half-brother. I couldn't face it. I was their over-protective mum; the one constant in their lives when their father was so often absent. I'd always been there for them. Even if they knew the full circumstances in which I'd had to give their brother up, what on earth would they think of me?

I still had a precious bundle of black-and-white photographs of Paul as a baby, in the nursery, with my mum, with me, with John, which I sneaked a look at every now and again. My mother also kept a set, although I had no idea if she studied them as often as I did. I only wished I'd kept the beautiful baby clothes she'd saved so hard for and brought to the hospital a few days after he was born, momentarily convincing me that she'd changed her mind.

No matter how many years passed, the pain of losing Paul had never left me. When I read in the newspaper one day that a middle-aged man called Paul from Wolverhampton was trying to raise money for a heart-bypass operation, I fretted for weeks that it might be him. I even asked John if he could discreetly check it out. 'He might not even be called Paul any more,' John pointed out. 'I know that's what he went to the foster parents as, but he was just a lad, remember, and they might have given him a different name altogether.' Wisely, he left well alone, realizing that I was clutching at straws.

It was a horrid thought that Paul might not bear the name I'd given him; the name I'd chosen specifically because of its links to me. Not that he knew it linked him to me – or did he? I often wondered how much his adoptive parents had told him. As time went on, I began to worry that Paul might die before he had the chance to find me. Or was he dead already? Had being given up by his mother damaged him in some way? Why hadn't he contacted me? Since 1975 the law had changed, allowing him to. Did he think I might be dead? The endless possibilities were always lurking in the back of my mind.

The legislation didn't yet allow for birth parents to trace their adopted children, only the other way around. That wasn't enacted until a few years later. It did, of course, occur to me to get in touch with him if and when the laws were changed. I wanted to so much but I didn't want to intrude; I was afraid also that he might reject me. Secretly I think I always hoped that he'd want to find me first. When he didn't, I tried to reassure myself that it meant he must be happy with his life and not need to look for his birth mother.

So quickly it seemed, the years had flown by and on my sixtieth birthday I suddenly found myself a pensioner. My son Paul, wherever he was, would be forty-three years old. The previous ten years had gone so fast. Would the next decade pass as quickly? What if he never tried to find me? What if I never learned his fate? Would I ever have the courage to look for him? I simply didn't know.

I had two wonderful boys who'd given me such immense joy, but I always knew I had another son out there somewhere. That sense of something missing never quite left me. The days that Johnathan and David were born were, without doubt, among the happiest of my life. Both my sons had turned into busy, successful and handsome young men. They'd met two fabulous girls I couldn't have picked better myself: Ashlie, a hard-working lawyer and successful partner in her firm, and Rozlynn, a bright young producer with the BBC. Both such good friends to me, they are indeed the daughters I never had. Johnathan was still running his own property business and David was in the media and public relations. Both were helping their father, David politically and Johnathan on the business side. Their lives were complete. None of them had any idea how gaping a hole I had in mine.

Another year of having to suppress my feelings passed, flying by as quickly as the previous few had. With a growing sense of panic, I felt as if I were running out of time. Then, in 2000, soon after John had celebrated thirty years as an MP, he heard out of the blue from friends in Chester city council that some reporters had been to the town hall making enquiries about a Prescott 'love child'. The rumour was that there was an estranged son of John somewhere and they were determined to find out if it was true. Not long afterwards, a small advertisement appeared in the *Liverpool Echo* asking for anyone who knew John from his seafaring days to come forward. A PO Box number was given. The handful of those from our past who knew the true story never said a word to anyone and contacted us immediately to warn us. Then, a little later, we heard that the reporters had gone through the records at Chester town hall and discovered that there was a child, but that it was mine.

Initially, I felt scared. My main concern was for the boys, who still didn't know a thing. It wasn't shame that had stopped me from telling them. If I'd been ashamed I wouldn't have hung on to Paul as long as I did. I was just always so afraid of what they would think. I was their mum, after all. Then, gradually, I began to feel excited and, dare I say, happy? Maybe this was our time. Perhaps now my Paul would be found and we could be happily reunited as so many others had been.

John and I discussed whether or not we should tell the boys straight away and decided not to. 'Leave things alone for the moment,' John advised. 'Let's wait and see. Nobody's going to talk so nothing may come of this and then you'd never have needed to tell them in the first place.' Although relieved for the boys' sakes, my heart sank a little at the thought. Peter Mandelson went to the Press Complaints Commission to try to put a stop to any further investigations on the basis that neither Paul nor the boys knew anything and it would be a gross invasion of their privacy if the story were to be published.

Six months passed, and then a year went by. I began to lose hope. Perhaps John was right. Maybe the reporters had been put off the scent. Or maybe they couldn't find Paul or – worse – they had and he didn't want to know me. The strain of waiting for news began to tell on me and, I think, on John too. Then, in May 2001, when we still had all the stress of not knowing and were having to cope with the gruelling schedule of another election campaign as well, the newspapers found a new reason to focus on the Deputy Prime Minister.

In all the years I'd known John, I'd never once known him to get into a fight. He wouldn't be one to back down, of course, and there were plenty of times he could have got into a punch-up, especially as a young man at sea and with angry strikers, but he rarely did. Despite the punch he threw at the singer who'd drenched us at the Brit Awards, my husband is not a violent man; indeed violence has always been something he has abhorred. He was given the nickname 'Thumper' at the House because he gives people a verbal thumping, not because he thumps them physically. Well, he hadn't until that point, anyway.

The first I heard of anything was when my mum rang. She always had the television on in the background for company and so she called up one evening and said, 'Pauline, you'd better switch on the telly and watch the news. John's got himself in a spot of bother.'

I turned on the TV and watched as John was filmed walking off the battle bus towards an election rally he was due to address in Rhyl, north Wales. He was accompanied by his chief of staff Joan Hammel and his press secretary Beverley Priest. Just as he was being led past a group of local farmers and pro-foxhunters protesting about high fuel prices and the ban on foxhunting, he was suddenly pelted hard on the head with an egg, which cracked and dripped down his neck. In fury, he lashed out at the egg-thrower with his left hand, pushing him away with a half-punch, half-thrust. Joan and Beverley were almost knocked over.

As I watched, aghast, the telephone rang again. It was John. 'I suppose you've heard,' he began.

'Yes, I'm watching it now. Are you all right, love?' I asked, seeing the slow-motion replay repeated on the television.

He sounded unusually shaken. 'I was expecting a bit of booing but not to be physically attacked!' he explained. 'I honestly thought I'd been stabbed. When I felt what I thought was blood dripping down my neck I did what anyone else would do. In self-defence, I hit the bloke I thought had stabbed me.'

What was so annoying, John said, was that the police knew there would be a demonstration waiting for him but did little to protect him, and shepherded him and his staff right past the waiting protesters. He was so close he could feel the heat of their anger. When the egg hit his head and the yolk dripped down his skin it was its warmth that made him think it was his own blood at first. He realized later that the man who threw it at him must have been holding the egg in his hands for a very long time, waiting for his moment. The police clearly didn't think to search any of those into whose path they were going to steer the Deputy Prime Minister. Although I'd cracked a couple of eggs on John's head in the past, I knew that an egg thrown that hard from close quarters can be a pretty effective and painful missile. If it had hit him on the temple, it could even have killed him. No wonder he lashed out. The headlines the next day, which renamed John 'Two Jabs' instead of 'Two Jags', could just as easily have read, 'Protester Attacks Pensioner'.

When John had hung up, I switched over to Sky News and watched political commentator Adam Boulton declaring that John Prescott should resign. That made me hopping mad, along with the fact that the egg-throwing incident came to completely overshadow the important launch of the Labour manifesto that day. John had no intention of resigning over the issue although he did tell Tony Blair he could take the job back if he wanted it; fortunately Tony refused and told anyone who asked him about the incident, 'John is John.' The public were soon behind my husband and an opinion poll said it actually boosted his standing among male voters. He received a mailbag full of letters from elderly ladies, businessmen and fellow pensioners saying, 'Good for you!' Sean Connery even wrote personally to congratulate him.

John declared that he would never apologize for lashing out at the man who hit him, even if he was supposed to set an example to the nation as Deputy Prime Minister. For John, it was a matter of principle. Since his earliest days below decks on the cruise ships he'd stood up to bullies and he wasn't going to back down now. He always joked, 'Tony said I should connect with the electorate, so I did!'

The incident also gave President Bill Clinton a chance for a ready quip. The next time he saw John he said with a smile, 'So, John, who have you punched today?'

Seventeen

BY THE SUMMER OF 2001, I HAD ALMOST SUCCEEDED IN PUTTING THE IDEA of being reunited with my lost boy from my mind. Then a television programme called *My Beautiful Son* was aired, starring Julie Walters. I was transfixed. There was a moment when the son returned to find his long-lost mother who gave him up for adoption and asks her: 'Do I have any other family?' She nods and says, 'Yes, you have two brothers and an uncle called Peter.' I could hardly believe my ears.

A few weeks later, we were staying with our dear friends Brenda Dean, the former trade unionist, and her husband Keith McDowell, at their holiday home in Falmouth, Cornwall. We'd been there less than a day and were standing in the window admiring the view as Keith pointed out his boat, which he was planning to take us out in later on that Friday. As ever, I had my camera in hand, and was snapping happily away when John's mobile telephone rang. Taking the call, he went into a corner and I heard him say quietly, 'Right ... right ... OK.'

He seemed unusually subdued, so I turned and took a photograph of him too. When he hung up, he gave me an expression that instantly told me something was wrong.

'What's the matter?' I asked.

Brenda and Keith stopped talking and looked at him too.

'The holiday's over. We'll have to leave,' he said.

'Why?'

'The media will be here within hours.'

'Why?' I asked again, feeling increasingly anxious. 'What's happened?'

He paused and stared at my face before saying, 'They've found Paul.'

I can't explain how I felt but I do remember the camera slipping from my fingers to the floor. I sat down very quickly and very hard and tried to catch my breath. Brenda grabbed my arm as I fell backwards into a chair, and was obviously concerned. I didn't know whether to laugh or cry but it was just the most wonderful feeling. I was in shock but a kind of ecstatic shock from the bombshell that had just come crashing into our lives. Most of all, I wanted to pack my bags and run to wherever my son was.

Then I managed to regain some control. As Brenda and Keith looked on perplexed, I heard myself say to John, 'No, no. We can't go. The press don't know where we are. Nobody does. We'll stay here.'

John nodded. He knew I was right.

Brenda finally broke the silence that followed. 'Er – who's Paul?' she asked.

Laughing and crying all at once, unable to speak, I sat trembling in a chair as my John told our friends all about the boy I'd given up for adoption more than forty years earlier. This was the first time in four decades that his name had been mentioned publicly. It felt so strange to hear it – Paul … Timothy Paul … *my* Paul … Tilly's baby – but it also felt so right. I was overwhelmed with relief. Congratulating me with kisses and hugs, Brenda and Keith were over the moon for me and couldn't have been kinder.

Then I called my mum. 'Are you sitting down?' I asked her. 'They have found my Paul!'

'Oh, Pauline!' she cried. 'My goodness!'

She was as happy as I was, although I could tell she was concerned for how it might all turn out for me, for Paul and for John, not to mention the boys, who still didn't know a thing. She was also very nervous at the idea of meeting her grandson again, I realized. For the first time I wondered if she, too, had shared my deep sense of guilt all these years.

Later that day, John learned a little more from his contacts in the media, chiefly that Paul was in the armed forces and had contacted the Ministry of Defence press office to let them know that the *News of the World* had doorstepped him. 'He's not a teacher then?' I said, trying to take in the news as it was drip-fed to me from across the years.

'No, but we should be able to find out more tomorrow.'

I don't think I slept a wink that night, in anticipation of what would happen next. Did Paul know whom I was now? How did he feel? What would he do with the information? What should I do?

Early the following morning John called Geoff Hoon, Defence Secretary, and asked him to find out what he could about the member of his armed forces who'd been approached by the media. I was so excited. I wanted to know everything but the response that came back staggered me.

'He's a lieutenant-colonel in the Royal Military Police,' John relayed to me, his hand over the mouthpiece as Geoff filled him in on the phone.

'No!' I was glad I wasn't standing up.

'He's got an MBE for his services in Northern Ireland and an OBE for commanding the Military Police in Kosovo ...'

'My God!'

'He was educated at Sandhurst —'

'You're winding me up, John!'

'No, I'm not.' John grimaced. 'I bet he's a bloody Tory.'

'Stop it!' I chided, reaching for the phone. 'Let me speak to Geoff.'

Geoff told me all that he knew about my talented son, who had also served in the Falklands and was now head of the Royal Military Police at Edinburgh Castle. He added, 'He must be a pretty bright chap, Pauline, because he's very young to have done all of this.'

I was over the moon.

Trying to decide what to do and extremely wary of making the first move and pushing Paul towards something he might not even want, we thought it best if Joan (John's chief of staff at the Commons) made the first call. She got the number of Paul's commanding officer from Geoff Hoon and the two of them acted as intermediaries. Paul told Joan how the most momentous news of his life had been broken to him on his doorstep a few days earlier.

'Do you know who your mother is?' a young female reporter from the *News of the World* had asked him bluntly. 'It's Pauline Prescott, the Deputy Prime Minister's wife. We're running the full story in two days' time.'

What a shock that must have been. What if he'd never even been told he was adopted? He said later that although he was tempted to slam his door in the reporter's face, he was so taken back and so curious about what she'd told him that he sat outside his house on the front wall with her for a while. He knew who John was, of course, but all he could remember about me was the story he'd read about us driving three hundred yards to the Bournemouth conference because of my hair.

When the reporter had gone, he went inside and looked me up on the Internet. Staring at a photograph of me on the computer, he said to himself, 'My God! That's my mother!' He found the whole concept staggering. Then he cracked open a bottle of champagne. When Joan relayed that part of the story, I couldn't help but smile. That's my boy, I thought.

'Paul sent you a message,' Joan told me. 'He sends his love and hopes this hasn't upset you too much.' I melted. Straight away he was thinking about me and my feelings. That spoke volumes.

Paul's other major concern, of course, was for his widowed mother Mary, who knew nothing of this momentous turn of events. He said she was in her eighties and not well. The news, he thought, might kill her. When I heard that, I could only imagine what that dear lady was about to be put through. She and her husband had only ever adopted one child and very late in life. Three years earlier, in 1998, she'd lost her husband Ted whom Paul had adored equally, and now this. My heart went out to her and to him for having to face her distress.

Having sought advice from the MoD Director of Communications (who asked him if he was drunk when he told him the news!), Paul managed to get the story postponed for his mother's sake. He agreed to cooperate with the *News of the World* if and when he and I were happily reunited further down the line. When Paul was first doorstepped on that Friday he was told that the newspaper had enough information to publish that Sunday. On the intervening Saturday he was at the Highland Games in Braemar near Balmoral; the Queen drove past and waved at him just as he was in the process of negotiating arrangements with the Press Complaints Commission.

How bizarre, he thought to himself, waving back to the monarch before faxing a copy of his terms to the *News of the World* from MacTavish's grocery store in the village of Braemar.

At our end, Peter Mandelson, Labour's spin doctor, was incredibly helpful. Separately, he too negotiated with the *News of the World* to buy us time. Peter arranged a similar deal with the newspaper that we would consider giving them an exclusive interview in two years' time, when we'd had time to get to know one another again. What it meant was that Paul could choose his moment to tell his adoptive mother Mary and we could choose ours to break the news to Johnathan and David. John said we had to do it straight away but I simply couldn't face it. One aspect of giving Paul up that had always haunted me was whether it would diminish me in the eyes of my other sons in some way. After so many years of waiting, wondering, I simply wasn't ready to face the disappointment I feared I'd see in their eyes, so John did it for me, something I will always be grateful to him for. I wasn't there but I gather that when he started to tell them that there was a child who'd been given up for adoption, they automatically assumed it to be his.

'No, no,' he told them. 'It's your mum's!' That information must have been quite devastating, especially for the elder, Johnathan, who suddenly had to get used to the idea of an older brother appearing out of the blue.

The boys came straight round to the house to see me after John had told them. Few words were spoken at first. We just hugged. One by one, they walked me round the garden and told me how happy they were for me.

'What do you think of me, though?' I asked. 'I mean, I'm your mum and I gave up my baby.'

'Don't be stupid,' they each said in turn. 'This doesn't change a thing. You're still our mum and we love you.' They were both amazing and continue to be. David was especially curious and couldn't wait to meet his half-brother. Johnathan, as is his way, was excited for me but didn't want to delve. He had always been very protective of me after years of being the 'man of the house' whenever John was away. To find out he wasn't my eldest son after all was a huge adjustment for him to make.

There was a big change for John, too. Another man had suddenly appeared on the scene – and one I'd been secretly besotted with long before John was even on the scene. My mother was very wise and she said, 'Be careful with this, Pauline. There's bound to be some jealousy. Don't ignore the other men in your life.' She knew I was on cloud nine and she needed to remind me to be considerate and careful with them, which I have tried to be ever since.

Still wondering who should make the first move and still fearing that Paul might not, I wrote my long-lost son a letter telling him how thrilled I was that he'd been found. Three weeks passed without any reply.

'It's because of who I am,' I told John unhappily. 'He doesn't want to rock the boat.'

John advised me to be patient, and once again he was right. Paul's letter arrived via John's office a few days later, and it was just wonderful, so wonderful. I must have read and reread it a hundred times. Through Joan, we arranged a time for him to call me at my home.

The morning of the telephone call I was so nervous I didn't know what to do with myself. I rose early and got myself as dressed up as if I were meeting him in person. I was home alone when the telephone finally rang.

'Hello, Pauline,' he said. 'This is Paul.' They were words I feared I might never hear.

'My Paul!' I cried. 'How wonderful to hear your voice. Are you OK? Do you feel all right about this?'

'Yes, fine,' he replied.

Top) Welcoming the Queen to Hull. A dream come true for a royalist like me. © Hull Daily Mail
Bottom Left) With John, Tony Blair and Gordon Brown at a Labour Party Conference in Brighton.
Being seen with you two they'll think I'm one of the beautiful people,' John joked. (Bottom Right)
ohn and I with our dear friend, the late singer, Marion Montgomery-Holloway.

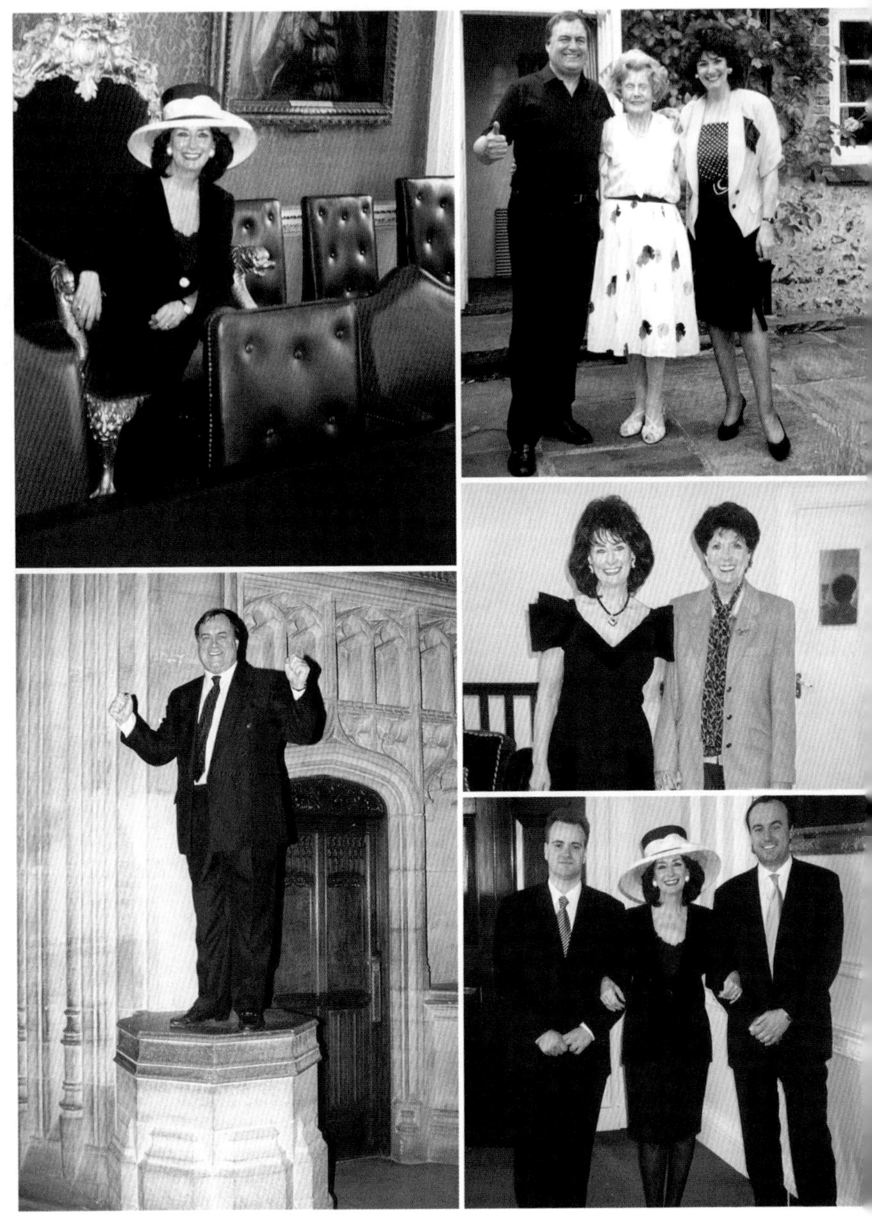

(Top Left) Queen for a day! (Top Right) John and I with Barbara Castle. (Centre Right) With Helen Sykes, the elegant owner of my favourite dress shop. (Bottom) A very proud moment for the boys and I – the first opening of parliament with John as Deputy Prime Minister. Trust John to climb atop Mrs Thatcher's plinth!

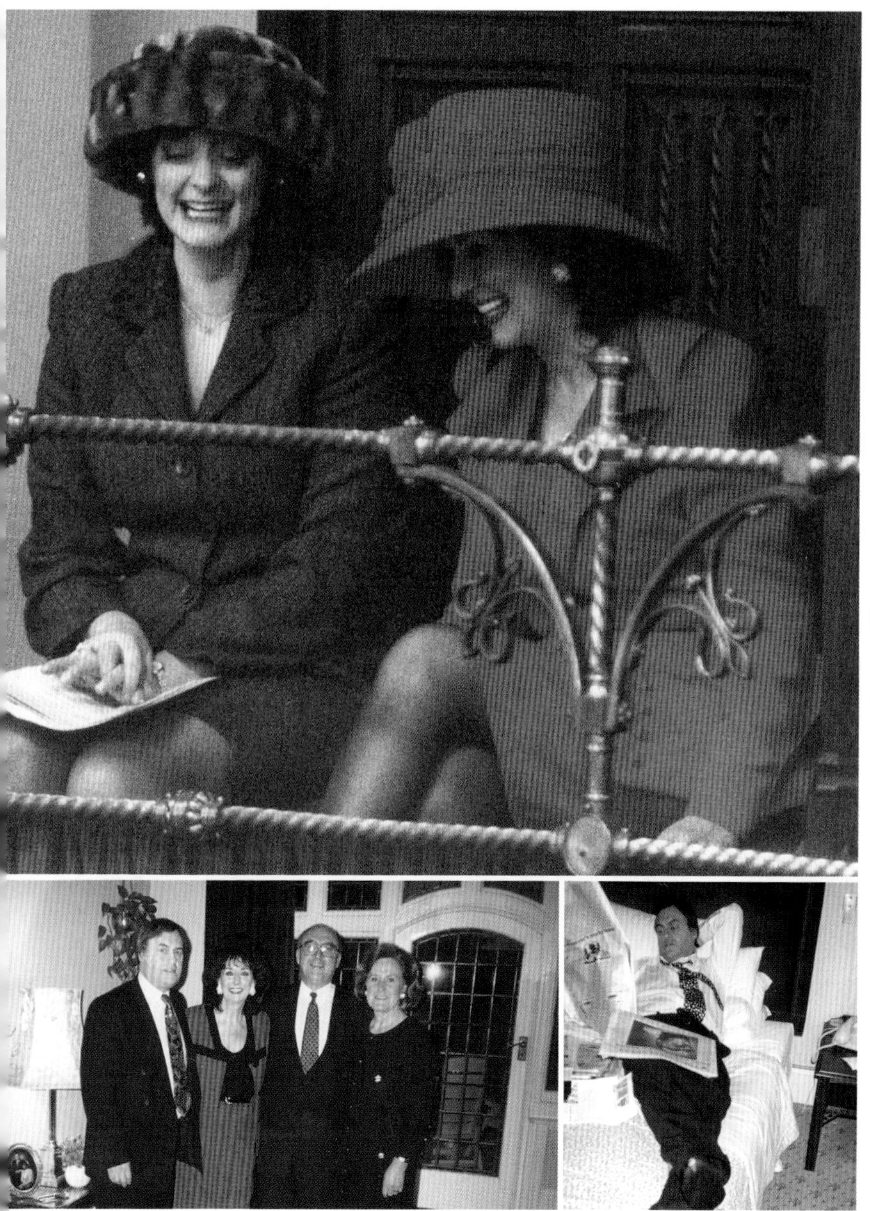

Top) Cherie and I giggling in the galleries of the House of Lords as we spotted old Lords struggling to stay awake! © Fiona Hanson/Press Association Images (Bottom Left) John and I with our dear friends John and Elizabeth Smith. (Bottom Right) Don't get too big-headed John Prescott - I know about the holes in your socks!

A British soldier is homeward bound...
THE RAILWAY SLEEPER
by Malcolm Greensmith
TRAIN
DEPARTURES
URGENT
A fine porcelain
collector plate edged with precious 22-carat gold

(Top Left) The first photograph I saw of Paul. It took my breath away. (Top Right) The first photograph that appeared in the press of Paul and I. Arthur said they were the happiest photographs he'd ever taken. © Arthur Edwards / The Sun / N.I.Syndication (Bottom Left) Another of my treasured pictures of Paul. He gave it to me on the same day that I handed him a porcelain plate I had bought depicting a soldier dozing on his kit bag (Bottom Right). The resemblance is uncanny.

Top Left) The Golden Girls – Mum and Auntie Ivy – at Dorneywood for Mum's ninetieth irthday. Happy memories. (Top Right) Mum and Paul getting acquainted at Dorneywood. his picture says it all. (Bottom) John and I on the day he was elected as Deputy Prime Minister. Vhat a proud moment!

(Top Left) New Year at Dorneywood with friends Frank and Janet, Laurie Holloway and John's former head of staff Joan Hammel. (Top Right) Paul's adoptive mother Mary, Paul and I at our first wonderfu meeting. (Middle Left) With Mum and my brother Peter. (Middle Right) Mum on her 92nd birthday. She passed away a few weeks later. (Bottom left) With friends Sally and Ernie at their ruby wedding anniversary party. (Bottom Right) Girls at the races! L-R: Janet Brown, me, Tanya Coburn.

The Quaintways Girls then and now. (*Top*) At Carol Fellows' wedding. L-R: 'Tilly' Tilston, as I was known then, 'Hancock', Alice Snell, Kath Hurley, Carol Fellows, Lynne Anderson and Gill Welch. (These are their maiden names). (*Bottom*) At my 70th birthday. L-R: Kath, Carol, Norma Hignett, Roz Caldecote, Trish Fields, Gill, me, Lynne and Alice.

(*Top Left*) David and Rozlynn's wonderful wedding at the House of Commons. (*Top Right*) On the same day, with all my boys: Johnathan, David, Paul and my brother Peter. (*Centre Left*) Another special moment at the House of Commons – Johnathan and Ashlie's beautiful wedding. (*Centre Right*) Johnathan and I at John senior's retirement party. (*Bottom Left*) At my beautiful granddaughter Ava Grace's christening. © *Brian Benson* (*Bottom Right*) John and I in residence at Dorneywood.

'Oh, you have such a lovely voice!' I said, surprised. 'There's no accent at all. I suppose it's from being with the military all these years.' There was a pause and then I asked, 'Tell me, Paul, have you had a happy life?'

'Yes,' he replied. 'I've been very fortunate.' Then he began asking all about me. He knew who John was, of course, although their paths had never really crossed. He'd spotted him once in Whitehall but he'd never been assigned to protect him. 'I was in a phone booth talking to a friend and he walked past with his bodyguards and I said to my friend, "Bloody hell! John Prescott just walked past!" I remember thinking he was much smaller than I'd imagined.'

After a lively conversation, I told him; 'I'm longing to see a photograph of you. Do you think you could send me one?' He promised he would and we signed off, agreeing to speak again soon.

For the next few days, I watched and waited for the postman until the envelope arrived in amongst a load of other mail. I dashed downstairs to receive it and tore it open on the front doorstep, unable to wait. Gazing down at this handsome man in military uniform standing on cliffs overlooking the sea in Cyprus, I gasped. The resemblance to his father was uncanny, but better even than that was the resemblance to my darling dad: Ernie the bricklayer, the ex-Royal Marine taken from us so tragically young. They had the same shape of face, the same cleft in the chin. I was speechless.

The next step was to arrange a meeting. A date was agreed when Paul would travel from Scotland to our house in Hull. The week before he was due, I was a bag of nerves and couldn't settle to anything. John and Johnathan kindly agreed to meet Paul at the station when his train got in from Edinburgh, before bringing him home to meet me. I must admit to having a sherry or two to steady my nerves, knowing that the three men were having a coffee and a chat at the station first to break the ice. When Paul eventually walked in, between my two Johns, I could hardly believe my eyes.

'Oh my! You're so handsome, and so tall!' I cried, before reaching up to hug his five-feet-eleven-inch frame. Choking, I told him, 'I don't know you as well as my other two boys, Paul, but I love you as much.' Only a mother could say that.

Clinging to each other in the hallway, we were almost oblivious to the fact that John and Johnathan had slipped quietly away. We wandered into the garden, clasping hands, both of us trying to keep ourselves together. I was so happy as I showed him around the place and then brought him inside to make him a cup of coffee. He gave me a fridge magnet which reads: *Hold on to your dreams because dreams really do come true.*

Sitting down opposite Paul in the lounge, I showed him the baby photographs I'd always kept tucked away. He'd never seen any photos of himself under the age of three, and was clearly moved. There were ones of him alone, me with him as a teenage mum, and some of him in the arms of my mother and with John – which probably surprised him the most.

Taking a deep breath, I said, 'Well, OK, this is it, Paul. You can ask me anything you like and I'll be as honest with you as I possibly can. I'll tell you everything I know.'

Gently at first, he began to probe.

'Who was my father?'

I found myself speaking the name I had never even told John.

'What happened?'

I explained how we'd met on a blind date but that his father didn't tell me he was married with a child. When I found out, I said, he promised to marry me.

'Then what?'

'He disappeared. Some officers at the base told my mother they didn't know anyone by that name. Later, they admitted he'd flown back to the States. I wrote to him at an address he'd given me but I never heard from him again.'

Then came the question I'm sure Paul most wanted to ask: 'Why did you wait until I was three to have me adopted?' He said that all the people he knew who'd been adopted had been so at a much earlier age. 'The only children that people didn't want to adopt and who were left until last were handicapped or had something wrong with them. I wasn't handicapped so I always wondered why I was left till last.' Nobody had ever told him it was because I fought to keep him for such a long time, so he'd always thought there must have been something wrong with him. Paul would counter now, though, that that was probably what drove him to achieve all he had in his life.

I explained everything I could. I spoke of St Bridget's and how the social services sent him away to a nursery so far away that I could only visit him occasionally. He wasn't sure if he could remember those visits but he did recall the teddy bear I bought him, and other presents. I told him he was so settled there that he even called one of the nursemaids 'Mummy'. Paul said he remembered that young nursemaid with great fondness. I felt unreasonably jealous about that, but I was glad he only had good memories of his time at the Ernest Bailey Nursery.

He couldn't remember being in hospital or John and me visiting him so I explained why he was initially placed with foster parents. A year later, I said, social services told me he was happy with his new family. 'I still wasn't able to have you at home with me. There seemed no alternative but to sign the adoption papers.'

Paul told me that he could remember Ted and Mary coming to visit him and taking him back to their house for short stays. Then he recalls a court hearing in Stafford where a judge in long red robes told him that he'd 'have a Mummy and Daddy for ever', before his new parents took him to a Beefeater restaurant to celebrate. Even though I found that incredibly painful to hear, I was pleased it was a happy memory for him. He said that red had been his favourite colour ever since and strangely was the colour of his Royal Military Police beret that he proudly wore for thirty years.

'I had to let you go,' I said finally, choosing my words carefully. 'I didn't want to. I was vulnerable but that's not an excuse. I tried to hang on to you as long as I could, but I didn't have any other choice.' He could see I was upset and he tried to reassure me but I told him the guilt would always be with me. 'The fact remains I gave my baby away, no matter how good the reason.'

Then Paul showed me some other photographs from his past. There was one of him in a little tent in the garden; another of him making sandcastles on a beach with Ted and Mary. There were outdoorsy snaps of him camping and playing games such as tennis. The images were super to see; this happy little boy of mine smiling at me from neat squares of paper that proved to me what a good childhood he'd had. When I learned that he was top of his class at school, I knew that his adoptive father had done him proud as I'd always hoped he would. Best of all, although Paul was very bright and spoke French fluently, he was quiet about it and not at all snobby.

When he told me he'd had such an incredible upbringing that he wouldn't have changed a thing about his life, I believed him. I only had to look at what he'd achieved. And despite the fact that he is so different from John, and votes Tory, my husband has grown to like and respect the boy he first met as a toddler. Seeing them together is a hoot, actually. They couldn't look more different and Paul teases John all the time about being diametrically opposed to him politically, although out of respect to John he did promise to give up foxhunting.

Paul had always known he was adopted. When he was twelve years old and going through some old papers of his parents in the attic, he came across some airmail letters they'd sent to each other during the war. Mary was in London during the Blitz and his father had served in the Royal Artillery in Europe.

'I wanted to know why they couldn't have children,' he said, 'although I never did find out. Then I unearthed some of my adoption papers and learned that my birth mother's name was Pauline Tilston. I saw something on a form that said my putative father was a US airman. I didn't know what the word "putative" meant so I went downstairs and looked it up in a dictionary. It said it meant "supposed", which – if it were true – meant I was half-American, I supposed!'

He'd kept the information about me and his birth father in his heart all these years, thinking that he'd wait until his parents were much older or maybe even dead before he'd try to find one or both of us. Paul always had such great sensitivity for his mother Mary, whom he had yet to tell and I had yet to meet.

I couldn't wait for Paul to see my mum again after all these years. From the moment I suspected I was pregnant at sixteen and told her the news, she had been my best friend and my confidante. Yes, she'd been tough on me about giving him up but it was, she always believed, in the best interests of me and my baby. Having arranged a date for the two of them to be reunited, I travelled by train to the terraced house in Chester that she'd not left since the day she married my father, and waited for Paul to arrive. After an initial hello, I'd promised to take them both to the Grosvenor Hotel in Chester for afternoon tea.

When I opened the front door of my parents' house in Boughton Heath and saw Paul standing in the doorway, leaning against the wall with a grin on his face, I was momentarily speechless. He looked uncannily like his father, who'd stood in the same doorway when I was a little girl, his airman's cap pushed to the back of his head, saying, 'Hi, Paula,' with that big smile.

'Well, here I am,' our son said.

'One military man may have left me but another came back,' I told him before leading him inside.

My mother, normally the epitome of no-fuss common sense, was surprisingly emotional to meet her grandson after all these years. Maybe it was his resemblance to her Ernie, I thought. Through her tears, she revealed for the first time the details of how she and Ivy had been taken into care with her brothers Albert and Joe when she was seven years old, after her father Joseph had died and her mother married a drunk. From the little she said of her time at the Bluecoat School in Chester, you could tell it had not been a happy experience. When I saw how difficult it still was for her to speak of her time in a home all those years ago, it almost broke my heart. Just as I had been keeping secrets from those I loved for much of my life, so, it seemed, had she.

Over the years, my auntie Ivy had tried to tell us that their childhood hadn't been happy, but then she'd always add a little fearfully, 'Don't tell your mum.' Now I learned, for the first time, that my mother's step-father was a violent man who'd thrown my grandmother to the floor and kicked her in the tummy when she was pregnant. My mother didn't say, but the implication was that he'd also been violent to them.

'I couldn't bear the idea of you being in a home too,' she told Paul. 'Your mum was my little girl and I had to protect her as well. When that nice couple came along and offered to take you, I knew that was the right thing to do. If I could have taken you in, I would. I hope you know that.'

Paul nodded and seemed to understand.

My mother's childhood experiences had clearly marked her, although I think they must also have made her into the tough little lady I'd always known her to be. Her memories must have shaped all her decisions about Paul and me, and I hadn't realized that at the time. I thought back to the time when Paul was little and my mother had told me over and over that it would be 'cruel, so cruel' to keep him in state care. She had seemed so certain of the fact that I had found it impossible to argue with her. It was only now, as I watched her weeping and stroking the hand of her lost grandson, that I fully understood.

Eighteen

THE NEXT FEW MONTHS WERE LIKE A DREAM FOR ME. THE AREA PAUL WAS in charge of for the Royal Military Police stretched all the way from Scotland to Yorkshire so he was able to visit; he came whenever he could. When John went away on business, he spent a weekend with me so that we could get to know each other even better.

A few days before he was due, I spotted an offer in the *Daily Mirror* for a porcelain plate depicting a young soldier dozing on his kitbag. It was called 'The Railway Sleeper' and had been copied from a famous painting that hangs in the Imperial War Museum. I thought, I bet my Paul looked a lot like that soldier when he was younger: the shape of his face, his hair tumbling down, the cleft in his chin. I sent away for this little plate as a gift for him.

Paul arrived for the weekend and I cooked him a meal and then afterwards we sat chatting in the lounge. 'I've got a little present for you,' I said, thinking of the plate.

'And I've got something for you,' he said, handing me a photograph of him to keep. After all those lost years, it was so wonderful to see his life unfolding before me in pictures. I looked down at the photograph and froze. It was of him in army combat kit, asleep on a folding chair somewhere after a hard day in Kosovo. It was a mirror image of that on the plate I was about to give him; he had his hand to his chin and his head tilted in just the same way. Talk about a psychic connection. How do you explain that?

It took Paul eighteen months to prepare his mother Mary for the news that he'd found me. He had tried to tell her that we'd been reunited on a number of occasions, but she'd always been quite unhappy about the idea and told him she'd be jealous if ever he did decide to look for me. He even took her to visit her parents' graves in Anglesey once and broached the subject there. 'You can look at these graves and know exactly who you are and where you come from,' he told her, 'but I have no idea who I really am. Can you see that I'd like to find out one day?' She told him that she couldn't.

When he did eventually break the news to her, when she was visiting him in Scotland, she was naturally very upset. She found how it had all come about incredible and always suspected that Paul had somehow made it all happen, despite his assurances that he hadn't. In time, though, she came to believe him and that was when he told me that he'd like to introduce us. Knowing how reluctant she'd always been about him finding me, I was terrified and thought, What am I going to say to her? I obviously wanted to thank her for being a marvellous mum and for giving him such a good life, but anything else seemed too contrived.

My friends Frank and Janet drove me over to Stafford and we stopped at a supermarket so that I could buy Mary a bouquet of flowers. I already had a little gift for her – a portcullis brooch from the House of Commons shop – but I thought of the flowers at the last minute. As we pulled into the driveway of her house, she was standing on the doorstep waiting, a little grey-haired lady with her hair pulled back into a bun. Paul told me later that she'd been just as nervous as me. Despite having a speech prepared, I didn't know what to say. We just took one look at each other and hugged, as Paul stood to one side.

Mary was very kind to me. She received me graciously and seemed to accept me so well. Paul led us both inside and we sat side by side in her lounge where I finally got to say what I had long wanted to: 'Thank you so much for giving Paul such a wonderful home.'

'We did our best,' she replied. I thought that was so lovely.

'You're Paul's mother,' I told her. 'You're the one who raised him and loved him for all those years. I'm not going to take him away from you. I couldn't, even if I wanted to.'

She smiled and seemed grateful for that. I think she needed to know that Paul wouldn't be giving me all his attention from now on and that he would still have time for us both. There was such a warm feeling between us as we sat and held hands. It must have been extremely difficult for her with me, a younger woman, coming along and staking some sort of claim on her son. Yet she never showed it. She was just so proud of Paul and he was adorable with her. They were clearly extremely close.

When Mary died a few years later, Paul invited John and me to the funeral. I took my cousin Anne along as well for moral support. It felt strange, sitting right behind Paul and Mary's two nephews in the church with all of Mary's friends and family around us. I did wonder if I should have been there but Paul made it clear that he wanted me to come, he had no doubts at all, so I went. I was warmly received by everyone but I kept in the background as much as I could. I was moved when Paul stood up and read a eulogy to Mary; it was a remarkable tribute to the woman he will always call his 'Mum' – and quite rightly so.

Afterwards, there was a reception at the golf club where Mary had been ladies' captain and Paul's father had also been a keen member for many years. I heard lots of stories there about Ted too. I would have so loved to meet him. By all accounts, he was a real English gent who took the trouble to raise his son properly and to give him all the things I would have wanted him to have. Ted and Mary were an amazing couple and I was incredibly lucky that it was they who took in my son and gave him such a wonderful life.

Telling John's mum about Paul being found was another hurdle we had to face. Having talked it over, we decided it would be best not to tell her over the phone so we arranged to go to her house in Pine Gardens, just down the road from our first house together.

I had such good memories of Pine Gardens. I'd loved our little home. As a blissfully happy newlywed, I had been so house-proud and really enjoyed taking care of my husband and baby Johnathan, with the help of my mum, John's mum, and friends and relatives who lived nearby. There had been a time when I never thought I'd leave Pine Gardens; I certainly never had any aspirations beyond its boundaries. Now I was returning to the neighbourhood as a very different woman, someone who had in the interim become the mistress of 'Prescott's Castle', Dorneywood, and a spacious apartment in Admiralty House. A sixty-two-year-old mother of three, I was accustomed to international travel, embassy living and dining with world leaders. Whenever I walked up to the front door of Phyllis Prescott, however, I was Pauline Tilston again and just as timid.

She invited us in for tea, which – as usual – she served in the Royal Albert country roses teapot, her little finger raised. It was like visiting Hyacinth Bucket. After some general small talk, John looked at me and took a deep breath.

'Mum, we have something to tell you,' he began.

'You're getting divorced!' she said, quick as a flash. By God, she was a tryer!

'No, we're not actually,' John replied testily. 'It's not that at all. Pauline's son has been found. The newspapers are on to it and it's all going to come out, but everyone's delighted about it.'

She paused and managed a smile. 'Oh … how lovely.' Looking directly at me, she added, 'I'm happy for you.' Turning back to John, she asked how this news might affect him and his career. All these years that had passed, all that water that had flowed under the bridge, and he was still her oldest boy who she felt needed protecting. I could relate to that.

John discovered later that it was Phyllis who had set the reporters on to Paul in the first place. His official biographer admitted as much a few years later. When told that there were rumours of a John Prescott love child, she was indignant on John's behalf and said, 'You're barking up the wrong tree.' She was only trying to protect her son, I suppose, but what did she think or hope might follow from such a leak? Divorce? Maybe. Or perhaps she just never got over the fact that in her opinion I wasn't good enough for John and let the news slip accidentally. John hardened towards her in the final years of her life but, whatever she may or may not have done, I have to say that from the day she threw us an engagement party and made our bridesmaids' dresses she tried to be kind to me.

Paul and I continued to feel our way with each other and I tried not to push myself on him. He always introduced me as 'my mother' and addressed me as 'Pauline'. Mary had been his 'Mum' for forty years and although I would love to hear him call me that one day, I know it doesn't come naturally to him.

It didn't really matter what name we used for each other anyway. There was so much to find out about his life and so much we both wanted to ask. But first there was the media to face. As agreed in a deal brokered by David and checked by Paul, the *Sun* broke the story and the *News of the World* would carry the full interviews and photographs. A reporter rigorously questioned Paul and me about every aspect of our lives and then Arthur Edwards, the famous Fleet Street photographer, turned up to take all the pictures. He declared afterwards that they were the happiest he'd ever taken.

Paul was incredible. Despite being in the Royal Military Police and naturally guarded because of the security aspects of his work, he cooperated fully and then had to cope with the unaccustomed glare of publicity into his private life. That was especially hard for him. Even when he and his girlfriend Liz split up there were stories written and reporters on his and her doorsteps, demanding to know more. One particular newspaper kept hounding Paul on the telephone, demanding that he tell them who his father was. And all because I happened to be married to someone in the public eye, which was nothing to do with what he and I were to each other. There were some lighter moments though, too, like the time we took him to the House of Commons for lunch and he bumped into former Defence Secretary Tom King and the Tory MPs Bill Cash and Patrick Mercer, all of whom he knew.

'What the hell are you doing with Prescott?' they asked.

'Er, he's my stepfather,' Paul had no choice but to reply.

Another time he had a meeting locally with a senior police officer and in general conversation mentioned that he'd been to Mr Chu's Chinese restaurant in Hull the previous night, although he didn't say with whom. 'Oh, that man Prescott goes there,' the policeman commented with a scowl.

I, too, had to face up to the media glare, which was something I'd always gone out of my way to avoid. Suddenly, I was faced with reporters outside our home and photographers lurking in all sorts of unlikely places, including restaurants and shops. What most amazed me was how many people read the slew of articles that followed publication of the *News of the World* story and who suddenly knew the secret I had kept locked in my heart for so long.

The unlikeliest people seemed to know everything about me – a shop assistant, the postman, even Prince Charles who, at a function I attended at the House of Commons, took me to one side with a smile and said, 'Please give my best wishes to your son.' At a Remembrance Day service in Whitehall, General Sir Mike Jackson, Chief of the General Staff and officially Paul's boss, told me that he knew Paul quite well and was very pleased for us both.

Strangers congratulated me in the street; others wrote tome in their droves, telling me how happy they were for us. So many people in a similar situation sent me the most moving letters, saying that despite our success they were still scared to try to contact their lost children. One lady who was in her eighties felt like me that she shouldn't intrude and was waiting to hear from her son first.

'I was caring for my mother when I had him. I couldn't look after him as well,' she told me. 'I wrote him a letter explaining all that so if he wants to find me he will.' I didn't have the heart to tell her that the social services almost certainly never passed her letter on.

I think my girlfriends Sally and Janet must have been the most shocked by the news. I told them both just before it hit the papers: Janet on the train on the way to Leeds, and Sally on one of our Beverley days out. They were both thrilled for me but I don't think they could believe that I'd kept such a secret from them for all those years.

'I couldn't tell anyone,' I explained. 'My boys didn't know and I couldn't risk them hearing it from someone else.'

Like the true friends they were, they gave me their love and support and told me that they couldn't wait to meet him.

The first time Paul and I went out alone together in public was to a dinner at a place outside Chester called Frogg Manor. John and I go there all the time and know John Sykes, the owner, very well. I knew that Paul and I would be well looked after, away from prying eyes.

Assuming that the owner knew about us because it was all over the newspapers by then and everyone else seemed to, I rang to book a table for two. 'I'd like a table by the window,' I told John. 'I'm bringing a nice young man in with me. You might see us holding hands or even sneaking the odd kiss, but if you do, try not to notice.'

'Don't worry,' he replied, his voice deadpan. 'Your secret's safe with me.'

All went well and we had a lovely evening together in our little corner. Paul presented me with a gorgeous silver Luckenbooth brooch, depicting two hearts entwined. I was so touched. All sorts of things about him surprised me, including the fact that he has some of my funny little mannerisms: like putting a hand on his hip when he's talking; speaking softly, as I do; and waiting until everyone else has ordered from a menu before making his choice.

Some of the things Paul told me about his life before I found him threw up some other uncanny coincidences. When John and I were courting we often used to go to Chester Zoo with friends as a fun day out. Ted and Mary used to take Paul there too and he also went on school trips to the zoo. We could have passed within a few feet of each other on any number of occasions and not even known. Was his face one of those I'd peer into and ask silently, 'Are you my Paul?' Did he look up into my face and vaguely recognize the nice lady who used to visit him in the home and bring him toys?

When Paul was older and working in the Royal Military Police in London, he used to visit an address in Rochester Row, just behind Westminster. Almost every time he went there, he'd spot a bag lady. She was a familiar down-and-out who wandered that neighbourhood. Each time he saw her, he said for some reason he always wondered if she might be his real mother. How sad, I thought.

'I lived all over the world and met all sorts of people and I never saw anyone else who made me think that,' he told me. 'Yet each time I spotted her in Westminster I couldn't help but think of you.' The strange thing was that he was probably less than a quarter of a mile from Admiralty House every time he was there; or I could have been closer still, in the Members' Dining Room of the Commons with John. The very thought that my son might have been within a few hundred yards of me in recent years sent a shiver down my spine.

As we ate dinner and chatted about all these coincidences at Frogg Manor, the owner John Sykes left us alone as requested. He said nothing about our visit until John and I went back there for dinner. 'You never told me that you had another son!' he said. 'I didn't know until someone said they'd seen your pictures in the paper. I honestly thought you were with a toy boy the other night. When you came in the next day with John, I nearly died!'

There were more surprises waiting. One of the people who'd discovered our story was Dorothy, Paul's former nursery nurse at the Ernest Bailey home, whom he'd always spoken of so fondly. Whenever I heard him talk about her I'd be grateful but more than a little jealous that she'd been there for him every day and I hadn't.

One of Dorothy's friends read one of the numerous articles about us and told her, 'Your Paul has been found. And you'll never guess who his mother is!' Dorothy wrote to me via John's office at the House of Commons and I then put her in touch with Paul. Once they were reunited, he realized to his delight that she'd never forgotten about him either.

'I'd love you to meet her,' Paul told me. I flinched inwardly. I agreed but secretly I didn't want to. Then one day a few months later, John had to go to a meeting in Chester so I went along with him. We stayed at the Mill House Hotel, owned by Gordon Vickers, our old friend from the Wall City Jazz Club days. John went downstairs early with his security men while I stayed in my room for breakfast. Not long after, he came back up to our room and said, 'You'll never guess what happened. A lady came up to me and introduced herself. She's on a weekend break with some girlfriends from the WI. She's Paul's old nursery nurse.'

I couldn't believe it. Dorothy was staying in the same hotel on the same day as me! She'd never been there before and was just a few rooms down from ours. It had to be Fate. I knew then that I'd have to face her and invited her to my room. I was so nervous, I think maybe even more scared than when I met Mary. This young woman had seen me visit Paul as an emotional and naive sixteen-year-old. She'd fallen for my boy, as did everyone who ever met him, but then she must have found out that I'd signed the papers to give him away. What would she think of me?

I don't know what I was worried about. Dorothy was kindness itself. The same age as me, she told me all she could remember about Paul's time at the nursery, where she'd worked as a sixteen-year-old nursery nurse. Paul was her first ever charge and he soon became a favourite of the staff. She couldn't have been more charming with me and she made me realize that what we shared was a deep love for Paul. We were thrilled to have met up again and I was so grateful that I could finally thank her for the special care she always took of my son.

Taking Paul to Dorneywood for the first time has to rank as one of the greatest days of my life. In all the years I'd been privileged enough to have access to such a grand house I'd wished I could share it with *all* my family. Now that dream came true.

He, of course, was far better accustomed to grand country houses than we were, having gone to Sandhurst and been based at Edinburgh Castle and elsewhere. He seemed very much at home in his surroundings, not at all fazed. The second time he came, we invited everyone we could to join us, including the boys and their girlfriends, my mum, Auntie Ivy, and John's mother Phyllis. This would be the first time that Phyllis ever met Paul, so I was dying to see how they got along.

I must confess to feeling immense maternal pride as I watched my tall handsome son walk up to the woman who'd been less than charitable towards him in the past. He shook her hand and kissed her on the cheek. We sat Paul next to her at lunch and I couldn't help but listen in to the conversation. As it turned out, they had a lot in common. Phyllis came from Chirk in North Wales, and Paul's mum Mary had originally come from that area too. Every time I tuned in, Phyllis was speaking very politely and nicely to my boy; she was clearly impressed by who he was and what he'd achieved in his life.

My mother sat back and watched it all with a little smile on her face. Like her, I tried not to gloat but I felt like crying, 'How about that then, Phyllis? That's my son.' It was a great moment.

We took lots of photographs and there is one special one of Paul with my mum that day that I will always cherish. They are sitting side by side, chatting and holding hands, just like a grandmother and her beloved grandson should.

In anticipation of Paul coming to Dorneywood, I'd asked him what sort of music he liked because we almost always had a little dance after dinner. He said he loved classical, Mozart especially, but that he also liked rock and roll. I bought a compilation album of music from the fifties and sixties and showed it to him. Running his finger down the list of songs, he stopped at one and hesitated.

'There's a song on here that's in the charts again now. It's the strangest thing but through the years every time I hear it I get very emotional. I have no idea why.'

'Oh?' I asked innocently. 'What's the song?'

'"Unchained Melody",' he replied. Looking at my shocked expression he asked, 'Do you know it?'

'Y-yes,' I managed. 'I used to play it all the time ... when I was pregnant ... with you.'

The words sprang instantly to mind, only now I realized they related even more to Paul than they ever did to his father:

Oh my love, my darling,
I've hungered for your touch a long lonely time.
And time goes by so slowly and time can do so much.
Are you still mine?
I need your love … God speed your love to me.

Nineteen

THE YEARS IMMEDIATELY AFTER MY REUNION WITH PAUL WERE FILLED WITH yet more highs and lows. Only a month after the story broke, our David was involved in a car accident that could so easily have killed him. The irony of nearly losing one son having just gained another was not lost on me.

It was late one night in September 2003, and David was overtaking a lorry in the fast lane of the M180, a few miles east of Brigg in North Lincolnshire. A producer and journalist on the BBC's *Look North* programme, he was heading home after work when his car plunged down an embankment, flipping over twice. The police and an ambulance were quickly on the scene and David was taken to Scunthorpe General Hospital but discharged after six hours. Perhaps because of all that was happening in our lives just then he didn't want to worry us so he asked his friend Colin to call us and let us know he'd been X-rayed and that he was all right.

Colin brought him home to us so that I could take care of him. When David walked through our front door, we saw he was absolutely ashen and clearly in great pain. We called our GP straight away and asked him to come and check him over. Roz, David's girlfriend, came over too and spent the night to keep an eye on him. Thank God she did because by the early hours he was seriously ill and couldn't even move. We called an ambulance and when the paramedics arrived, they told us that David's lungs were filling with fluid.

He was rushed to the Royal Hull Infirmary where the true nature of his injuries was finally revealed. He had four broken ribs and numerous spinal fractures. He was lucky to be alive. My mind flashed back to John's accident on the Humber Bridge and the fear that he might never walk again.

Fortunately, my prayers were answered a second time and after a long spell in hospital and several weeks' rest and recuperation afterwards, David was gradually able to make a full recovery from his injuries. Look North had a special bulletin wishing him well and filmed him when he eventually emerged from hospital, leaning on Roz. We'd been blessed once more.

David and Roz had a little house in Beverley and, soon after he was well again, he asked me to go there one afternoon and help him with something. Roz was really busy studying for an exam at the time but at David's request I turned up on her doorstep to tell her I'd been shopping locally and was a bit fed up so I'd thought I'd pop in to see her and cheer us both up. I could tell she didn't really want me there because she was working so hard but, bless her, she still invited me in. Then I said, 'Oooh, let's watch Dave's programme on the telly.' She must have thought me very pushy.

I switched the TV on just in time to see the weatherman Paul giving the nightly forecast. He was a good friend of David and we watched with interest. When Paul finished his report, he announced, 'There's a little something our producer would like to say now.' Roz looked at me but I just shrugged my shoulders innocently.

David came on screen next and looked straight to camera. 'Roz,' he said. 'I love you dearly. Will you be my wife?'

She couldn't believe it. Seeing my grin, she suddenly twigged that my visit had all been part of a master plan. Before she could say anything, Paul the weatherman piped up, 'Now, Roz, before you say yes think very carefully. He could end up looking like his dad.' Cheeky monkey. Despite Paul's warning, Roz rang David and accepted his proposal on live TV. He came home within an hour and they had their photograph taken for the newspapers. The headline in the *Sun* the next day was 'Wedding Prezza'. What a fabulous thing for David to have done. I was thrilled to have been a small part of it. And, oh, how much more romantic than being shoved into a train toilet.

The happy couple were married at Westminster Cathedral a few years later. Roz is a Catholic and so David converted. John was right all along; the boys would make up their own minds about religion once they were old enough. It was a fabulous wedding and a wonderful occasion. We went to St Stephen's Crypt at the Houses of Parliament for a blessing afterwards. Mum was sitting watching with me when Johnathan whispered, 'OK, we've done the Catholic cathedral and we've done the Anglican chapel, so now we've got half an hour.'

'What for?' I asked.

Johnathan laughed and said, 'The rabbi's waiting!'

He had proposed to his wife Ashlie in just as romantic a fashion as his brother. John and I were giving them a tour of Number 10 Downing Street when Johnathan slipped Ashlie into the Cabinet Room, sat her in the Prime Minister's seat, and got down on one knee. She came out to tell us a few minutes later, and to excitedly show us the ring. He'd told her to pack a little case to stay in London but whisked her off to

Paris instead. I knew that years of living at home alone with me watching romantic movies would pay off. Johnathan and Ashlie were married at the Commons, in a beautiful ceremony in the crypt which both my mother and John's mother were able to attend, along with Paul. He was brand new to the family then but Johnathan treated him like a brother, allocating him his own table, just as he had David, and his generosity of spirit touched me greatly.

Paul had always said that he had no interest in trying to trace his father, and I accepted that. It wasn't that he bore him any malice; he just knew that Mary would be upset all over again if he did. Once she died, though, his view changed.

As he had told Mary that time he took her to visit the graves of her parents, he didn't know anything about his family history. All through his life, when people had asked him his medical background and whether there were any hereditary conditions in his family, he'd had to reply that he didn't know. Having met me, he'd uncovered one half of the picture and learned that my family generally lives to a ripe old age, but there was still another half of him that felt unknown. Paul did some research and – being the only person left alive in the world other than me who knew his father's full name – he found an address for a man he thought could be the right one.

Anxious about how I might react, he told me, 'I don't think I'm going to make contact; I just want to see where he lives and maybe spot him at the house to see what he looks like.'

I honestly didn't mind for my sake. The only person whose reaction I was worried about if Paul ever decided to make contact with his father was my husband. Ever since I'd met John in Chester when Paul was a baby, he'd never wanted to know a thing about Jim. He hadn't asked me any questions about the father of my child and I'd always wondered if he might be a little jealous of the man who had first stolen my heart. What would he think now if Jim came back on the scene, through Paul? How would that make him feel? I had to tell myself that I was being overprotective and what was most important in all this was what Paul needed to do. He'd lost the only father he'd ever known. His mother was dead. He was a middle-aged man himself and he needed some answers. I told him, 'It's up to you, Paul,' adding, 'If you were ever to meet him I'm sure he wouldn't remember me, anyway. I was an unsophisticated little girl back then.'

Paul flew to the States as planned and, picking up a hire car at the airport, drove to the neighbourhood he'd identified. Having driven past the address once to see what it was like, he spotted a grey-haired man in a baseball cap on the front lawn. Acting on a whim, Paul came up with a sudden plan. He let some air out of his front tyre a few blocks away and pulled up outside the house with the tyre all but flat. As he'd hoped might happen, the man saw him and offered to help. They soon got chatting. Having realized Paul was English, the older man volunteered the information that he'd been stationed in England in the early fifties. He staggered Paul by telling him he'd had a 'great girlfriend over there'. That was when Paul knew it had to be Jim.

As the two men talked, Paul had to be careful what he said because he knew so much more about Jim than Jim could possibly know about him. He also had to keep his emotions tightly in check, which was fortunately something he'd learned to do as part of his military training. He admitted afterwards that it was hard. The two men chatted for some time, and Jim offered Paul a beer. He still sang, Jim said, and then he offered to play Paul some of his songs. It seemed he still had the musical talent that had first so impressed me. Sitting side by side in the front seat of his car listening to the music with his dad, Paul couldn't believe the lyrics of one song, which told of a girl who woke up one day to find the man she loved gone.

Thanking his father for his help and asking for a memento photograph of them together, Paul set up his camera, resting it on the roof of the car. Jim posed innocently with him in front of his own house before Paul drove off. A few blocks away, he stopped his car and breathlessly rang me from his mobile phone. It was during the 2005 election campaign and John and I were en route to a rally in London when I took the call.

'I've just met my father,' Paul blurted.

'You're joking! What? You've spoken to him?'

'Yes. I even sat in his car. He doesn't know who I am but he's a really nice guy and he spoke about you.'

'Paul, you're just saying that!'

'No, really. He said his girlfriend was called Paula.'

'You're kidding. I didn't think he'd even remember who I was!'

'Well, he does and I have a photo of him to show you.'

I was gobsmacked.

After our chat, Paul went back to his motel to discover that his camera had jammed. There was no photograph after all. Determined not to leave the States without at least a picture of his father, he went back the next day with a bottle of wine as a 'thank you present' and asked for one more shot 'to finish off the reel'. His father didn't seem overly suspicious and even gave Paul a copy of his CD.

A few days later, Paul flew home. The next time we met he pulled out the photograph he'd taken of the two of them and presented it to me. I took it in my hands and drew a sharp breath. 'Oh my God!' I cried. 'That's him!' Privately I thought, That's you, you bugger! Even though he had aged and greyed, he was unmistakeably my 'Jim' from Chester, circa 1955.

Paul gave me a copy of the CD and when I listened with him to the song he'd heard and realized what the lyrics were about, I came to appreciate that – for good or bad – Jim hadn't completely forgotten me.

Paul didn't say what he was planning to do about further contact with his father and I didn't pry. It was up to him. He left it a while and then he wrote a letter to the address he had and told him who he really was. His father told one of his daughters, who contacted Paul via the Internet. He said later that he'd thought it a bit fishy when Paul came back the second day and asked for a second photo. Putting two and two together, the ex-airman wondered if it were possible that the handsome man who'd drunk his beer and listened to his music might just be the son he'd never met.

Paul decided to fly back to the States and meet his father properly, which was a much more emotional prospect. I was happy for him but asked, 'Please give Jim a message for me, would you?'

'Of course,' Paul replied, his face suddenly serious. 'What's the message?'

'Gotcha!' I said and Paul laughed.

The two men have now been happily reunited and Paul did indeed pass my message on. Apparently Jim was in hysterics when he heard what it was. Paul has also met the half-brothers and -sisters he never knew he had. When he first stepped off the plane they were waiting and immediately saw the family resemblance. Paul now knows all he needs to know about his medical history, genetic make-up, and how long his father's side of the family tend to live. He tells me they are good, uncomplicated people; the types who wear baseball caps and have ready smiles when they ask, 'Wanna beer?'

Paul's father told him he had divorced his first wife when he returned to the States, as he'd always told me he would, but then he'd married again. His second wife had recently died and he'd lost a son to cancer so now, with Paul, he felt as if he'd been given something back. He admitted that he knew my mother and Harry had gone to the base to look for him but that his commanding officer had given him no options. Summoning him to his office shortly afterwards, he'd told Jim I was pregnant and ordered him to leave immediately. There was no time to pack; a fast car was waiting outside; he just had to get in and fly back to the US. That's what they did then. They protected their own.

One day, when Paul was visiting his father in the States and they were at a family barbecue and talking about me, Paul decided on a whim to call me long distance. After a brief chat, he asked me if I'd like to speak to Jim. I hesitated but then I said, 'If you want me to, Paul – if you feel the need – then I will.' After a few seconds, he handed the telephone over.

For the first time in fifty years I spoke to the American airman who'd broken my heart as a teenager. I can't say that it was an entirely comfortable feeling. I resisted the temptation to ask him if he still had my bronze medal for tap dancing. We were extremely civil to each other, and I could tell he was as delighted as I was to be reunited with our son. I found myself thanking him for accepting Paul so warmly into his family. This man had left me fifty years earlier to figure out what was best for Paul all by myself. I'd done what I had to do. As I spoke to him across the miles and across the years, I found myself wondering if he shared any of my guilt.

My mother always said everything happens for a reason. Paul had a super life with Ted and Mary, and being unable to have a child of their own they were blessed to have shared their lives with him. He and I have been happily reunited and, having lost the only family he thought he'd had, he's now in touch with his real father and his various half-siblings and has a large extended family all over the world. Like me, he has no regrets that the newspapers found him, even if the way in which it was handled was so brutal. The reporter who knocked on his door wrote to him after we'd been reunited and told him how happy she was that it had all worked out in the end. What he hasn't enjoyed one little bit is all the publicity that went with the discovery of who I was. An incredibly private individual, an officer and a gentleman in the real sense of the words, my Paul has moved on now, the story's out and he has no intention of ever being in the media spotlight again.

'I might even write my own life story one day, Pauline,' he told me jokingly one day. 'Do you want to know what I'd call it?'

I nodded and smiled.

'*Mothers Are Like Buses* ...' he said with a wink.

Knowing what I now know about Paul and about Jim, I can't help but imagine sometimes how different all our lives might have been. If Jim had not abandoned me, I could have ended up having a quiet but relatively uneventful life in the States and, although I'd have kept Paul, I'd never have known the excitement and privileges that I've known as John's wife. Nor would I have experienced the joy of being mum to Johnathan and David. And what of Paul, had the tables been turned and he'd been able to stay with John and me? I wonder what he might have become. A trade union leader? An MP? Prime Minister even? Who knows? It would certainly have been a very different existence to the one he had.

I hope Paul thinks that it all worked out well in the end too. In my heart, I believe he does. When I'd finished speaking to his father that time on the telephone, our son came back on the line afterwards and I could hear from the tone of his voice that he was delighted.

'Thanks, Pauline,' he said, his voice a little choked. 'Now the circle feels complete.'

Twenty

THE RINGING OF THE GATE INTERCOM WOKE ME FROM A DEEP SLEEP. Rolling over to answer it, I peered at the clock and saw that it was just past six in the morning. 'H-hello?' I said into the phone, my mind racing. Who would be at the gate at this hour? Especially when I was alone in bed.

'Mrs Prescott?'

'Yes?'

'This is the police. Stay in your room. Lock the door and stay in your room.'

'What?!' I sat bolt upright, peering around me in the half-light of an April morning. 'Why?'

'There are a number of men on your roof.'

'What?!' I said again. 'How is that possible? We've got armed police outside.'

'Yes, but they got past.'

'Well, how many are there?'

'About a dozen. Now please just stay in your room until we can get to them.'

I could feel my panic rising. 'But – but Della's in the house!' I cried. 'One of John's staff. She's in the turret room.'

The voice hesitated. 'OK then, go and get her, but quickly. Take her back to your room and lock the door.'

I put the phone down and pulled on my dressing gown. Staring at the picture windows that were a special feature of the bedroom, I feared for a moment that men in black might come smashing feet first through them as they did in the movies. These people must have had ropes and ladders to get up on the roof. How did they manage it? What did they want? Who were they? Did they know John was away on the campaign trail? Or was it me they were after?

Summoning my courage, I opened my bedroom door and ran to Della's room. Throwing open the door I found her standing in the middle of the floor, half asleep in the red tartan winceyette pyjamas we'd laughed about before she went to bed.

'Della!' I cried. 'Quickly, come with me!'

She looked at me in a daze and pointed to the window. For some reason she was wielding a toothbrush as if it could protect her against intruders. 'There's a ladder,' she said. 'People are climbing about on the roof.'

'I know,' I replied. 'Hurry now. The police said we have to lock ourselves in.'

She still looked dazed so I grabbed her hand and led her across the landing to my room. Locking the door behind us and wedging a chair up against the handle, we sat huddled together on the bed, waiting for our next instructions from the police. Ever since John had become DPM we'd had two armed police sitting in their car just inside our gate night and day during any election campaign. I couldn't imagine how the men on the roof could have slipped past them. Maybe they'd drugged the policemen, or worse. Maybe they'd taken them hostage. Was that what would happen to us?

'They must have been SAS-trained,' I whispered as we heard voices shouting from below the window and others answering from the roof.

'What do they want with us?' Della said. We stared at each other for a moment, two women alone in a large empty house, neither of us able to voice our fears. For almost half an hour, we sat there, holding hands and trying to remain calm.

When John first joined the Cabinet, the Special Branch had come to our home to advise us on what we should do to keep ourselves safe from possible intruders. On their advice, we had wire meshing erected all the way round the garden, double glazing installed and panic buttons put in almost every room. The high brick wall at the front of the house was gated and a security telephone installed. I became quite a security buff, and John says our house is like Cell Block H. I've even locked him in the extension before now. He was working late in his office and I forgot that he was home. I fell asleep and woke to hear him shouting and banging on the door. 'Pauline, darling, you've locked me in,' he said – or words to that effect!

Despite all the security we'd had installed, I tried not to think how John's job might make us a target for terrorists or cranks. I didn't want to live in fear and, although I'd been made aware of the risks, the measures we'd taken made me feel secure. Besides, I'm not a panicky person by nature. I'd lived alone in that large house for years without ever calling the police or hitting any button. This was different, though. My sense of security had been shattered by that early morning call. My home had been invaded; my sleep and my private life disturbed. I was frightened, angry and upset.

When the telephone rang again, Della and I nearly jumped out of our skins. I picked up the receiver gingerly, afraid that it might be the men on the roof demanding to be let in.

'Hello?'

'Paul? It's John.'

I was so relieved to hear his voice. I'd been trying to track him down for half an hour. 'Oh, John, love, we've been invaded!'

'I know. The police called me, but you're not to worry, these people are just making a protest over some daft thing.'

'A protest? Why? Who are they, John? And what are they doing on our roof?'

'Didn't the police tell you? It's bloody Greenpeace!'

'Greenpeace? You're kidding!' I held my hand over the cradle and told Della, who shook her head in disbelief and, I think, relief. 'What do Greenpeace want with us?'

'God only knows but, listen, just do as you're told and stay put until they can get them down. OK?'

Once Della and I knew that we weren't in imminent danger, we were finally able to relax a little. Sadly, I no longer had a Teasmaid so I couldn't make us a cup of tea, but I did have some water and a packet of Rich Tea biscuits which would have to keep us going. Thankfully, there was an en suite bathroom.

From the sanctuary of the bedroom, we could hear a helicopter circling low overhead and a police loud hailer ordering the demonstrators to come down. We tried to tune into the news to see if we could get a reporter's view of what was happening. The protest went on and on – they were up there all day – and I couldn't believe that we'd been left stranded a few feet below with nothing more than a dry biscuit to sustain us.

The protesters, on the other hand, were fully catered for and highly disciplined. We watched in disbelief as items were pulled up to them on ropes from their helpers below. They had climbing gear, shelter and provisions. They could be planning to stay there for a week, for all we knew. The longer it went on, the angrier I became. 'This is my home!' I wanted to yell through the ceiling. 'Get off my bloody roof!'

I rang the boys to let them know I was all right. Johnathan was on a train and advised me to stay calm. I rang Paul because I knew he'd know what to do from a military point of view. His advice was to remain in my room and keep down. Out of the window, we could see the house surrounded by police with dogs. Across the street, there was all manner of TV crews and journalists' cars. It looked like they were having a jolly day out. I was furious.

It wasn't until lunchtime that Special Branch officers decided it was safe to enter the house and came to tell us we could come out. Della and I got dressed and went down to the lounge, where we sat and watched the rest of the drama unfold on the television news. The front of our home was featured in all the news bulletins. The protesters had erected solar panels and unfurled a huge banner which read: *Oi, 2 jags! Hit targets not voters.* Outside, the helicopter still circled and police dogs with armed officers patrolled the grounds. There was no suggestion that we leave the house and I wouldn't have wanted to anyway. No protester was going to drive me from my home.

I couldn't believe that it took another five hours to get them down from the roof. When the police finally persuaded the men and women to abseil down the walls at five o'clock that afternoon, they warned me to stay away from the windows.

Bugger that! I thought, I want to see these people who've caused us so much grief! I pulled back the curtains and watched as the four men and four women were taken away one by one, but sadly none of them caught my angry scowl.

We learned later that not only had the protesters somehow slipped past the guards in the early hours but that when they were discovered and police guns were drawn, they claimed they were unarmed so the officers reholstered their weapons. John challenged the police on that, asking why they'd let them carry on climbing to the roof. The response was that the protesters were part of 'a peaceful movement'.

Peaceful? Della and I had been genuinely frightened. She admitted later that until we found out exactly who they were she even thought she might die. The experience left me scared in my own house, which was not acceptable. They must have planned the whole thing to perfection. A few weeks before, we'd seen some people across the road from the house taking photographs, but we'd ignored them, thinking they were journalists. The police said afterwards that what they were probably doing was making a note of how many courses of bricks led to the roof because the ladders they used reached precisely to the two highest turrets.

Five months later, I had to relive the whole ghastly experience when I was summoned to give evidence at the trial of the eight protesters in Hull Crown Court. They'd pleaded not guilty and elected for trial, of course, which would get them maximum publicity, but which meant that I had to stand in the witness box. I was extremely nervous about having to face them but then I thought, Why should they get away with it?

My daughter-in-law Ashlie briefed me on what to do and how to behave in court. She said the district judge was in charge and I should address all my responses to him, giving only 'yes' or 'no' answers. I asked her how long I was likely to have to give evidence for and when she said ten minutes I thought I could just about manage that. I was getting over the flu and felt really grotty but I was determined to have my say. The media were there in force once more and Della and I were due to give evidence one after the other.

I was first up so when it was my turn, I told the court exactly what had happened from my point of view. I said how I'd been woken by the police, and how Della and I had at first feared for our lives. Then the barrister for the defence stood up to cross-examine me. He fired question after question at me. Ten minutes passed, then twenty. I was feeling so horrible I kept having to sit down. The barrister tried to suggest that Della and I were exaggerating how frightening the whole experience had been. That's when my tough streak kicked in. I looked at him and thought, You think you're a clever little so-and-so, don't you?

He asked me if I knew what the Greenpeace movement stood for so I told him, 'I should think I do know what Greenpeace stands for. My husband swam up the Thames quite a few years ago protesting on their behalf about nuclear dumping at sea.'

The barrister said that Greenpeace was a peaceful organization, to which I replied something to the effect of, 'When a group of people storm my house in the early hours of the morning and climb on to the roof in what can only be described as a military operation, then quite frankly that to me is an act of terrorism. It's made me extremely nervous in my own home and that should not be tolerated.' Turning to the eight people in the dock, I said, 'It was clearly a well-organized operation and they must have known I was there alone, because my husband was on the campaign trail. That really was cowardly. It was terribly intimidating. Dreadful.'

The judge could see I was on a roll so he kept his head down and let me go on. I told him that I was a private person and had felt violated.

After that, I began to enjoy myself, even though I was in the stand for almost an hour. Every time the barrister asked me a question, I pretended I couldn't hear him, which is the one thing lawyers hate. 'Sorry,' I said, 'can you speak a little more clearly? I didn't catch that.'

Ashlie said to me afterwards, 'You didn't!'

When the trial was over the protesters were each given a community service order, which probably meant nothing to them, plus they got the publicity which I'm sure is what they really wanted. What I've been left with is a new paranoia about security and an enduring dislike of barristers. Still, I had my day in court.

Twenty-One

JOHN'S FATHER BERT DIED IN 2001, AGED NINETY. IT WAS THE END OF AN ERA. He and John had had their differences over the years and John had been especially hurt whenever Bert spoke to the media about him, but in the end they made their peace.

After his cremation, at which John recited a funny poem Gordon Vickers had written for the event, the family scattered his ashes at the finishing post of the Chester Roodee racecourse. It was, John said, the closest Bert would get to it after a lifetime of money wasted on the ponies. The bottle of champagne we'd bought along to toast him popped itself before we were even ready but, as someone said, that was typical of Bert – he couldn't wait for a free drink.

Phyllis Prescott, that proud Welshwoman, died of cancer a couple of years later, in April 2003. In her early nineties, she was terribly ill with it, poor thing, and fought bravely, keeping her dignity to the end. She managed to stay in her own home with carers, but it was terrible to see such a strong and beautiful lady suffering so. John seemed to handle his mother's death quite well, despite the enormous influence she'd had on him over the years, but then men don't show their feelings in the same way women do.

Having been told of her passing, we went to Chester to see Phyllis, where the undertakers had laid her out in her bedroom. I was taken straight back to my father's death when I was a little girl and the idea of a body being visited by friends and family in its own home.

'Come up and see her, Paul,' John said to me.

I hesitated, thinking back to my dad's face under the white gauze cloth and the sweet sickly smell in the room. 'It's all right, love,' he assured me. 'She looks like she's sleeping.'

I went up and sat with John and his siblings around the bed where Phyllis lay just as he had said. One by one, we each began to tell stories from her life: our personal reminiscences of a woman who had been so many things to so many people. I spoke of the many kindnesses she had shown me and the beautiful outfits she had made me over the years. John recalled Labour Party fundraisers in the garden; the barbecues he'd helped host when he came back off the ships; and the family holidays at the party conferences. Ray, Adrian, Vivian and Dawn shared their memories too. Strangely, it ended up being a lovely chatty occasion.

'Let's spray her with some of her favourite Chanel No. 5,' I suggested and we found the bottle and sprayed it all around the room to mask the funereal smell. Then we chose what we knew was a favourite suit for her to wear and prepared her for her final rite of passage: a local funeral attended by many and a wake afterwards in her garden, just like those fun parties she'd thrown over the years. Before she died, she'd asked for her ashes to be scattered over her parents' grave in Wales so John and his siblings went and carried out her wishes on their own.

Phyllis had been at John's side when he was sworn in as an MP; she was in the gallery on his first day in the House of Commons; she was with him when he was made a freeman of the city of Hull; she had been at every family, political and celebratory event. She pretty much chose our home; she encouraged and supported our children. She was, as John has often said, in many ways the Prescott chief whip. A formidable wife, mother and mother-in-law, she had an indomitable spirit and a tremendous sense of style. To this day, I often think of her and smile.

In later life, John was looking through his family records and worked out that he'd been born seven months after his parents married. I think he was as shocked as I was that the woman who'd been so disapproving of me had almost had her own illegitimate child. Then I realized that maybe that was the reason she found it difficult to accept me – my experience reminded her too sharply of her own.

A few years before she died, Phyllis had taken me to one side at a party we held in Admiralty House. 'Now, I never disliked you, Pauline,' she said firmly, 'I didn't. You've been a good wife and mother. I was just upset about losing John. He was the head of the family, you know.' It was the closest I was ever going to get to an apology from her and I took it gladly, pleased that we had made our peace.

Phyllis's death made me dread once more the day when I would lose my own mother. She was in her eighties when John's mother died; arthritic and irritated by aches and pains but still living in the same house and managing largely on her own, with the help of her guardian angels.

She'd been fitted with a new hip and we'd had a lovely new kitchen installed for her while she was recovering in hospital. She could no longer travel to Hull by train and only came when John could pick her up but she still kept appointments at 'The House of Hair and Beauty', enjoyed lunches with girlfriends and trips out in taxis. She loved to watch *Coronation Street* and adored the television presenter Paul O'Grady, who shared her wicked sense of humour. She also liked to watch the Last Night of the Proms and particularly enjoyed the way they always finished with 'Land of Hope and Glory'. She was determined to remain in her own home and hoped to be well enough to do so until the end. I remember crossing the road with her in Beverleyonce when she spotted a couple of old ladies in wheelchairs. 'If I ever get like that, Pauline,' she said, 'shoot me.' She'd have hated to be really infirm and dependent on people to that extent.

I still spoke to her two or three times a day to see how she was, phoning her mid-morning, at lunchtime, and then often in the evening as well before she went to bed. She'd chatter on about her day and her friends and what she'd seen on television or read in the newspaper, and I'd soak it all up happily. One of the last times I saw her, I gave her some pearl earrings as a gift but she was cross and told me off.

'They're far too expensive, Pauline,' she said. 'You shouldn't be buying me presents like this at my time of life.'

'Go on, Mum, put them on,' I told her with a smile. 'You deserve them.'

On Wednesday, 3 November 2005, when she had just turned ninety-two, I rang her at midday as usual. I reminded her that it was my 'Thelma and Louise' day in Beverley with my friend Sally. Mum had loved Sally ever since she'd found out that she was the one who'd processed her claim against the Ideal Laundry for her accident.

'Well, have a lovely day, Pauline,' she said. 'Take care of yourself and give my love to Sal.'

By the time I got home after a nice lunch and an afternoon traipsing round the shops, I was very tired and fell asleep on the settee. When I woke up, it was too late to ring Mum so I decided to call her the next morning. The following day, the telephone rang early, waking me. This was the call I'd been dreading. It was Freda, Mum's friend and neighbour. She told me that she couldn't get a reply when she knocked on

Mum's front door an hour earlier, so she and Maureen used their key and found her dead upstairs. She'd fallen out of bed and was on the floor. Mum had always said she wanted to die in her sleep and, it seems, she did. Maureen said a little prayer over her and then Freda rang me.

I had lost my best friend in the whole world and I felt bereft. If only I hadn't fallen asleep. If only I'd made that phone call and bid her a last goodnight. I never got to say goodbye to my mum; I never sent my final love to Rene, that tiny human dynamo. I've felt so guilty about that ever since. Visiting her the next day in the funeral parlour, I held her little body to mine, kissed her face and told her I loved her. She was so cold and I knew she was gone but it made me feel better that I said goodbye. My brother Peter flew in from the home he'd retired to in Spain after a lifetime in the aerospace industry and the two of us stood shoulder to shoulder at her coffin and recalled happier times.

Mum had once said of my father in death, 'He never hurt you when he was alive, and he certainly won't hurt you now.' Looking at her, so peaceful and neat, I wasn't afraid any more.

For the funeral, we dressed her in a favourite black velvet suit with a cream blouse and I put on her new pearl earrings. We gave her a lovely send-off with all her friends and smothered her coffin in her favourite white lilies. We played a song by Nat King Cole she especially loved called 'Smile'. The lines, 'Smile, though your heart is aching, Smile, even though it's breaking', summed up her life and, in many ways, mine.

The vicar gave her a wonderful eulogy, adding, 'Rene will be up in heaven now and if there's a front step there, she'll be cleaning it.' She was cremated and her ashes interred with my dad at Blacon Cemetery. Peter and I had a new headstone made in black granite with silver lettering.

Auntie Ivy wasn't well enough to attend the funeral, sadly, being too frail, but her daughter Anne came. Dear Ivy, a year younger than my mum, died almost exactly a year later in her nursing home. The Golden Girls were reunited again.

Clearing out Mum's house a few weeks after she died, I came across an old set of black-and-white photographs in a drawer. They were copies of the pictures of baby Paul, taken at the nursery and at the hospital. They were dog-eared from years of being held in my mother's hands.

The first Mother's Day after she'd died, Paul came to spend some time with me. Having been raised by the Church of England Children's Society he was a diligent churchgoer, so he went off to the local church that Sunday evening. Halfway through the service, the lights suddenly went out. The hymn being played at the time was 'Guide me, O thou great Redeemer', a Welsh one and a favourite of his adoptive mother Mary. He'd even had it played at her funeral. When he came back to the house, he couldn't get in via the electric gates because the same power cutthat had extinguished the lights in church had locked them, so he ended up climbing over the gate.

Sitting in our living room later, he said to me, 'There's definitely something weird about this Mother's Day. I bet you any money you like that your mother will contact us too before the day is out.'

A few minutes before midnight, I looked up at the clock and said, 'Well, she hasn't made contact yet.' At that precise moment, an Easter card on the mantelpiece took off of its own accord, it seemed, and came floating down to a table by the side of the fireplace, making us jump. The card landed right next to the last photo of my mother, taken a few weeks before she died. We looked at her photo, looked at each other and couldn't help but laugh. Paul was right. Mum was still with us, still watching over us. What a comforting thought.

Several weeks later, I had a powerful dream in which my mother appeared to me at the side of the bed. She was so bright, in full Technicolor. I jumped out of bed and said, 'Mum! You've come back to me!' I hugged her and could feel her warmth. I told her, 'Oh, you're lovely and warm. How are you?'

'I'm fine,' she said.

'Mum, I love you and I miss you,' I said but then she disappeared. Everything went dark for a moment and the last I saw of her, she was sitting on the edge of the settee on the other side of the room as if she were just about to leave and then that was it. I woke up and shook John to tell him. 'Mum came back to me!' I said, and I explained my dream.

'She was in the departure lounge,' he said sleepily before rolling back on his side.

'Yes, yes, that was it!' I cried, sitting up wide awake. 'She came to say goodbye to me before she went to the other side.' Even though I feel her around me all the time, I know now that the next time I will see her is when I pass over.

I told my brother what had happened, adding sheepishly, 'Peter, you'll think I'm mad.'

He shook his head. 'No I don't, because Dad came back to me.' I was amazed. Peter told me he was at our family home in Boughton Heath not long after Mum had married Harry when our father came to him. 'I saw Dad at the bottom of my bed and it wasn't even in the middle of the night – it was in the morning. He didn't speak but he looked at me and he was happy and I knew he was saying goodbye. I told Mum and Harry but they dismissed it and said I probably had a hangover.'

Peter and I both loved the idea that our parents came back to us to say goodbye, in their own way. It doesn't matter if anyone else believes us; we both take great solace from the thought.

Twenty-Two

IT WAS A THURSDAY NIGHT LIKE ANY OTHER: 27 APRIL 2006. JOHN WAS IN Barcelona at a European Union conference and was due home the following day. I'd just washed my hair in preparation for glamming myself up the next day and was looking forward to seeing him.

My week has always been geared up to the day John comes home. When he's away the house is neat and tidy, quiet, calm, with all the loo seats down. It usually takes me a day or two after he's gone to get it straight and to let it breathe again. The moment he walks in, it becomes his office and every surface is liable to become cluttered with documents and files, books and papers. First in the house are his security staff, then his driver who'd 'love a coffee, thanks', then John himself: tired, hungry and – more often than not – grumpy with it. Surprise, surprise.

This particular Thursday, it was around nine o'clock and I was upstairs with my wet hair wrapped in a towel when the bell at the gate rang. I remember thinking, Gosh, who on earth's that at this time? I wasn't expecting a soul. When I checked the surveillance camera I was surprised to see it was John. As far as I knew, he was in Spain; he hadn't called to tell me he was coming home early. Pressing the buzzer, I released the gate and went downstairs in my dressing gown to greet him.

The first strange thing that happened was that the security staff came in, dumped John's washing and walked straight out without saying a word. His wonderful driver Allan Hall didn't even get out of the car. Then John walked into the hall, his face deadly serious.

'Hello love, what are you doing home?' I asked cheerily.

'Let's go up to the bedroom,' he said, heading for the stairs.

I giggled. 'Oh, John,' I said, 'how nice. I love a man who comes home and orders me upstairs!'

He said nothing as he led the way into our bedroom with its soft cream hues – a colour scheme I'd chosen as a haven of calm in what often seems the madness of our lives.

'Sit down, Paul,' John said, his face like granite.

I sat on the dressing-table stool and looked up at him, forcing a smile. 'You look so serious,' I said, still half laughing. 'You don't want a divorce, do you?'

'No,' he said, staring at the carpet. 'But you might once you've heard what I've got to say.'

My heart did a flip. An affair, I thought immediately. He's going to tell me he's had an affair. In those few seconds before he actually spoke, I ran the entire scenario through in my head. It had to have been at the office Christmas party – a fling after he'd had one too many drinks. He wasn't a drinker. It was probably a quickie in a cupboard; that sort of thing.

'I've had an affair,' he said, speaking the words I never thought I would hear him say.

No. Not my John. Not the man whose life and bed I'd shared for the last forty-five years. Not the boy who once saw his father kissing another woman in the street and was so affronted he went to the police station to report him. Not the John I thought I knew; this bright, impassioned man of the highest principles.

I shook my head, unable to believe what he was saying.

'It'll be all over the newspapers tomorrow.' He paused. 'I'm so, so sorry, Pauline. You don't deserve this.' He looked terrible; his skin was grey and his face bore the saddest expression I had ever seen. He sat down on the edge of the bed as if his legs would no longer support him.

'Who?' I asked. My mind sped through all the possibilities. Some tall, leggy blonde, most like. That would be his type, wouldn't it? Or would it? What was his type? Glamorous, attractive? Younger than me, probably. I felt sick to my stomach.

'Tracey,' he replied, his voice breaking. 'Tracey, in my office.'

I looked up. 'Tracey Temple?' I couldn't take that in at all. Not Tracey. She was the last person I would ever have suspected. She was my friend. She was in her mid-forties and had accompanied me to various functions; she'd joined us in Southampton when I'd opened that new terminal. She and I had always got on so well, laughing and joking together whenever I went into the office adjoining John's apartment at Admiralty House. Oh God, the apartment. Had they done it there?

'How many times?' I heard myself asking. Did I really want to know?

'Not many.'

'But how long?' My mind raced ahead of his reply. A week? A month? Longer? No.

'About two years.'

'What?' I was on my feet. 'Two years?' I was so shocked. 'Two years?' As if saying it out loud made it any easier.

How could he have kept this from me for two years? I felt such a fool. Pacing, shaking my head, I found it impossible to take in. 'Were you in love with her?' I asked. My heart was thumping against my ribcage as I waited for his answer.

'No!' He shook his head vehemently. 'Nothing like that. That didn't even come into it. There were no feelings involved at all.'

Somehow that made me feel better.

'It's over anyway,' he continued. 'It ended a while ago ... She finished it.' I knew he was being honest then, but I dearly wished it had been the other way round. I suppose she felt she was just being used. But she was still on his staff. I'd spoken to her only a few days earlier. What were they both thinking? How could he have done that and still looked me in the face?

I started pacing again and John stood to block my path. 'You need to pack some things,' he told me. 'We'll go to Dorneywood. The media will be on their way. All hell's going to break loose.'

I rounded on him as my anger started to kick in. 'I'm not going anywhere!' I cried. 'If you think I'm fleeing my home in the middle of the night, you don't know me very well, John Prescott. You go. I'm staying. I've done nothing wrong.'

He grabbed my arm, but I jerked away. 'Don't touch me!' I cried. 'Just go.'

No amount of pleading could make me change my mind. He knew that. Telling me again and again how sorry he was, he finally left the room and hurried down the stairs. I heard the front door shut behind him. I heard his official car start up and pull out of the driveway. I held my breath until the gate clicked closed behind him.

Going downstairs, taking one step at a time and gripping the banisters for support, I sat as still as I could in the lounge for a while to try and stop myself shaking. What had he done? Why? The betrayal cut me like a knife. We were a unit: John, me and the boys. We always had been. That's what marriage meant to us. I had stayed home and provided the secure base from which he could go out and achieve all that he had. Now this driven, intelligent and loving man had swept all that aside.

Where exactly had it all taken place? In his office? In the car? In the bed Della and I had bought together? How many times? Was this the first? What about all those attractive European women he'd worked with in Brussels when he was an MEP? Or the other women in his office? My mind tramped back and forth over all the possibilities. Why hadn't I suspected anything? Had everyone been laughing at me behind my back while I foolishly thought that we'd had one of the most enduring marriages in politics? What should I do? I couldn't think clearly.

In normal circumstances, the first person I would have called would have been my darling mum. That tiny firecracker of a woman had been my rock as long as I could remember, but now I had lost her too. The grieving process had already taken its toll and I'd been physically as low as I'd ever been in my life. There wasn't a day went by when I didn't think of her, or miss our thrice-daily telephone calls. Now, when I needed her more than ever, when I wanted her to tell me what to do about the son-in-law she'd always adored, she wasn't there. In that dreadful first hour after John broke the news to me, I had never felt so alone.

Pulling myself together, I tried to imagine what Mum would say if she were still alive. 'Stand firm,' she'd have told me. 'You're as good as anyone else and better than most. Head high, shoulders back, Pauline. Whatever happens, keep your pride.'

My pride? That had gone out of the window along with my self-esteem.

The boys. I had to call the boys. They needed to hear this from one of us, not from anyone else. But how would I tell them? What could I say? All I could think of was to come straight out with it and say something like, 'I'm in shock. You won't believe it. Your father's had an affair.'

Thankfully, Johnathan called me first, on his mobile. He was on his way to the airport for a business trip to the States. It had completely slipped my mind. He told me he already knew because John had called him on the way home to confess to me. I could tell our elder son was as shaken as I was. He dealt with Tracey all the time whenever he was helping John or needed to know his schedule. As always, though, his first thought was for me. 'How are you, Mum? I'm so sorry. I'll cancel America and come up.'

'Don't cancel anything,' I told him, sounding a lot stronger than I felt. 'You go. I know how important this is for you.' Then I called David. He and Roz assured me they'd drive up overnight from London and be with me first thing in the morning. I rang Paul then, who didn't really know what to say. John was relatively new to his life and he'd already had so much to deal with – and now this. He sent me his love and support.

'Don't worry,' I told them all. 'I'll be fine.'

Putting down the phone I listened to the sounds of the house all around me. I could hear the echoing silence in the bedroom where John had just shattered my world. I listened to the ticking of the clock above the mantelpiece. A blackbird sang its evening song out in the garden we'd so loved to sit in.

Where would John be now? Probably only fifty miles away or so, speeding back down the motorway, alone with his guilt in the back of his Jag. I sat on the sofa, still trembling from head to toe, imagining every mile between us. Frightened and alone, I wondered if the widening gap could ever be bridged.

Locking myself away in my home, I waited for the media onslaught. At dawn the first TV crews and cameramen began staking their claims outside. Through the voile security curtains, I could see men and women laughing, joking, sharing bacon sandwiches and coffee in polystyrene cups. By eight o'clock, there was an entire press circus on my doorstep, with television and camera lenses trained on every window. Some reporters even tried to climb over the gates.

At nine o'clock, the builders arrived to start work on our hall and bathroom; it was a refurbishment we'd been planning for months. John had joked that we'd need a grand opening of what he called 'Paul's damn toilet!' I think everyone assumed I'd cancel the builders but there was no way I was going to stop them coming. It was going to be business as usual. Strange as it sounds, the installation of my brand-new loo became my salvation. The builders were my bodyguards in the midst of all the mayhem and highly protective they were too. The completion of a project I'd been arranging for some time was the only thing I had to look forward to. Not that the media didn't capitalize on the event. One photograph they took of my plumber George carrying in a new lavatory had the headline: *Everything's going down the pan at the Prescotts.*

Putting on my make-up each day and refusing to dress in sackcloth and ashes, I apologized to the builders and our neighbours for the media scrum and tried to carry on as if nothing had happened. With David and Roz at my side and Johnathan and Ashlie in constant contact, I kept myself busy making endless rounds of tea, coffee and sandwiches, always with the crusts cut off (standards must be maintained), helping to supervise the workmen and trying to make light of the fact that my heart was secretly breaking.

Cherie Blair called me; I was somewhat surprised. How was I, she wanted to know, from a woman's point of view? Then Alastair Campbell rang. Others followed, even Harriet Harman, one of the women in the Cabinet John calls 'the Sisters'. They all expressed their concern and wondered which way I would turn. Whatever I decided about staying with John or leaving him could make or break his future and have a serious ripple effect on the government. They'd only just survived the scandal of Home Secretary David Blunkett's affair with a married American journalist and his subsequent resignation over alleged improper behaviour. They didn't need another. I didn't know what I wanted to do yet, so I told them I needed more time. I could tell they were worried which way I was going to swing.

Meanwhile, the media scrutiny intensified. By then, there were huge vans blocking our road. Cameras were placed on gantries and swung high over the gates. I had to close all the curtains and lock the doors. I felt vulnerable and lonely, even with my workmen there to jolly me along.

I don't know what I would have done without David and Roz, Johnathan and Ashlie. Our friends Sally and Ernie and Frank and Janet were also a constant presence. Frank, who is a big man, went out and told the reporters hanging off the gates to 'clear off!' Ashlie sent me little poems each day. One read, *God does not rain on the flowers to make them miserable. He does it to make them grow.* My neighbours sent cards asking if I was all right and conveying their blessings. Everyone protected me as best they could and acted as intermediaries and counsellors. Their love and support was like a great big comfort blanket. I kept reminding myself what my mother would have said, had she still been alive: 'You're not the first, and you certainly won't be the last.' The difference was that my marriage crisis was being played out in the public eye.

The telephone never stopped ringing. Reporters urged me to tell them my side of the story. Offers came through the post. Johnathan called when he could get through from the States, and told me that the story had even made it over there where people mostly knew John for hitting that protester. The newspapers here kept printing a picture of John at a staff Christmas party in 2004 lifting Tracey off her feet and into his arms. He held a party each year for his secretaries and political and security staff and this had been at one of them, apparently. He'd always go to such trouble, helping out in the kitchen and making sure everyone had a nice time. John was good like that – he took the time to thank people who worked for him and who'd helped him over the years.

I rarely went to those parties, which were usually too close to Christmas for me to travel all the way to London, but I was entrusted to buy little gifts – usually something funny and nautical. I'd happily wrap them for him and enjoy hearing about the party afterwards. To see that picture of him and Tracey at one of those parties hurt me so deeply. What little gift had I unknowingly wrapped for my husband's mistress that year? Della and Joan had been there, along with John's drivers Allan and Nigel, who took turns to sit in my kitchen most Fridays. They must have had an idea. Who else knew? Yet what could they have done about it if they did?

In the privacy of my room, I agonized over the years of our marriage and the details John had left out about him and Tracey. Was this really his first affair? How many more might there have been? He'd promised me that it was and that there had been no others, but could I believe him?

My mind was shooting all over the place. I couldn't sleep. I couldn't eat. I was driving myself crazy with doubts and fears.

John had been so handsome when I met him and always a little flirty, but I'd never had any cause to suspect anything before now, even though he'd travelled abroad for months at a time and been away at university. People often think that relationships like ours can't be as good as they seem but I honestly believed that ours was. He'd never been one to fuss me in public, but he was always kind and considerate in private. He loved to plan surprises and I'd never wanted for anything. I guess power is an aphrodisiac though, both for the person who has it and for those around him who feel they're in the heart of government. I'd definitely noticed that women had become more flirtatious with him since he became DPM. I'd seen them giggling in his presence but they were just being girls, weren't they? Nothing more than that. Or so I thought.

Tracey was his diary secretary in the Admiralty House office adjacent to his apartment. She'd joined the team about three years before and I got along with her fine, as I did with most of his staff. I became quite close to these girls because I spoke to them almost every day. They gave me John's itinerary each week. They'd tell me where he was and what he was doing. If I was attending a function and needed to know how to dress or what was expected of me, Tracey or one of the other girls would find out. If we were going to something like the State Opening of Parliament, she'd walk in with me ahead of John to keep me company until he came in with the other ministers, and then she'd slip away discreetly. She was just a nice little Cockney girl, smartly dressed and friendly. I'd certainly never had any problems with her.

John had been surrounded by attractive, powerful women all his life – on the ships, in the Council of Europe, in his office and in Parliament.

Many of them were absolutely stunning but I honestly never worried. He was my John and that was that. None of our close friends had ever broken up or even had affairs. It never occurred to me that John might stray. He was away from home so much. I wouldn't have had any peace of mind if I'd fretted about that sort of thing. I had to trust him.

Once the affair was public knowledge, John stayed locked away in Dorneywood and then at the home of Alan and Diane Meale in Mansfield, Nottinghamshire. He rang the house almost every day to speak to me but I refused. David would relay his messages to me. Eventually, our younger son – ever the diplomat – sat me down and told me that John and I would have to talk some time. 'Why not start on the phone?'

I couldn't imagine being able to speak to him but I eventually agreed, mainly to keep David happy. My daughter-in-law Ashlie, a divorce lawyer, tried to prepare me for what to expect. 'You're going to experience so many emotions all at once,' she said. 'You're going to be angry. You're going to want to cry. Don't keep it all bottled up, Pauline. Let it out. Go with the emotions as they hit you.' Sound advice.

The workmen had gone for the night and David and Roz went out and left me in peace. I downed a glass of you-know-what and then, at the allotted time, I rang Alan and asked to speak to John. As soon as I heard my husband's voice on the other end of the receiver, everything came pouring out of me: all my rage and distress. I blew my top and told him exactly what I thought of him. I wouldn't even allow him to respond. He just listened in silence while I ranted. 'You damn fool! How could you do this to us? Why? I might have expected this if things weren't right in our marriage but we were so good together. What were you thinking? How could you?' Then I slammed down the phone.

Each day, the newspapers were filled with more and more revelations. Determined to read every word that the media were printing about me, my husband and my family, I forced myself through Tracey's version of events, sold to the *Mail on Sunday* via celebrity agent Max Clifford. In an 'exclusive' published just three days after John had broken the news of his affair to me, she claimed that their relationship had started at an office party in 2002 and that in the intervening years she had been 'seduced and used for sex' both in his office and in our apartment. She said she felt 'abandoned' by John and the government since the story broke and had been made a 'scapegoat'. She even issued a video statement advertising her story in which she said how much she loved me and that I was her friend. 'I never wanted to hurt her and I never wanted to break up the marriage,' she declared. It was nauseating. She went into graphic detail about how she'd go from the office to John's flat claiming she'd forgotten some important papers and that's when it happened.

The most hurtful thing of all was to see a photograph I had never seen before, taken while I was in Spain with Paul so that he could finally meet my brother Peter. The photo had been taken at the October 2003 remembrance service at St Paul's Cathedral in honour of British soldiers killed in Iraq, which the Queen had attended. John was pictured walking into the service with Tracey at his side. I couldn't believe the way she was looking up at him adoringly. It was like that famous photo of Bill Clinton and Monica Lewinsky. At the time I'd had no idea he was even taking her. The papers quite wrongly quoted other ministers who were there as saying they couldn't believe he'd taken Tracey because they didn't even take their wives and no one else took members of staff, although Tony Blair and John did.

In her version of the story, Tracey claimed that it was her birthday that day and afterwards, they'd gone straight back to his flat for sex, which the media made much of as inappropriate. What really cut me to the quick though was the fact that not only had John taken his mistress along – which looked like a little treat for her (almost as if she were seeing what it would be like to be me) – but that he had walked into the service at her side.

I read every word and examined every photograph. Everyone said I was just torturing myself but I had to know what everybody else was reading in order to deal with it. I felt violated after so many years of being such a private person. I hated to think that people who didn't even know us were talking about the state of our marriage and what I should or shouldn't do. I watched an episode of a TV show in which someone said I must have known and implied that I was blind or stupid if I didn't.

At home, life went on. People still needed feeding and taking care of. I was somehow managing to look after them all without breaking down every five minutes. In urgent need of some groceries to cater for the workmen, my friends and family, I decided to brave the world and slip out to Asda. The men were worried for me. My decorator Bernard offered to go instead and said, 'Pauline, write me a list.'

'No,' I replied firmly. 'That's really kind but you've got work to do. I'll go. I can't hide away for ever.' My only concession to privacy was the dark glasses hiding my eyes. I thought I'd slipped past the press but someone must have followed me because my photograph appeared in the papers the following day with my trolley loaded and my sunglasses on. Some commentators cruelly suggested that I had dressed specially, which I hadn't. I'm always smart. I didn't dress any differently to normal.

One columnist was particularly horrid and claimed I was 'all glammed up'. I thought, You horrible woman. That was one of the hardest things I ever had to do. It was as though I'd done something wrong by going out and yet it took all my strength.

A week later, I did dress up to brave Beverley and then Hull. Sally was away on holiday so I went on my own. I dreaded going into Hammonds, where I'd once worked. I knew all the girls there and I thought they'd be embarrassed. They couldn't have been lovelier. Everyone asked me how I was. After that I made a point of visiting all my favourite shops and the place where Sally and I go for lunch. The kindness of the staff and of complete strangers, some of whom stopped to hug me in the street, gave me the strength to carry on.

Coming home to a house without John was the hardest part. He had repeatedly tried to speak to me again and had begged to be allowed to come home, but I'd refused on both counts. Part of me wanted to sit him down and have him tell me everything. I wanted to know the truth, not all the rubbish I was reading in the papers. But another part, at that moment a larger part, never wanted to see him again. My self-esteem had hit an all-time low. Whatever else I'd done as a wife I had always tried to look my best, keep myself trim, and be the best wife John could possibly have by his side as he continued his important national work. I'd made an enormous effort to do that. And for what? So he could go off and sleep with another woman? I'd look in the mirror and think, What's wrong with me? What didn't I do that he had to go elsewhere?

One newspaper commentator claimed that if I had lived in London with him, things might have been different. I asked myself that question too, but knew that the answer was no, it wouldn't. If a man's going to be unfaithful, he will be. Of course you can make it easier for them by being far away but no matter where I'd lived John had always travelled widely. Then I reminded myself that some of the most stunning and powerful women in the world have been cheated on. A well-wisher told me that, in her experience, any man will cheat on his wife if he is given the opportunity to do so. It saddened me to think that my John was now the same as every other man.

Twenty-Three

AFTER HOLDING OUT FOR ANOTHER WEEK, I FINALLY SUCCUMBED TO DAVID'S insistence that John and I should meet. I knew he was right. I'd have to face him sooner or later. David and Roz prepared us a cottage pie for lunch and then left the house. John was due to arrive soon after breakfast. As the time drew near, I started shaking all over and asking myself if I'd be able to handle the confrontation. Would I go to pieces? Then I heard my mum in my head saying, 'Sit down, Pauline. Write a list of all the things you want to ask him. Stay calm.'

I told myself I needn't be afraid. John had a way with him; he'd always been able to reassure me. He made sense of things and I'd always trusted him to do that. I wanted him to make everything right again. We were a team; we'd always been a team. He had a great big job but I knew he couldn't do it without me keeping the wheels rolling. That was my job. Now, as I waited for the doorbell to ring, I honestly didn't know if I could do it any more.

When the bell rang, I opened the door to a man I barely recognized. I had never seen him look so terrible. He came in and sat down in the lounge, the image of someone who was gutted and ashamed. He looked so very, very sad and kept saying, 'You never deserved this, Paul.'

Despite how awful he looked, I refused to feel sorry for him and didn't give him any sympathy. I wanted to know every detail. First of all, I asked him if all the things I'd read in the newspapers were true. Other women had come forward, claiming to have been involved in liaisons with him. A hotel owner somewhere said John had slipped off to a bedroom with another of his female members of staff. A stewardess said he'd tried something with her on a plane somewhere. John denied everything. He didn't even know half these women, he protested. People were making money out of his misery by telling lies.

I asked him question after question and he answered them all unflinchingly.

Did he love her?

No.

How many times had they had sex and over what period?

Not *many*.

It was all so sordid.

Where? In our bed?

No.

Oh, I so wanted to believe that– it was such a fabulous bed. Della and I had chosen it; trying it out in the store with people looking on as we lay side by side in fits of laughter.

John was a defeated man. He owned up to everything, just as he'd admitted everything to the Mirror's Kevin Maguire when Kevin rang him to confirm the affair in the first place. Even so, the temptation for me to throw it all back in his face was enormous. I was so angry and upset but he just sat there and let me shout at him. That was almost as shocking as anything else.

At one point, needing some air, I jumped up and went to run from the room. As I pulled open the door, the handle came clean off in my hand, something that had never, ever happened before. I looked at John and he looked at me and neither of us said a word. He stood up and tried to get the handle back on for me while I waited, but we were trapped. We couldn't escape. Standing there, side by side, eased the tension a little.

My mother had always told me that, no matter what, I was never to walk away from my home. Looking up, I half laughed and half cried, 'I know you're in here, Mother!'

I was convinced that the handle coming off was my mum's way of telling me, 'You've finally got him in that room, Pauline, don't you dare run out and don't you let him out until this is sorted.'

So many of my friends had already said, 'My God, if your mother were still alive she'd give John a piece of her mind!' She'd always adored him and claimed he had a heart as big as a bucket but she would have been furious and deeply disappointed in him. She would also have told me that the one thing nobody could take away from me was my dignity.

Reminding myself of that, I pulled myself together and turned back to face John. His face still crestfallen, he told me once more that he planned to resign as DPM. I knew there had been many calls for him to do so since news of the affair broke, but I wouldn't hear of it.

'Oh no, you don't!' I said furiously. 'You've worked too hard for this. We all have. There's an election coming and you must finish what you started. You don't give up now.' I could tell he just wanted to have the whole problem go away, but I knew that wasn't the answer. I told him, 'It would be the end of your political career and, anyway, that's a coward's way out. We've been with you all the way. Running from this now would not only show your guilt, it wouldn't be fair on me and the boys.'

When John eventually managed to fix the door handle and get us out of the room, we sat down in semi-silence to eat the lunch David and Roz had prepared for us. Neither of us had much appetite and it felt so strange, sitting at our dining-room table together breaking bread as if nothing had happened. When it was over, John looked even more exhausted. 'I'm going to go and have a lie down, if that's all right,' he announced wearily and went upstairs. I didn't suppose he'd slept much in the previous weeks.

I cleared up and pottered around downstairs until David and Roz came back and asked me how it had all gone. Still, John slept on. He must have been shattered. When it was time for me to go to bed I went up to our bedroom and, to my surprise, found him in our bed and not in one of the spare rooms where I'd assumed he'd be. I thought, You cheeky bugger, Prescott!

There were plenty of other places I could have gone, but if anyone was going to leave our marital bed it was John, not me. I knew of old that I'd never wake him once he was so soundly asleep so I had no choice but to slide into the other side. My 'Berlin Wall' of hats was nothing compared to the invisible barrier I erected between us. I don't remember sleeping much as I spent most of the night making sure that the icy space between us remained just that.

John has never left my bed since.

People have asked me if I have forgiven him and the answer is that I haven't because to forgive is to condone. I have accepted that the affair happened but I've made the decision not to throw all of our lives in turmoil over what he did. I've moved on. I didn't want revenge or, worse, to find myself acting out of spite. There were two high-profile marriages that came to an end around the same time as we hit our problems and in both cases the focus appeared to be on moneyand what people could get out of it. I thought how sad that was: that all your years as a happily married couple boiled down to nothing more than pounds, shillings and pence.

Rightly or wrongly, I felt John deserved a second chance. He gives his all to everything he does, 101 per cent. Now that dedicated focus has turned to me and our marriage. He listens to me much more. He doesn't take me for granted. I never wanted for anything before but, boy, I can get away with murder now! 'Go on, love, you buy it,' are not words that I thought I'd ever hear fall, let alone frequently, from my husband's lips.

Nobody could have been more deeply ashamed than John Prescott that he did this to me and the boys. The shame will be with him for ever. To have done what his father did and had an affair is so out of character and will eat him up because he has a good heart. If anyone could turn the clock back it would be my John. But he has done his job very well and – up until the day he began an affair – he has been a diligent worker, a devoted Labour Party member, a loving husband and a terrific father to our boys. It wouldn't have been fair to have thrown all that away out of revenge.

It has taken me a great deal of soul-searching and all my courage to get through this, but I have been helped by my wonderful friends and amazing children. I have surprised myself actually because I remember when MP John Profumo's wife the actress Valerie Hobson died in 1998. John and I were on our way back from Dorneywood when I read her obituary in the newspaper. I turned to John and said, 'I don't know how she could take her husband back after what he'd done. I know I couldn't.' That was certainly how I felt at the time; little did I know that I would end up doing exactly that.

What I couldn't and wouldn't do was what some other political and celebrity wives have somehow managed to do in the same situation, which was to pose as a happy family over the garden gate days after the affair is leaked. Fortunately no one ever asked me. The first time John and I were seen out together was several weeks later when we went to the village hall in Sutton to vote in the local elections. It was the first opportunity for the media to take photographs of us together so when we came out, they were all there waiting, as I expected them to be. The local police kept them back but I could see them across the road. A lady I didn't know came up to me, handed me some flowers and gave me a kiss, which was so kind. The warmth of people towards me has been just wonderful. As I accepted the flowers, some of the reporters called out, 'How are you, Pauline?'

Looking up, I smiled for the cameras and said, 'I'm fine, thank you,' which is just what my mother would have said. Under my breath, I was tempted to whisper, 'No thanks to you lot!'

What upset me deeply as well were all the horrid things the press said about John after the affair – this proud, brilliant and caring man. They tried to use every new sordid twist and turn to finish him off. John was already so sad and disappointed in himself and it hurt us both when all sorts of unsavoury stories came crawling out of the woodwork. At a time when we were trying to mend our marriage we had rubbish like that to contend with. John personally challenged most of the stories with the editors concerned and the Press Complaints Commission. He was able to prove that he wasn't where many of the reports claimed he'd been on certain dates, and that others could back him up, but that didn't make it any easier on him when I made him justify each new 'revelation' to me.

The press even jumped on John for playing croquet at Dorneywood a couple of months after the affair came out. Tony Blair had gone abroad and John was on a long-booked away-day for his staff. I was there too, sitting quietly in the garden while he and his team worked through some new government policy on transport or the environment. Dorneywood was designed to be a place of rest and relaxation for government ministers so when they had finished their brainstorming session, John and his team emerged from the house and played a game of croquet together on the lawn. The set had been donated to Dorneywood some years earlier by the Tory minister Ken Clarke.

A photographer must have been in the bushes because a blurred picture of John leaning on a croquet mallet appeared in a Sunday newspaper soon afterwards, criticizing 'Two Jags' Prescott for enjoying himself at the taxpayers' expense. He couldn't win. He and his team could have gone for a walk, played cards or had a swim in the pool and no one would have batted an eyelid, but for some reason the fact that a working-class Labourite was playing an upper-class game when he was 'supposed to be running the country' became big news. If it had been a Tory minister, I'm sure no one would have cared.

In February 2007, a so-called drama-documentary called *Confessions of a Diary Secretary* was aired on prime-time television. John couldn't bear to watch it and didn't want me to but I had to, even though it was farcical. God knows where they got their material from but, in it, they claimed John had set Tracey up in a flat and that she'd cooked dinner for Tony Blair and Gordon Brown. Most of it was nonsense, but I felt compelled to watch it with our friends Frank and Janet, just to see what people were saying about us.

The first Labour Party conference in the September after the affair was going to be my toughest ever to face, although I never for one moment thought that I wouldn't go. John asked me rather sheepishly, 'Are you coming to conference in Manchester this year?' and I told him, 'Of course!' I'd never missed one and I wasn't going to start now. It was probably my biggest challenge yet, knowing that all eyes would be on me, the media lenses trained on my every expression, waiting for me to crack or grimace or cry. John had apologized to me a hundred times over but then he decided to make a separate, public apology to the party. When I heard that, I almost backed down. I wasn't sure I could sit through that. Then I reminded myself that I'd done nothing wrong and if I wasn't there as usual, it would be commented on, so I went, sitting in the front row with Cherie by my side.

He had originally planned to apologize at the end of the conference but Alastair Campbell told him to get it in first, so that people weren't kept waiting. Up he stood, in what was undoubtedly the hardest speech of his life, and as the television cameras switched between me sitting in the front row and John on the podium, he apologized.

'Conference, Tony started his speech by saying thank you. I want to start mine by saying sorry. This party has given me everything and I've tried to give it everything I've got. I know in the last year I let myself down, I let you down so, Conference, I just want to say sorry.'

I managed to sit stock still, my face as blank as I could manage for the flashbulbs, until it was over. A ripple of applause echoed around the hall as I blinked back the tears. Cherie, sitting to my right, clapped enthusiastically along with everyone else. Now, at last, we could really move on.

I have been inundated with letters and cards expressing sisterly solidarity and support throughout the affair and afterwards. I tried to reply personally to as many as I could because each note that someone somewhere took the time and effort to write and post meant so much to me and helped me get through it.

Many women have written to me to ask how I can forgive John. They seem to think I am too placid but I'm not a Goody Two Shoes, I am tolerant. There is a difference. Admittedly, I didn't always realize that John was taking me for granted but now if I think he is, I don't let him get away with it.

The truth is that I am one of a dying breed: a traditional wife. John would never have married anyone else, especially after the strong influence of his mother Phyllis. Nor could he have achieved all that he has in life without a good solid base. And I don't see being a traditional wife as a bad thing. On the contrary, living in the constituency I've had the best of both worlds. In between being a housewife and mother, I have travelled widely, been treated kindly and met world leaders. My time at home has been just as rewarding. As my mum always said, you reap what you sow and I've certainly done that with my boys, of whom I'm so enormously proud. What could be more rewarding than seeing your children grow up? And to have Paul in my life again, too, so that I can be a part of all that he has achieved. If I had to start again, I wouldn't change a thing, apart from giving up Paul. I would still live in the constituency and bring the children up there. I wouldn't have had my life any different. No regrets.

My relationship with John has recovered now, although it took a while. The secret is not to remain bitter and not to seek vengeance. I was just very sad and disappointed and terribly let down. The disappointment will probably never leave me, but from day one John made the effort and is still trying to make it up to me. Truth is, he will probably spend the rest of his life trying. He does everything he can to please me and keep me happy. He'll tell anyone who'll listen that he married 'the most beautiful girl in the world'. Always thoughtful, he continues to send me flowers and gifts, and he arranges surprise dinners or little trips away just as he did when he was a young steward.

Our first holiday after the affair was to a villa near Barcelona, where things slowly began to get better between us. Then he took me to London to meet up with his staff, so that I could let them know everything was all right. They each told me they never suspected a thing. Afterwards, he took me to lunch at the House of Commons, a public show of unity for his colleagues that I wasn't especially looking forward to. John did manage to make me laugh, though. As we walked through the Members' Lobby, he spotted the empty plinth which was waiting for a new bronze statue of Mrs Thatcher. Jumping up on to it with the agility of a man half his age, he stood there posing while I snapped a quick photograph.

After lunch, John and I went back to the apartment at Admiralty House. He wasn't sure if I'd even set foot in it again after what had happened there with Tracey but I knew I'd have to. It wasn't easy but if I hadn't gone there she'd have won, wouldn't she? I'd made that apartment into a haven for us and we had so many happy memories of our time there. Once I'd made the decision to carry on with John, which I did the day he came back home, I went to stay there quite soon afterwards. I deliberately didn't leave it too long. It was like laying a ghost to rest.

John's relationship with the boys is as close now as it ever was even though he will always be deeply ashamed of letting them down. After all, he was their hero. I know they each rounded on him privately for what he'd done and I know he has apologized to them personally but I am glad that they've found it in their hearts to accept that apology. It was especially hard for Paul, who'd only just become part of the family and didn't quite know how to react. As for me, I have accepted that our marriage and everything we've built up over the years is worth holding on to. Not fighting for to the detriment of my dignity, but holding on to.

There are a few other things I have learned along the way. You have to let your family and friends close to you, even if you feel like pushing them away. You need a good sense of humour. If that goes, you've had it. My mum always said everything happens for a reason. The reason with us may be that the whole experience has made me stronger and John that little bit softer. In many ways we are better together now than ever before. I know he's proud of me and I'm certainly proud of him.

People say if he could do it once, he could do it again, but I have absolutely no fear of that. Apart from anything else, he knows that if he ever did, that would be the end. I wouldn't go through all that again. I wouldn't have any pride left in myself if I did. Mind you, I have kept a few letters from women telling me what to do with him if ever he does try anything. Some of the suggestions are positively eye-watering!

Twenty-Four

AFTER THE MOMENTOUS AND TRAUMATIC EVENTS OF 2006, I COULDN'T imagine what the next year would bring. Little did I know that it would herald the end of an era for John and for me, and that our lives were about to change for ever.

But before those events even began to overtake us, I had reason to count my blessings once more. In June 2007, John – who'd been under enormous strain both at work and at home for several months – joined Johnathan, Ashlie and me in Barbados. We three were already out there at Johnathan's holiday home and John came because he'd been invited there as part of the two-hundredth anniversary of the abolition of the slave trade. It was a long flight and he was so hot and bothered when he arrived that he decided to sleep out on the veranda, with only a towel thrown over him. Having had dinner with the Prime Minister of Barbados, who'd been to Hull a few months earlier to open a museum in honour of William Wilberforce, John flew home, leaving me to spend a few more days with my son and daughter-in-law. By the time John got back to Hull, he had a bad cough and cold, I'm sure from sleeping outside for three nights in a row. Typically, he refused to stay in bed and insisted on getting up and boarding his usual train to London. During the journey to King's Cross, he took a turn for the worse and by the time he reached his destination, his security men had summoned an ambulance. Doctors at University College Hospital diagnosed pneumonia and moved him to a high-dependency ward because of his age and the fact that he is diabetic.

Joan Hammel called us in Barbados to tell us the news. Johnathan and I flew home on the first available flight and rushed straight to the hospital. Sitting by my husband's bedside over the next few days, I tried not to think of the possibility that he might not pull through. He was not only seriously ill; he was weakened by jet lag, exhaustion and stress. Despite all that had happened the previous year, I had never stopped loving John. When I stared into his face as he inhaled oxygen through a mask, I could still recognize the dashing young 'Hollywood waiter' who'd swept me off my feet under the Eastgate Clock. I had made the decision to stay with him; I hoped and prayed that he would now make the decision to stay with me.

John being John, of course, shook off the pneumonia in record time, annoyed that it had impeded on his work schedule. He was still very weak but when he had 'turned a corner', as the hospital announced to the press, he insisted that I go home and get the house ready for his return. I'd picked up a bug on the plane home anyway and was feeling dreadful. He issued a statement to let everyone know that his condition was now stable and that he was sitting up and joking with hospital staff. Having discharged himself from hospital a week later, he threw a party at Admiralty House for all the nursing staff who'd cared for him and then went straight back to work.

There was no time for any convalescence. He was immediately embroiled once more in the ongoing tussle for power between Tony Blair and Gordon Brown. The promise Tony had made Gordon all those years before, that he would step down one day and let Gordon take over, was about to be kept at last. John, tired of playing piggy-in-the-middle, had threatened to resign to trigger a leadership election on at least two previous occasions. He'd always said that when Tony stepped down he would too, even though he could have stayed as DPM under Gordon. In June 2007, that day finally came. Privately, and especially after he'd been through so much and only just recovered from his pneumonia, I was relieved.

One of the hardest things about him stepping down as DPM, though, was losing access to the Admiralty House apartment. John had already agreed to give up Dorneywood the previous year after all the fuss over him playing croquet, a decision which had caused me much heartache. In a statement, he said that, like other Cabinet ministers before him, he'd used the house as a place to relax and to work. He added, 'But I am well aware that my use of it is now a subject of public controversy and criticism and a matter of concern amongst some MPs and the Labour Party. I have accepted that my continued use of Dorneywood is getting in the way of doing my job in government. I have told the Prime Minister that it is my personal decision that I no longer want to be the official resident.'

No one had enjoyed the use of those two wonderful places as long as we had. At Dorneywood especially we were treated so well. Ian the butler and his wife Barbara had always made us welcome from the minute the wrought-iron gates swung open and we headed down the long gravel drive, sighing with relief. Barbara was a marvellous cook and not only made wonderful meals, she dressed the house beautifully with flowers. At Christmas, it looked like something out of a magazine.

On our farewell visit to Dorneywood we lay in bed that final morning and waited for the usual knock on the door as Ian came in with our breakfast tray. We had a last bittersweet day in those unique and historic surroundings. When we left, Barbara and Ian, the security men Gary and Chris, and the rest of the staff stood by the door as we gave them each a little something and thanked them for their ten years of service.

Leaving Admiralty House a few months later was just as difficult. Even now, when I ride past in a taxi I long for that view and the spaciousness of the place. Lord Malloch-Brown of the Foreign Office had it after us and now Peter Mandelson has use of it, I hear. I hope they each enjoyed it as much as we did. I must admit to being very hurt when it was reported in the press that the apartment needed a 'deep clean' after we'd left. I'd spent several days on my hands and knees scrubbing that place spotless before we moved out. Some of the fixtures and fittings were undoubtedly tired and needed refurbishing and there was nothing I could do about ingrained limescale marks in the washbasins or bath, but everything else was as clean as it could be, bearing in mind it hadn't been redecorated in several years.

Johnathan found us a modern new flat near Lambeth Palace in London, which we use quite a lot these days. It is fabulous, central and conveniently located for everything we have to do. It can't compare to Admiralty House of course, but Johnathan helped me choose the furniture and we've made it very comfortable. We can sit in the lounge and gaze out across the river Thames to the Palace of Westminster. I love people to ask me what the time is so that I can look up and check the hands on Big Ben.

When John stepped down as DPM, he also announced that he would step down as an MP at the next general election. That was quite a decision after thirty-seven years in politics, but as I told him, 'This is playtime now.' He also decided to get rid of the trappings that went with the

DPM job, including his security staff, which he could have held on to for much longer. He insisted he wanted to relinquish the past and start afresh. He also gave up his official car although he could probably have had a driver for life. After so many years of sitting in the back of the car with all the extra leg room, I still prefer to sit there so John now sits up front driving while I'm behind him like Lady Penelope in *Thunderbirds*. Sometimes I think he wishes he still had a driver – especially when he got nicked for doing 35 mph in a 30-mph zone on one of his first solo journeys to London.

He's still firing on all engines – well, almost all! He doesn't seem to feel the need to slow down despite being in his seventies, although I have noticed that he tires more easily. I do travel with him sometimes, although I wouldn't want to be doing it all the time. One thing I will do is take him up on his promise that when he's fully retired he'll take me to visit all of the ships I've launched. I haven't been a very good godmother to them so far, even if my thoughts have sailed with them.

He still spends much of the week away on business or in London, and has so many fingers in so many pies that he is far from bored. I think he'd really like to develop his work on the environmental side, as he did with Al Gore in Kyoto. Al certainly still welcomes his input. I can never imagine John not working at something. He doesn't do relaxation very well. I dread going on holiday with him now because after just a few days he starts to get twitchy.

When John stepped down as DPM, all the Labour lords and baronesses threw a little thank-you party for him in appreciation of what he had done. He was very grateful for that, not least because it proved that he had regained everyone's trust and respect. There are suggestions that he could become a lord himself along with so many of his friends like Betty Boothroyd, John Evans, Peter Snape and Tom Pendry. I think that would be lovely thing: an honour and a privilege and a fitting end to a fascinating career. Best of all, I'd become Lady Prescott and be sleeping with a lord. Now, there's a thought.

Once he'd stepped out of the political limelight, John decided to write his autobiography and have it published to coincide with his seventieth birthday. This was a huge leap for the man who had always shied away from publicity about his personal life. His thinking behind it was that others had written books about him in the past and that more would undoubtedly follow, so he might as well set his own story down for the record.

The big revelations of his book would obviously be his take on the political machinations behind the closed doors of Number Ten and the rivalry between Tony and Gordon, but the stories the media would inevitably focus on most closely would be his affair, his battle with bulimia and my reunion with Paul. Entitled *Prezza: My Story: Pulling No Punches*, his autobiography was published in 2008. In it, John said of me: *She's had a lot to put up with, God knows, but she's supported me through thick and thin and shown the maturity and wisdom that I sometimes lacked.* He added:

> I owe my whole career to her ... for going out to work when I was a student, and always believing in me when others didn't. I can't apologize enough to her for what I did. It did teach me a terrible lesson ... I let down Pauline and the boys, and put them through so much.

That meant the world to me.

He spent his seventieth birthday signing copies of his book in a supermarket in Hull and giving away pieces of a giant birthday cake that the publishers had made for him. 'I'm not one for parties,' he told a TV crew who were filming him at the time, adding with a scowl, 'I'm a miserable bugger.'

After his book came out, John was approached to do some after-dinner speaking. His initial reaction was, 'I'm not going to do that; it'll be like singing for my supper.'

I was cross. 'For God's sake, John,' I said. 'It's a compliment that people ask you. You've been Deputy Prime Minster. You've done some incredible things. You stood in for Tony I don't know how many times at Prime Minister's Question Time. You've got so much to say.'

'Would you like me to do this, then?' he asked, showing me the invitation from a company specializing in the tourist trade in the Mediterranean.

'What?' I said. 'Fly to Monte Carlo? Stay in a hotel looking across at the royal palace?'

After some thought, I said with a smile, 'Well, somebody has to do it.'

So off we went, although of course John doesn't do anything half-heartedly. Instead of just speaking after the dinner, which was all that he was expected to do, he joined in the entire conference – all day. We went to another one in Cyprus and he did the same thing. What is so great about these events is that people get to see him in an entirely different light. They think that this bombastic self-opinionated man will come along, but it's not so. He takes an interest, asks questions, gets involved in all the discussions and they really seem to value his contribution. I hope it is something he will get the opportunity to do more of, quietly and in his own way shattering some of the popular myths about him.

Once John stepped down, I have to admit my chief reaction was one of relief to be out of the recent limelight. 'Thank goodness,' I said. 'Now the cameras will be turned on someone else, and we won't have to go through all of that again.' Public speaking didn't involve me and all I had to do was go along and enjoy the ride. Then John was approached about making a television series on class in Britain. He jumped at the chance and I was quite pleased too, thinking that it would be a perfect opportunity for him to air his deep-held views on the unfairness of the system. When the producers told him that they wanted me to be in it as well, his heart sank. 'She won't do it,' he told them. He was right; I didn't want to do it at all, even though John and the boys were urging me to step into the public arena.

'Oh no,' I told them, horrified. 'They only build you up to knock you down and I don't need that at my time of life. As I've said before, it's playtime now.'

Johnathan and David were especially in favour of me giving it a go. They reiterated what a great opportunity this was for John. Other television work could well follow, they said, opening up a whole new future. It could also boost our pension, Johnathan reminded me, and he knew because he looked after all our finances. We weren't wealthy like many of John's fellow MPs because he'd turned down almost every directorship and business proposition offered to him in favour of 'getting the job done'.

Under pressure from all sides, I finally agreed to take part in the pilot for the programme, although I had serious reservations about it and was terribly nervous. John was clearly excited about the whole project and as soon as we started filming, he really came into his own. I think he's a natural on camera, especially when he's caught off guard.

He never advised me how to behave during the filming, probably because I'd told him firmly, 'I'm not going to say anything. I'll let you do all the talking.' But on day one John said something and before I knew what I was doing I suddenly interrupted him with, 'Now, that's not exactly right.'

The producers seemed to love my interjection and encouraged me to say more. As we both began to relax in the company of the crew, chatting on the swing seat in our garden or playing croquet on the lawn, I came out of my shell and began to express my views, which I'd never before aired. Despite his permanently grumpy expression, I could tell that John rather liked the idea of me finding my voice in this way and there developed a sort of light-hearted one-upmanship between the two of us.

The pilot of the series was shown to the BBC and they loved it. John told me, 'They're thrilled but they insist you're in the series as well. Apparently, you stole the show.'

I was horrified at first but then I realized that John was secretly rather chuffed about it. To have done things like this before he stepped down as DPM might have caused him embarrassment but suddenly he didn't have to worry. After more persuasion from the boys, I said, 'Well, OK, I'll do a couple of programmes, but I hope to God we don't come across like Neil and Christine Hamilton. I'd die.'

The film crew we'd come to know before turned up once again at our home and before I really knew what they were asking me to do, I found myself giving the nation a guided tour of our smart new downstairs loo. 'I believe you should call it a lavatory,' I said, thinking back to my *faux* pas over the words 'flat' and 'apartment'. 'There's an awful lot of snobbery about that,' I added.

I told them all about launching ships – 'There's a knack, you know' – and then they filmed me making sandwiches for lunch while John watched. As usual, I wore disposable plastic gloves for hygiene and cut the crusts off. 'I'm working class and yet my mum taught me how to make sandwiches like this,' I said to camera.

'Your mum never even saw smoked salmon,' John snorted. 'She made doorstep sandwiches for your bricklayer dad.'

Holding up a bread knife, I pointed out that his mother Phyllis owned a Royal Albert tea service. I threatened, 'Don't come too close, John Prescott.'

John was brilliant as he explained his remarkable journey through the class system and how he'd been obsessed with class most of his life. Having grown up in the industrial North with strong union connections, he'd gone to sea as a servant to the upper classes before turning to politics. Despite his father Bert's lifelong insistence that the Prescotts were working class to the end, John reiterated that he had become middle class when he was created an MP, adding with a wry smile, 'I no longer keep coal in the bath; I keep it in the bidet.'

He told the story of how he had always been portrayed in the media as a class traitor, ridiculed for playing croquet, and even suffered the indignity of having a perfectly innocent photograph of him drinking beer doctored so that the beer was replaced with champagne. As if!

When the producer asked me on camera what I missed most about John being DPM, I admitted, 'It was a privileged life and I did enjoy the security. Travelling was very different. At airports, there was always a car waiting and there was none of that standing by the wheel for your luggage. We're back in the real world now.' Mind you, as John always says, at least we don't have to worry about anyone but ourselves now.

Travelling with the film crew all over the country was quite different again and a lot of laughs. We visited people from all walks of life; John went to Rugby School and to see a couple with nine children living on benefits in Rochdale. He attended the Hay-on-Wye Literary Festival (where he jokingly claimed he'd never read a book), went out to dinner with a minor celebrity, and to meet some young girls from a council estate in Lewisham who didn't know who Gordon Brown was. The highlight for me was meeting the seventh Earl of Onslow. As we were greeted at the door of his Surrey home, I turned to the camera and whispered, 'How do you tell a lord his zip's down? Do you curtsey first?' I never did find the right moment.

We were shown around Clandon Park House, Lord Onslow's ancestral home, now owned by the National Trust, and then invited to a beautiful lunch with several of their lovely friends, all laid on by Lady Onslow. A Tory hereditary peer, Lord Onslow told us what it was like to be born into the aristocracy and educated at Eton and the Sorbonne in Paris. He claimed to have friends from all walks of life and said that he believed the class of one's birth was largely irrelevant. Suddenly, I found myself asking John, 'Excuse me, can I say something please?' before proudly telling Lord Onslow the story of my happy reunion with Paul and how he had become a Tory-voting army officer despite his unusual origins. It was quite ridiculous really, asking John's permission to express my point of view, but it somehow felt right in that situation.

Lord and Lady Onslow were extremely nice and gave us a fabulous day. Before we went home, he assured me that John would love being in the House of Lords. 'When people start addressing him as "my lord" his view will change, believe me,' he said.

'Well, it would be nice to be going out with a lord,' I confided.

'What do you want to be Lady Prescott for?' John interrupted. 'You're a lady already.'

I enjoyed making the class programme much more than I imagined I would. John and I became good friends with the producers Amanda Blue and Suzanne Lavery. When the last scene was finally filmed, I was allowed to say, 'It's a wrap!'

The programme was entitled Prescott: *The Class System and* Me and was aired over two one-hour slots on BBC Two in October 2008. To my amazement, not only was it extraordinarily well received, but many of the media commentators focused on me rather than on John. I was dubbed 'the Cleopatra of Hull' and 'Joan Collins of the North'. The *Daily Mail* announced, *A new TV star is born*, adding, *Pauline Prescott is in a class of her own*. It was certainly a bit of a giggle and I was quite chuffed.

The press were less kind to John whom one commentator said looked like *a bulldog who swallowed a wasp*. Another cruelly said he had not just one chip on his shoulder, but a whole chip shop, *in case he gets peckish*. In contrast, they said, I had *a cheery disposition, northern wit, elegance and good manners*. They said I wore *a knockout outfit* but added – rather unkindly I thought – that my hair *hadn't moved since 1963*. Thinking of my 1961 wedding-day hairspray incident, though, I had to laugh.

Columnist India Knight was the sweetest to me. She said I was *the kind of woman who can put on her own lippie in three seconds flat and in the dark if she had to. She'd rather give up her trusty eyeliner forever than read a poxy self-help book*. How true.

To our great surprise, our programme won the Channel 4 Politics in the Media Award, beating competitors like *Have I Got News for You*. John's book had also been nominated in the Political Book of the Year category but lost out to Hugo Young's take on thirty years in politics. When they announced at the awards ceremony that our documentary had won, I said to John, 'You go and collect it. I'm not going up,' but by the time he reached the podium, it seemed the entire audience was stamping its feet and chanting my name. I had no choice but to join him.

If I was ever worried about the glare of the cameras, it was too late now. Offers started flooding in from the unlikeliest places. The producers of *Have I Got News for You* asked me if I would consider chairing an episode. I laughed and said I was very flattered, but no thank you. Someone else suggested that I become the new host of *Blind Date*. That would have been a lot of fun, I'm sure, and my mum always said I reminded her of Cilla Black, the way I fooled around and made her laugh.

'What would you like to do, then?' people asked. 'How about a fashion programme? Do you cook?' I didn't know which way to turn.

Johnathan told me, 'Mum, you may actually like doing some of these things!' He, David and Paul all encouraged me to 'give it a go'. Whatever I did, I knew that I couldn't take the pressure of making a television programme on my own, although never say never, I suppose. John and I were asked to do quite a few things together, Mr & Mrs style, but they didn't appeal to me. It's not about money; to do something just for financial reward is ridiculous and has backfired on many. If an idea comes up and we're comfortable with it, then great. Armed with that thought, we agreed to do another programme called *The North/South Divide*, which was in a similar vein to the class-system programmes but focusing on the differences between the North and the South. It aired in October 2009 and I, at least, was largely well received.

As for what happens after this, well, watch this space. Lights, camera, action, I say. I accept now that for the first time the focus could be as much on me as on my husband. John is rather miffed that when the paperback version of his book came out the publishers had changed the hardback jacket photo of him to one of us together as a young couple, dancing at the Wall City Jazz Club. Invitations have started coming through the door for 'Pauline Prescott and Guest'.

'They don't want to know about me any more,' John moans. 'It's all about you now. I even got a bloody letter the other day addressed to Mr Pauline Prescott.'

I know one thing: when the class programme was so well received I was approaching my seventieth birthday, which somehow seemed significant. I realized then that the previous ten years had flown by so quickly and that in ten years' time I'd be in my eighth decade. So now I've got to the point where I just don't care any more. Whatever I do, I'm determined not to take such a back seat in what will probably be my final years. If I have something to say, I'm just going to come out and say it. When I'm up against the wall, I will fight back.

Even now, new things are still coming my way. People have approached me about doing some after-dinner speaking on the interesting people I've met and the ships I've launched. They want me to talk about finding Paul and what it's like to be a political wife. I never in a million years thought I could do anything like that. I didn't think anyone would be interested. Yet everyone's been so warm and friendly. They clearly see more potential in me than I see in myself. Maybe I have yet to peak?

One of my favourite Tony Bennett songs is 'The Best Is Yet to Come' and that seems to sum up my life. Now, when anyone asks me, 'What are you going to do, Pauline?' my response is always the same: 'Who knows?'

Twenty-Five

THE YEAR JOHN ANNOUNCED HE'D BE STEPPING DOWN AS AN MP AT THE next general election, our son David decided to stand for selection as the next Labour Party candidate for the safe seat of Hull East.

The idea of David taking over the reins was very exciting for us all. He'd been deeply political from an early age, from even before telling Barbara Castle that his father wasn't famous enough. The lovely Della ran as a Labour candidate too, which made the whole campaign feel even more like a family affair.

We were so very proud of David, who worked his socks off. Roz used to drive him up here and they'd often leave London at 5 a.m. To get around the constituency, he decided to buy a second-hand bicycle. I'd always been overprotective and hated the boys going out on their bikes as children. I complained to John, 'I got them safely through their childhood and now he's buying another bloody bike!'

David wouldn't let me fuss. 'Mum! How old am I? You've always been too clingy and now I know why – because of Paul.'

'Why get a bike though?' I tried to reason. 'There's a Jag in the garage doing nothing.'

David was horrified. 'If you think I'm driving around in my dad's Jag, you must be crazy.'

I told him he could park the car at the end of the road and then walk round knocking on doors and handing out leaflets and that nobody would even know, but he wouldn't have it.

We were both deeply disappointed when David wasn't selected. Della wasn't either. The job went to Karl Turner, the son of a friend of John, and we wish him well. It would have been wonderful, though, to have had the son who was born just as John became an MP being selected as the next candidate just as John stepped down. It would have felt like a handing over of the baton. I passed on my mother's maxim to David that all things happen for a reason. 'You wait and see,' I told him.

As it turned out, poor Roz was seriously ill after that and David had to take a lot of time off work to care for her, which he wouldn't have been able to do so easily if he'd been the Labour candidate on top of setting up his own PR company. Fortunately, Roz made a full recovery so my mother was right: everything does happen for a reason. When the time is right, David will step back into the political spotlight again and pick up the Prescott baton. As John celebrates forty years as an MP this year, David will celebrate his fortieth birthday. The timing could be perfect. They already work together on their Go Fourth campaign to secure a fourth term for Labour. He's transformed my husband into a blogger and tweeter, or a cyber warrior as some commentators have called him.

Paul left the Royal Military Police and his experience meant he was immediately offered an international consultancy job. He accepted and moved to the other side of the world. He has been living and working abroad ever since. I miss him not being in the same country as me but we speak all the time on the telephone and visit each other whenever we can.

Johnathan, as always, is working incredibly hard and currently divides his time between the UK and China. He has played a key role in our family for many years, looking after our personal and financial affairs. Since John stepped down as DPM, he has also become our unofficial 'manager', handling all our media negotiations, for which we are extremely grateful. The great legacy that John has left behind will not be lost on the next generation.

Within a year of David's attempt at being selected, John and I became proud grandparents to Ava Grace, the first child born to David and Roz. We are thrilled to bits. When I hold my tiny granddaughter in my arms, I cannot help but feel grateful that she has been born into a stable and happy relationship and will know such love and care her whole life. It is only one generation on and yet things are so very different.

Having a grandchild is the most incredible feeling and quite different to having your own children. Even though I gave birth to three strapping sons, to begin with I was nervous of holding little Ava because she was so perfect. I was afraid that by even breathing on her, I might spoil her in some way. Now I can't get enough of her and even John is melting. Recently, I caught him in her room making little cooing noises over her cot. He'd always wanted us to go on and have a daughter after the boys but for some reason it never happened, so now he has the little girl he'd always wanted. Like him, I can hardly wait for the coming years; to watch her grow into her own person and see what she becomes. If she turns out anything like her parents, then we will be blessed.

In February 2009, I celebrated my seventieth birthday with a party at Mr Chu's, our favourite Chinese restaurant in Hull, organized by the owner, our dear friend Jack Chu, and his lovely wife Qi Jia. Roz had prepared another birthday video for me, this time to the soundtrack 'More Than a Woman'. The roll call of people they had interviewed took my breath away.

Rodney Bickerstaffe, tongue in cheek, opened the tributes with: 'You are smart, elegant and beautiful; in equal measure all the things that that sixteen-stone lump lucky enough to be your husband isn't. The world is a much better place having a sparkler like you. You're a cracker. Have a great day.'

Others who were kind enough to speak to camera and wish me a happy day included Gordon and Sarah Brown. Gordon said, 'You're such a great friend and everybody loves you.' His wife sweetly said she didn't believe I was seventy. Sarah is such a warm and caring woman and a great mum. And, wow, that speech she made introducing Gordon at his first conference as Prime Minister! Not many could carry that off so well and everyone loved her for it.

Della spoke of the years of fun we'd had together, especially whenever she came to stay. Alastair Campbell said hundreds of Facebook fans had contacted him to ask if he could reach me for them. He kindly added, 'The truth that those of us have known for a very long time is that the Prescott who counts will finally emerge. You're the real star of the family. It's not too late to stand for office. Get on the greasy pole and climb up it. You're a woman of the people.'

The video moved me to tears, of course, but not quite as much as the *Book of Love* put together by my daughter-in-law Ashlie, in which she'd asked everyone who meant something to me to write a little note or tell an anecdote. She then pasted them all into an album, decorated it with photographs and beads, ribbons and coloured paper. I shall treasure it always.

As well as messages from the Quaintways Girls reminding me of my matching umbrella covers and homemade frocks, plus so many old friends from way back like Sally and Ernie, Frank and Janet, she'd asked Johnathan, David and Roz to contribute, along with Paul. Their wonderfully warm and open letters to me still bring tears to my eyes. My brother Peter, who'd recently undergone a heart operation, wrote: *To my very best friend and the most loving person I know.*

John carefully wrote out his letter, sealed it and placed it inside the album. No one but me has ever seen that cherished example of how loving and romantic he has been to me since his days as a young steward. He signed it, 'Your loving husband, John'.

At the party attended by my closest friends and family in the place where we've celebrated most of our big family events and entertained the likes of Gordon Brown and Tony Blair, I stood up and thanked everyone for coming. I thanked John for generously hosting such a wonderful party, and my sons and their wives for all their love and support through the years.

Then I turned to a special group of friends, sitting in a row: the Quaintways Girls. Eleven of us have remained in touch more than fifty-five years on. There was Norma Hignett who first got me the job at the salon and who's come through breast cancer; and Barbara Hill, John's old girlfriend, who went to the States to marry her American, Harry. There was Rita Starkey, who married an Italian called Luigi; and Trish Fields with the wonderful voice, who sadly suffered a rare type of throat cancer and can no longer sing but is still such a trooper. There was Carole Fellows and Lynne Anderson, Jill Welsh and Roz Caldecote, Cath Hurley and Alice Snell. We'd all started out as juniors in the salon on the opening day. They'd laughed with me when my overall stuck out over my skirt, they'd fussed me when I was pregnant, and they were my partners in crime at all our fashion shows and the fun nights out we had dancing at the jazz club.

We've helped each other through the good and the bad times, from serious illness and bereavement to the births of children and grandchildren. Doubtless we have more joys and trials yet to face. I've been to countless parties and events at their homes and in return I've been able to invite them to Admiralty House, Downing Street and the House of Commons. Like most women, we love to go out on our own. If our husbands tag along we're put out to say the least – unless they pay! We enjoy a good giggle, which we can't have when our men are around. No matter where we are or what we're doing, the Quaintways Girls revert back to being the silly teenagers we were when we first met. It's quite wonderful.

At that milestone event to mark my seventieth birthday, it was those women above all others who understood the sorrows and the joys of my life. Just as we used to when we were young girls earning only a few pounds a week, they'd all chipped in to buy me a present. They gave me an exquisite crystal lily vase, which I cherish.

Addressing them in front of everyone else at my party, I beckoned my firstborn son to get up and stand next to me. The Quaintways Girls rose to their feet as one, clapping and cheering as Paul gave me a hug and I fought back tears of happiness and pride. Johnathan and David quickly joined us as John watched proudly from the back. This was my life. These men were my family. All of us together again, at last.

Holding Paul's hand tightly, I cleared my throat. 'Girls,' I said. 'There's someone I'd like you to meet. It's been more than fifty years and you've all been very patient but here he is. It's Tilly's baby ...'

Epilogue

ONE THING JOHN PRESCOTT PROMISED ME, RIGHT FROM THE START, WAS that when I married him I would never be bored. He has certainly kept that promise.

Even in older age, life continues to bring daily surprises. We were shopping in London's Oxford Street recently when an anti-Israeli protester came running towards us with a placard, shouting about Palestinian rights. John tried to grab him, yelling, 'Come here!' but he ran off. Not long afterwards, we were sitting in John's Jag in Beverley one hot sunny day, eating ice cream with the door open for some fresh air. A local youth shouted something rude at us and before I could stop him, John had jumped out of the car and chased after him. Fortunately for them both, the lad got away. He is an old so-and-so, it's true, but he's my old so-and-so, isn't he?

People see my husband as such a serious character and of course politics is a serious thing, but the truth is that he also has a much softer side. At a party celebrating his years in politics at the Willow Dockers Club, he was moved to tears by the tributes paid to him, as he was at several of the farewell parties held in his honour.

One of the things that really sums up John Prescott for me is that his favourite film is *Billy Elliot*, with its harrowing tale of triumph over adversity, set against a gritty northern backdrop. He admits that he sees himself in the lad who rose up against the prejudices of his community to say, 'This is what I am and this is how I want to live my life.' He has seen that film on at least six occasions and can quote entire extracts from the dialogue. Each time he sees it he gets emotional.

Thanks to that hidden sensitivity, coupled with the steely drive and determination that form the backbone of the man I married almost fifty years ago, I've had a wonderful marriage and a very privileged one. I am still so immensely proud of what he is doing and what he's achieved. He has never lost his political passion and that has helped me to a far greater understanding of the world than I would have had if I'd stayed as a hairdresser in Chester.

Because of him, I have done a great deal of travelling and met so many fascinating people. I have knocked on doors throughout numerous campaigns and sat through umpteen party conferences. I've made more cups of coffee during marathon speechwriting sessions than I care to remember, and have tried to sleep through John's endless practising of their delivery. I've launched ships and flown in private jets. I've lived in houses that even millionaires couldn't buy. I've met the Queen and had lunch with the Prince of Wales, who signs letters to my husband, 'Yours ever, Charles'.

In June 2009, I was named Political TV Personality of the Year at the Alternative Parliamentary Awards held each year at the House of Lords. There was a cocktail and canapé reception on the terrace at the House of Commons and I thought I'd just been invited along to represent John and the team who'd helped make the class documentary. Then somebody suddenly announced that they had a special award for television personality of the year and that I'd been nominated, along with political commentator and *Strictly Come Dancing* star John Sergeant and Diane Abbott, MP. I was so surprised when I won. They presented me with the most wonderful cartoon of me lying on a chaise longue in a slinky red evening gown, while John, dressed as a butler and looking even more grumpy than usual, serves me champagne from a tray. I love it!

Not to have done all that I have done might well have been boring. Through John, I have been given a unique perspective on a remarkable life. There have been so many good things that have happened, and you have to take the bad with the good. Without a doubt, the happiest moments of my life have been getting my second chance with Paul, watching our sons Johnathan and David marry two wonderful girls, and seeing John become Deputy Prime Minister. The saddest were losing my wonderful mum and dad.

Now I'm approaching my own old age with the hope that if I end up with a walking stick in one hand, I'll be carrying a glass of something fizzy in the other. I have to agree with John's unique summing up of what has been an incredible seventy-odd years. 'We don't have a life ...' he says with a characteristic grimace, '... we have a bloody soap opera!'

Acknowledgements

THIS BOOK WOULD NOT HAVE BEEN POSSIBLE WITHOUT THE SUPPORT, encouragement and professionalism of a wonderful team of people. Special thanks must go to Annabel Merullo and Caroline Michel of Peters Fraser and Dunlop, and to Rhian Williams of FirstMarch.

Thanks also to Belinda Budge and Carole Tonkinson at HarperCollins for their unstinting enthusiasm, to Richenda Todd for her impressive editing skills, and to the numerous sales, art and editorial staff who beaver away tirelessly behind the scenes.

A great big thank you to my writer Wendy Holden. It has been an absolute privilege working with her. We bonded instantly. We laughed. We hugged. We cried. This book would never have been written without her. I know we'll be the best of friends for ever. We have to be – she knows too much!